Race, Work, and Family in the Lives of African Americans

Race, Work, and Family in the Lives of African Americans

Edited by
Marlese Durr and Shirley A. Hill

ROWMAN & LITTLEFIELD PUBLISHERS, INC.
Lanham • Boulder • New York • Toronto • Oxford

ROWMAN & LITTLEFIELD PUBLISHERS, INC.

Published in the United States of America
by Rowman & Littlefield Publishers, Inc.
A wholly owned subsidary of The Rowman & Littlefield Publishing Group, Inc.
4501 Forbes Boulevard, Suite 200, Lanham, Maryland 20706
www.rowmanlittlefield.com

PO Box 317
Oxford
OX2 9RU, UK

British Library Cataloguing in Publication Information Available

Library of Congress Cataloging-in-Publication Data

Race, work, and family in the lives of African Americans / edited by
  Marlese Durr and Shirley A. Hill.
    p. cm.
  Includes bibliographical references and index.
  ISBN 0-7425-3466-9 (cloth : alk. paper) — ISBN 0-7425-3467-7
    (pbk. : alk. paper)
  1. African Americans—Social conditions—1975– . 2. African
  Americans—Economic conditions. 3. African American families.
  4. Work and family—United States. I. Durr, Marlese, 1953–.
  II. Hill, Shirley A. (Shirley Ann), 1947–.
E185.86.R247 2006
306.85089'96073—dc22   2005028998

Printed in the United States of America

♾™ The paper used in this publication meets the minimum requirements of
American National Standard for Information Sciences—Permanence of Paper
for Printed Library Materials, ANSI/NISO Z39.48-1992.

Contents

Introduction

Family and work are major, integrally related dimensions of social life which affect the well-being and success of family members. As social institutions, family and work are also avenues where social inequality may be understood as a major element in the distribution of social, cultural, and economic resources and sites where inequality is perpetuated, negotiated, and contested. Our reader focuses on the family, work, and entrepreneurial experiences of African Americans in contemporary society. In understanding continuing patterns of racial inequality, numerous scholars have noted how marginal labor market positions and family instability intersect. Our focus on African Americans allows us to navigate the examination of this inequality and highlight elements of disparity. In our volume, we will explore issues of gender, work and family, look at the micro- and macrolevel factors that shape these experiences, and show the impact that social policies and institutions have on the lives of African Americans.

The historic notion of black families as weak and ineffectual, reiterated in the infamous Moynihan Report of the 1960s, was vehemently refuted by revisionist scholars of the civil rights era. This scholarship made a vital contribution to our understanding of racial inequality, allowing scholars to shift their focus from cultural pathology to structural barriers of inequality, such as racism, employment discrimination, occupational segregation, and social and cultural segregation. In the ensuing decades feminists, especially women of color, articulated the "matrix of domination" approach which recognizes race, class, and gender as intersecting dimensions of inequality that affect employment opportunities, social mobility, and family well-being. But more important, this research described how these barriers affected black families' well-being. Given black men's inability in most instances to cross racial employment boundaries and become the sole wage earner for their families, scholars began to bring into focus the work-family roles of African American women. This work illustrated how they were empowered by their labor market standing and it commended their community and social activism.

Protest during the civil rights era demanded an end to segregation and greater opportunities for African Americans, and prior to the 1970s, such progress seemed inevitable. As the civil rights era drew to a close, African Americans appeared poised to advance toward economic, social, and cultural equality. College attendance reached historically high rates, civic integration grew as opportunities to obtain leadership roles in community and neighborhood associations appeared, and equal opportunity legislation afforded new chances to become upwardly mobile in the public and private sectors. Doors seemed to be opening, yet in the 1970s the wage gap between black and white men had again begun to climb. Within two decades, a demise of gains achieved during the civil rights movement began to slowly emerge as rates of unemployment and welfare dependency among African Americans soared, and black families were again being described as "in crisis." In his 1978 book *The Declining Significance of Race*, William J. Wilson addressed the issue of growing racial inequality in an era of greater opportunity by arguing that, despite a historic legacy of racism, class had become more important than race in determining blacks' progress. In later work, Wilson, along with other scholars, noted that the absence of viable labor for black men was tied to neighborhood deterioration, higher rates of crime, and—important for our purposes—lower rates of marriage and family stability.

Despite these dramatic changes, revisionist-era scholarship on black families still seemed wedded to the myth-refuting "strengths perspective." While such perspective was admirable in challenging the notion of family pathology among blacks, few scholars seemed able to analyze the 'new' post—civil rights black family. Most continued to focus on the cultural adaptability and strengths of African American families, and challenging the notion that they were pathological. Even the emergence of the race-gender-class dynamic spawned by feminists of color and theorized as intersectionality theory or multiracial feminism did little to address the institutional barriers African Americans faced in the labor market and society-at-large. While Wilson provided key insights on the reasons for continuing racial inequality, his 'masculinist' approach focused almost exclusively on the connection between employment and marriage among African American men, thereby grounding the family-work connection in Eurocentric patriarchal values and negating black women's breadwinning status. Yet studies have shown that black women have also experienced a decline in their labor market positions.

At the approach of the century, our search for new scholarship on the more contemporary forces that were affecting African Americans—for example, deindustrialization, down-sizing, displacement welfare reform, a declining sentiment in favor of affirmation action, and class polarization—led to our coediting a special volume of *Gender & Society*. In that volume, titled "African American Women: Gender, Relations, Work, and the Political Economy in the Twenty-first Century" (August 2002), we compiled a set of six fresh, timely, previously unpublished articles that are now being recognized as a valuable contribution to the literature. We examined how the historic gender roles and identities of black women were being reconfigured by changes in work, family, and community. In this volume we build on that special edition with the publication of readings focusing on the family and work experiences of African Americans, in an age of continuing inequality.

I

RACE AND COLORISM:
THE FAMILY-WORK INTERFACE

The goal of Part One is to describe race, racism, and colorism as the context in which black people negotiate their lives, including work and family relationships. It contains three articles which discuss how black men and women have had to accept marginalized positions in the labor market—jobs which have been described as penalizing black men yet empowering black women. Herring's recent article in *Contexts* documenting continuing racial discrimination in employment and the need for affirmative action is the lead article. Eduardo Bonilla-Silva critiques various approaches to theorizing racism and offers his own theory of racialized social systems. On a more interpersonal level is the article by Thompson and Keith on skin color—a growing area of research among scholars. Studies show that skin color is an important predictor of self-esteem and marriageability for black women, but not black men.

1

Is Discrimination Dead?

Cedric Herring

To hear much of the political and legal debate in recent years, one might imagine that the issue is whether or not discrimination *in favor of* African Americans is justified. But it is employment discrimination *against* African Americans, though illegal, that is still at work in America.

In November 1996, Texaco settled a case for $176 million with African American employees who charged that the company systematically denied them promotions. Texaco originally vowed to fight the charges. But when irrefutable evidence surfaced, Texaco changed its position. *The New York Times* released a tape recording of several Texaco executives referring to black employees as "niggers" and "black jelly beans" who would stay stuck at the bottom of the bag. Texaco also ultimately acknowledged that they used two promotion lists—a public one which included the names of blacks and a secret one which excluded all black employee names. The $176 million settlement was then the largest amount ever awarded in a discrimination suit.

Much has changed in American race relations over the past 50 years. In the old days, job discrimination against African Americans was clear, pervasive, and undeniable. There were "white jobs" for which blacks need not apply, and there were "Negro jobs" in which no self-respecting white person would be found. No laws forbade racial discrimination in employment; indeed, in several states laws required separation of blacks and whites in virtually every public realm. Not only was racial discrimination the reality of the day, but also, there was widespread support among whites that job discrimination against blacks was appropriate. In 1944, 55 percent of whites admitted to interviewers that they thought whites should receive preference over blacks in access to jobs, compared with only 3 percent who offered such opinions in 1972.

Many blatant forms of racism have disappeared. Civil rights laws make overt and covert acts of discrimination illegal. Also, fewer Americans admit to traditional racist beliefs than ever before. Such changes have inspired many

This chapter was originally published in *Contexts: Understanding People and Their Social Worlds* 1(2): 13–18, 2002.

scholars and social commentators to herald the "end of racism," and to declare that we have created a color-blind society. They point to declines in prejudice, growth in the proportion of blacks who hold positions of responsibility, a closing of the earnings gap between young blacks and young whites, and other evidence of "racial progress."

However, racial discrimination in employment is still widespread; it has gone underground and become more sophisticated. Many citizens, especially whites who have never experienced such treatment, find it hard to believe that such discriminatory behavior by employers exists. Indeed, 75 percent of whites in a 1994 survey said that whites were likely to lose a job to a less qualified black. Nevertheless, there is clear and convincing evidence that discriminatory patterns against black job-seekers exist.

In addition to the landmark Texaco case, other corporate giants have made the dishonor roll in recent years: In 2000, a court ordered Ford Motor Company to pay $9 million to the victims of sexual and racial harassment. Ford also agreed to pay $3.8 million to settle another suit with the U.S. Labor Department involving discrimination in hiring women and minorities at seven of the company's plants. Similarly in 1999, Boeing agreed to pay $82 million to end racially based pay disparities at its plants. In April 2000, Amtrak agreed to pay $16 million to settle a race discrimination lawsuit that alleged that Amtrak had discriminated against black employees in hiring, promotion, discipline, and training. And in November 2000, Coca Cola Company agreed to pay more than $190 million to resolve a federal lawsuit brought by black employees. These employees accused Coca Cola of erecting a corporate hierarchy in which black employees were clustered at the bottom of the pay scale, averaging $26,000 a year less than white workers.

The list of companies engaged in discrimination against black workers is long and disturbing. Yet, when incidents of discrimination come into public view, many of us are still mystified and hard pressed for explanations. This is so, in part, because discrimination has become so illegitimate that companies expend millions of dollars to conceal it. They have managed to discriminate without using the blatant racism of the old days. While still common, job discrimination against blacks has become more elusive and less apparent.

HOW COMMON?

Most whites think that discriminatory acts are rare and sensationalized by a few high-profile cases, and that the nation is well on its way to becoming a color-blind society. According to a 2001 Gallup survey, nearly seven in ten whites (69%) said that blacks are treated "the same as whites" in their local communities. But the numbers tell a different tale. Annually, the federal government receives about 80,000 complaints of employment discrimination, and another 60,000 cases are filed with state and local Fair Employment Practices Commissions. A major study found that about 60 percent of blacks reported racial barriers in their workplace in the last year, and a 1997 Gallup survey found that one in five reported workplace discrimination in just the previous month.

The results of "social audits" suggest that the actual frequency of job discrimination against blacks is even higher than they (blacks) are aware of. Audit studies test for discrimination by sending white and minority "job-seekers" with comparable resumes and skills to the same hiring firms to apply for the same job. The differential treatment they receive provides a measure of discrimination. These audits consistently find that employers are less likely to interview or offer jobs to minority applicants. For example, studies by the Fair Employment Commission of Washington, D.C., found that blacks faced discrimination in one out of every five job interviews, and that they were denied job offers 20 percent of the time. A similar study by the Urban Institute matched equally qualified white and black testers who applied for the same jobs in Chicago. About 38 percent of the time, white applicants advanced further in the hiring process than equally qualified blacks. Similarly, a General Accounting Office audit study uncovered significant discrimination against black and Latino testers. In comparison to whites, black and Latino candidates with equal credentials received 25 percent fewer job interviews and 34 percent fewer job offers.

These audit studies suggest that present-day discrimination is more sophisticated than in the old days. For example, discriminating employers do not explicitly deny jobs to blacks; rather, they use the different phases of the hiring process to discriminate in ways that are difficult to detect. In particular, when comparable resumes of black and white testers are sent to firms, discriminatory firms will systematically call whites first and repeatedly until they exhaust their list of white applicants before they approach their black prospects. They will offer whites jobs on the spot but tell blacks that they will give them a call back in a few weeks. These mechanisms mean that white applicants go through the hiring process before any qualified blacks are even considered.

Discriminatory employers also offer higher salaries and higher status positions to white applicants. For example, audit studies have documented that discriminatory employment agencies will often note race in the files of black applicants, and steer them away from desirable and lucrative positions. A Fair Employment Commission study found that these agencies, which control much of the applicant flow into white-collar jobs, discriminate against black applicants more than 60 percent of the time.

Surprisingly, many employers are willing to detail (in confidence to researchers) how they discriminate against black job-seekers. Some admit refusing to consider any black applicants. Many others admit to engaging in recruitment practices that artificially reduce the number of black applicants who know about and apply for entry-level jobs in their firms. One effective way is to avoid ads in mainstream newspapers. In one study of Chicago, over 40 percent of the employers from firms within the city did not advertise their entry-level job openings in mainstream newspapers. Instead, they advertised job vacancies in neighborhood or ethnic newspapers that targeted particular groups, mainly Hispanics or white East European immigrants. For the employer who wants to avoid blacks, this strategy can be quite effective when employment ads are written in languages other than English, or when the circulation of such newspapers is through channels that usually do not include many blacks.

Employers described recruiting young workers largely from Catholic schools or schools in white areas. Besides avoiding the public schools, these employers also avoided recruiting from job training, welfare, and state employment service programs. Consequently, some job training programs have had perverse, unanticipated effects on the incomes and employment prospects of their African American enrollees. For instance, research on the impact of such training programs on the earnings and employability of black inner-city residents found that those who participated in various job training programs earned *less per month* and had *higher unemployment rates* than their counterparts who had not participated in such programs.

WHO SUFFERS?

Generally, no black person is immune from discriminatory treatment. But there are some factors that apparently make some more vulnerable to discrimination than others. In particular, research has shown that African Americans with dark complexions are likelier to report discrimination—half do—than those with lighter complexions. Job discrimination is also associated with education in a peculiar fashion: Those blacks with more education report more discrimination. For example, in a Los Angeles study, more than 80 percent of black workers with college degrees, and more than 90 percent of those with graduate-level educations, reported facing workplace discrimination. Black immigrants are more likely than are nonimmigrants to report discrimination experiences, residents of smaller communities more than those of larger ones, and younger African Americans more than older ones. Rates of job discrimination are lower among those who are married than they are among those who are not wed. Research also shows that some employment characteristics also appear to make a difference: African Americans who are hired through personal contacts less often report discrimination, as do those who work in the manufacturing sector and those who work for larger firms.

Discrimination exacts a financial cost. African Americans interviewed in the General Social Survey in 1991 who reported discrimination in the prior year earned $6,200 less than those who reported none. (This penalty is in addition to $3,800 less than whites that blacks earned because of differences in educational attainment, occupation, age, and other factors.) A one-time survey cannot determine whether experiences of discrimination lead to low income or whether low income leads to feeling discriminated against. But multivariate research based on data from the Census Bureau that controls for education and other wage-related factors, shows that the white-black wage gap, i.e., "the cost of being Black," has continued to be more than 10 percent—about the same as in the mid-1970s. Moreover, research looking at the effects of discrimination over the life course suggests that there is a cumulative effect of discrimination on wages such that the earnings gap between young blacks and whites becomes greater as both groups become older.

HOW CAN THERE BE DISCRIMINATION?

Many economists who study employment suggest that job discrimination against blacks cannot (long) exist in a rational market economy because jobs are allocated based on ability and earnings maximization. Discrimination, they argue, cannot play a major role in the rational employer's efforts to hire the most productive worker at the lowest price. If employers bypass productive workers to satisfy their racism, competitors will hire these workers at lower-than-market wages and offer their goods and services at lower prices, undercutting discriminatory employers. When presented with evidence that discrimination does occur, many economists will point to discriminators' market monopoly: some firms, they argue, are shielded from competition which allows them to act on their "taste for discrimination." These economists, however, do not explain why employers would prefer to discriminate in the first place. Other economists suggest that employers may rationally rely on "statistical discrimination." Lacking sufficient information about would-be employees, employers use presumed "average" productivity characteristics of the groups to which the potential employees belong to in order to predict who will make the best workers. In other words, stereotypes about black workers (on average) being worse than whites make it "justifiable" for employers to bypass qualified black individuals. In these ways, those economists who acknowledge racial discrimination explain it as a "rational" response to imperfect information and imperfect markets.

In contrast, most sociologists point to prejudice and group conflict over scarce resources as reasons for job discrimination. For example, racial groups create and preserve their identities and advantages by reserving opportunities for their own members. Racially based labor queues and differential terms of employment allow members to allocate work according to criteria that have little to do with productivity or earnings maximization. Those who discriminate against blacks will often use negative stereotypes to rationalize their behavior after the fact, which, in turn, reinforces racism, negative stereotypes, and caricatures of blacks.

In particular, labor market segregation theory suggests that the U.S. labor market is divided into two fundamentally different sectors: (1) the primary and (2) the secondary sector. The primary sector is composed of jobs that offer job security, work rules that define job responsibilities and duties, upward mobility, and higher incomes and earnings. These jobs allow their incumbents to accumulate skills that lead to progressively more responsibility and higher pay. In contrast, secondary sector jobs tend to be low-paying, dead-end jobs with few benefits, arbitrary work rules, and pay structures that are not related to job tenure. Workers in such jobs have less motivation to develop attachments to their firms or to perform their jobs well. Thus, it is mostly workers who cannot gain employment in the primary sector who work in the secondary sector. Race discrimination—sometimes by employers but at times by restrictive unions and professional associations that fear that the inclusion of blacks may drive down their overall wages or prestige—plays a role in determining who gets access to jobs in the primary sector. As a consequence, African Americans are locked out of jobs in the primary labor market, where they would receive higher pay and better treatment, and they tend to be crowded into the secondary sector. And these disparities compound over time as primary sector workers stay mired in dead-end jobs.

An alternative sociological explanation of African American disadvantage in the U.S. labor market is what can be referred to as "structural discrimination." In this view, African Americans are denied access to good jobs through practices that *appear* to be race-neutral, but work to the detriment of African Americans. Examples of such seemingly race-neutral practices would include seniority rules, employers' plant location decisions, policy makers' public transit decisions, funding of public education, economic recessions, and immigration and trade policies.

In the seniority rules example, blacks are hired later than whites because they are later in the employers' employment queue (for whatever reason), operating strictly by traditional seniority rules will ensure greater job security and higher pay to whites than to African Americans. Such rules will virtually guarantee that blacks, who were the last hired, will be the "first fired" and the worst paid. The more general point is that employers, themselves, do not have to be prejudiced in implementing their seniority rules for the rules to have the effects of structural discrimination on African Americans. Unequal outcomes are built into the ability to make the rules.

These same dynamics apply when (1) companies decide to locate away from urban areas that have high concentrations of black residents; (2) policy makers decide to build public transit that provides easy access from the suburbs to central city job sites but not from the inner city to central city job sites nor from the inner city to suburban job sites; (3) public education is funded through local property tax revenues which may be lower in inner city communities where property values are depressed and higher in suburban areas where property values are higher and where tax revenues are supplemented by corporations that have fled the inner city; (4) policy makers attempt to blunt the effects of inflation and high interest rates by allowing unemployment rates to climb, especially when they climb more rapidly in African American communities; and (5) policy makers negotiate immigration and trade agreements that may lead to lower producer costs but may lead to a reduction in the number of jobs available to African Americans in the industries affected by such agreements. Again, in none of these cases do decision makers need to be racially prejudiced for their decisions to have disproportionately negative effects on the job prospects or life chances of African Americans.

WHAT CAN BE DONE?

Employment discrimination, overt or covert, is against the law; yet, it clearly happens. Discrimination still damages the lives of African Americans. Therefore, policies designed to reduce discrimination should be strengthened and expanded, rather than reduced or eliminated as has recently occurred. Light must be shed on the practice and heat must be applied to those who engage in it. There are some modest steps that can be taken to reduce the incidence and costs of racial discrimination:

1. Conduct more social audits of employers in various industries of various sizes and locations. In 2000, the courts upheld the right of testers (working with the Legal Assistance Foundation of Chicago) to sue discriminatory employers. Expanded use of evidence from social audits in law suits against discriminatory employers provides more information about discriminatory processes, better arms black applicants, and provides greater deterrence to would-be discriminators who do not want to be exposed. Even when prevention is not successful, the documentation from social audits makes it easier to prosecute illegal discrimination. As in the Texaco case, it has often been through exposure and successful litigation that discriminatory employers mended their ways.

2. Restrict government funding and public contracts to firms with repeated records of discrimination against black applicants and black employees. The government needs to ensure that taxpayer money is not used by discriminatory

employers to carry out their unfair treatment of African Americans. Firms that continue discriminating against blacks should have their funding and their reputations linked to their performance. Also, as the law suits over this issue continue to mount, defense of such practices becomes an expensive proposition. Again, those found guilty of such contemptuous activities should have to rely on their own resources and not receive additional allocations from the state. Such monetary deterrence may act as a reminder that racial discrimination is costly.

3. Redouble affirmative action efforts. Affirmative action consists of activities undertaken specifically to identify, recruit, promote and/or retain qualified members of disadvantaged minority groups in order to overcome the results of past discrimination *and* to deter discriminatory practices in the present. It argues that simply removing existing impediments is not sufficient for changing the relative positions of various groups. And it is based on the premise that to be truly effective in altering the unequal distribution of life chances, it is essential that employers take specific steps to remedy the consequences of discrimination.

4. Speak out when episodes of discrimination occur. It is fairly clear that there is much discrimination against African Americans that goes unreported because it occurs behind closed doors and in surreptitious ways. Often, it is only when some (white) insider provides irrefutable evidence that such incidents come to light. It is incumbent upon white Americans to do their part to help stamp out this malignancy.

Now that there are laws forbidding racial discrimination in employment, stamping it out should be eminently easier to accomplish. The irony is that because job discrimination against blacks has been driven underground, many people are willing to declare victory, and thereby, let this scourge continue to flourish in its camouflaged state. But if we truly want to move toward a color-blind society, we must punish such hurtful discriminatory behaviors when they occur, and we should reward efforts by employers who seek to diversify their workforce by eliminating racial discrimination. This is precisely what happened in the landmark Texaco case, as well as the recent Coca Cola settlement. In both cases, job discrimination against African Americans was driven above ground, made costly to those who practiced it, and offset by policies that attempted to level the playing field.

REFERENCES

Dickinson, Katherine P., Terry R. Johnson, and Richard W. West. 1986. "An Analysis of the Impact of CETA Programs on Participants' Earnings." *Journal of Human Resources* 21:64–91.

Feagin, Joe. 2001. *Racist America: Roots, Current Realities, and Future Reparations.* New York and London: Routledge.

Fix, Michael, and Raymond J. Struyk. 1993. *Clear and Convincing Evidence: Measurement of Discrimination in America.* Washington, DC: The Urban Institute.

Gottschalk, Peter. 1997. "Inequality, Income Growth, and Mobility: The Basic Facts." *Journal of Economic Perspectives* 11:21–40.

Herring, Cedric. (ed.). 1997. *African Americans and the Public Agenda: The Paradoxes of Public Policy.* Thousand Oaks, CA: Sage Publications.

Kirschenman, Joleen, and Kathryn M. Neckerman. 1991. "'We'd Love to Hire Them, But . . .': The Meaning of Race for Employers." Pp. 203–32 in *The Urban Underclass,* C. Jencks and P. Peterson (eds.). Washington, DC: Brookings Institution.

O'Connor, Alice, Chris Tilly, and Lawrence Bobo (eds.). 2001. *Urban Inequality: Evidence from Four Cities.* New York: Russell Sage Foundation.

Thomas, Melvin, Cedric Herring, and Hayward Derrick Horton. 1994. "Discrimination Over the Life Course: A Synthetic Cohort Analysis of Earnings Differences Between Black and White Males, 1940–1990." *Social Problems* 41:608–28.

Wilson, William Julius. 1996. *When Work Disappears: The World of the New Urban Poor.* New York: Vintage Books.

2

What Is Racism?

The Racialized Social System Framework

Eduardo Bonilla-Silva

What is racism? For most people, the answer to this question is very simple. Racism is prejudice, ignorance, or a disease that afflicts some individuals and causes them to discriminate against others just because of the way they look. This commonsense view on racism is not much different than the definitions developed by social scientists. For example, anthropologist Ruth F. Benedict, one of the first scholars to formally use the notion of racism, defined it as "the dogma that one ethnic group is condemned by nature to congenital inferiority and another group is destined to congenital superiority."[1] Similarly, van den Berghe defined racism in his classic 1967 study as "any *set of beliefs* that organic, genetically transmitted differences (whether real or imagined) between human groups are intrinsically associated with the presence or the absence of certain socially relevant abilities or characteristics, hence that such differences are a legitimate basis of invidious distinctions between groups socially defined as races."[2] Despite some refinements, current use of the concept in the social sciences is similar to Benedict's and van den Berghe's. Richard T. Schaefer in his popular textbook on race and ethnicity defines racism as ". . . a *doctrine* of racial supremacy, that one race is superior."[3] Hence, analysts as well as lay people, regard racism as a phenomenon fundamentally rooted at the level of ideas.

I label this dominant perspective as idealist because, as idealist philosophy, it assumes that ideas are the root of social action. From the outset, however, I want to stress that my point is not that the ideas that individuals hold on racial matters are irrelevant. My argument instead is that the narrow focus on ideas has reduced the study of racism mostly to psychology which has produced a simplistic schematic view of the way racism operates in society.

This chapter was originally published in the author's book, *White Supremacy and Racism in the Post–Civil Rights Era*, Boulder, CO: Lynne Rienner, 2001.

First, racism is defined as a set of ideas or beliefs. Second, those beliefs are regarded as having the potential of leading individuals to develop prejudice, defined as attitudes toward an entire group of people. Finally, these prejudiced attitudes may induce individuals to real actions or discrimination against racial minorities.

In contrast to this idealist view, I advance a *materialist* interpretation of racism rooted on the fact that races in racialized societies receive substantially different rewards. This material reality is at the core of the phenomenon labeled as racism. Actors in superordinate positions (dominant race) develop a set of social practices (a racial praxis if you will) and an ideology to maintain the advantages they receive based on their racial classification, that is, they develop a *structure* to reproduce their systemic advantages. Therefore, the foundation of racism is not the ideas that individuals may have about others, but the social edifice erected over racial inequality. Eliminate racial inequality and the practices that maintain it and racism and even the division of people into racial categories will disappear.

Before elaborating my theorization, however, I review a few of the most significant critical perspectives on racism developed by American social scientists.[4] Because of the analytical relevance of these interpretations, I offer below a short formal review of each of these perspectives.

REVIEW OF CRITICAL FRAMEWORKS TO INTERPRET RACISM

The Marxist Perspective

For Marxists class is the central explanatory variable of social life and class struggle is viewed as the main societal dynamic. Hence, Marxists regard other social divisions and possible sources of collective action (e.g., gender- or race-based struggles) as "secondary contradictions" or as derivations of the class structure.[5] Not surprisingly then, the orthodox[6] Marxist position on race is simple and straightforward: racism is an ideology used by the bourgeoisie to divide workers. For instance, Albert Szymanski defines racism as,

> [A] legitimating ideology for an exploitative structure. Racist ideology propagated in the media, educational system, and other institutions, together with the actual distribution of relative petty advantage within the working class serves to disorganize the entire working class including the ethnic majority, thereby allowing capital to more effectively exploit most majority group workers.[7]

One of the first Marxist-inspired analysts on racial matters was black sociologist Oliver C. Cox. In his impressive *Caste, Class, and Race*,[8] Cox defined racism or race prejudice as "a social attitude propagated among the public by an exploiting class for the purpose of stigmatizing some group as inferior so that the exploitation of either the group itself or its resources or both may be justified."[9] This social attitude or ideology emerged in the fifteenth century as a practical consequence of the labor needs of European imperialists. In Cox's words:

> The socioeconomic matrix of racial antagonism involved the commercialization of human labor in the West Indies, the East Indies, and in America, the intense competition among businessmen of different western European cities for the capitalist exploitation of the resources of this area, the development of nationalism and the consolidation of European nations, and the decline of the influence of the Roman Catholic Church with its mystical inhibitions to the free exploitation of economic resources. Racial antagonism attained full maturity during the latter half of the nineteenth century, when the sun no longer set on British soil and the great nationalistic powers of Europe began to justify their economic designs upon weaker European peoples with subtle theories of racial superiority and masterhood.

Cox labels the antagonisms that emerged out of European imperialism as "racial," but does he recognize that certain aspects of social structure are racial in nature? Cox, as all Marxists, argues that race relations are not truly racial. Thus, for Cox, European imperialists justified their exploitation of the people and resources of the New World in racial terms but essentially established "labor-capital profit relationships" or "proletarian bourgeois relations."[10] Racial exploitation is viewed as a special form of class exploitation. According to Cox, the racial component of these class-based relations stem from the fact that blacks were proletarianized in their entirety (as a people) in contrast to whites who experienced a partial proletarianization. Given that the racial aspect of societies is not deemed as real, Cox concludes his *Caste, Class, and Race* by suggesting that racial minorities should strive toward assimilation, follow white working-class leadership, and ultimately struggle for socialism alongside white workers. The lack of any critical race viewpoint is amazing considering that Cox, a black writer, wrote this book at a time of great white working-class hostility toward black and minority workers and that he himself suffered the effects of racial caste in academia.

Another popular Marxist view on racism is Edna Bonacich's split labor market interpretation.[12] The twist in Bonacich's approach is that instead of regarding race relations and racism as fundamentally orchestrated by the bourgeoisie, she suggests they are the product of intra–working-class frictions resulting from a labor market split along racial lines. Bonacich argues that a split labor market exists when there is "a difference in the price of labor between two or more groups of workers holding constant their efficiency and productivity"[13] According to Bonacich, the United States has had a split labor market since slavery with blacks as the cheaply priced labor segment. After the abolition of slavery, Bonacich claims that black laborers remained at the bottom of the labor market due to a "difference in labor militance" compared to white workers. For Bonacich, white workers—whether old stock or immigrants—had greater levels of class consciousness than blacks. Although she is aware of the fact "that a number of 'white' unions openly excluded blacks while many others discriminated more covertly," she insists that the lesser degree of black involvement in labor unions was the reason for their utilization as cheap laborers by capitalists in the post–World War I period.[14]

What about the well-documented history of white working-class racism? Bonacich reinterprets this history as white workers' resistance to the "threats" (e.g., strike-breaking, displacement, lowering the wage rate, etc.) posed by blacks. In her view, this "resistance"[15] involved the total exclusion of blacks from unions and castelike occupational divisions. Significantly, Bonacich has little to say about the labor threats posed by the millions of European immigrants to white American workers. Although she believes that black and white workers coalesced between 1940 and 1960, she argues that the counter-offensive launched by the bourgeoisie (plant relocations and automation in the past and down-sizing today) extended the life of the split labor market. And because blacks were very vulnerable at the outset of the coalition period, the policies of the capitalists disproportionally hurt blacks and contributed to the creation of a "class of hard-core unemployed in the ghettos."[16]

The orthodox Marxist view on racial matters has many limitations.[17] First, orthodox Marxists regard racism and racial antagonism as products of class dynamics. Regardless of whether the antagonism is viewed as fostered by the bourgeoisie (Cox, Szymanski) or as the product of intra–working-class strife (Bonacich), racial strife is viewed as not having a real racial foundation. Second, racial strife is conceived as emanating from false interests. Because the unity of the working class and the impending socialist revolution are a priori Marxist axioms, racial (or gender-based) struggle is not viewed as having its own material basis, that is, as based on the different material interests of the actors involved. Consequently racism is regarded as "ideological" or "irrational" and the racial struggles of blacks as divisive. (Although Bonacich views the conflict between black and white workers as "rational," she interprets them as rational in *class* terms.) Finally, given that racial phenomena are not deemed as independent, most Marxists shy away from performing an in-depth analysis of the politics and ideologies of race.[18]

The Institutionalist Perspective

The institutionalist perspective emerged out of the struggle of racial minorities in the United States in the 1960s.[19] In contrast to the liberal view on race relations, which blames the ills of racism on poor whites, proponents of this viewpoint argue that racism is societal and that it affects all white Americans. According to Kwame Ture (formerly known as Stokely Carmichael) and Charles Hamilton in their book *Black Power,* racism is "the predications of decisions and policies on considerations of race for the purpose of subordinating a racial group and maintaining control over that group."[20] Furthermore, they suggest that a distinction should be made between individual racism or the overtly racist acts committed by individuals and institutional racism or the racial outcomes that result from the normal operations of American institutions. Mark Chesler developed the most succinct definition of racism produced by any author in this tradition: the prejudice plus power definition. In Chesler's words, racism is "an ideology of explicit or implicit superiority or advantage of one racial group over another, plus the institutional power to implement that ideology in social operations."[21] In its most radical version (Ture and Hamilton), institutionalists see racism as an outgrowth of colonialism and institutional racism as the contemporary expression of this historical event. Therefore, since radical institutionalists argue that blacks are politically, economically, and socially subordinated to whites, they advocate for blacks' national liberation.

The institutionalist perspective has contributed to dispel some of the myths perpetuated by the dominant paradigm on racism. Researchers inspired by this perspective have gathered data to show the systematic disadvantages that blacks suffer in economic, educational, judicial, political, and even in the health system. Their findings have forcefully served as clear and convincing evidence of the pervasiveness of racism.[22] Moreover, their assertion that all whites receive advantages from the racial order and their forceful advocacy for challenging all institutions, politicized more than one generation of activists and academicians to fight racism wherever it may be and in whichever form it operates. This perspective, therefore, helped to move the discussion about race in academic and nonacademic circles from the realm of peoples' attitudes to the realm of institutions and organizations.

Nevertheless, despite its valuable political contributions, this perspective does not pose a serious theoretical challenge to the dominant conception of racism in the social sciences. Theoretically, this perspective is just a mélange claim in which everything can be interpreted as "racist."[23] More significantly, despite its institutional label, this perspective still grounds racism at the ideological level thus failing to challenge the root problem of the dominant perspective. This ideological grounding of racism is evident in the following quotation from Ture's and Hamilton's book:

> Institutional racism relies on the active and pervasive operation of *anti-black attitudes and practices*. A sense of superior group position prevails: whites are "better" than blacks; therefore blacks should be subordinated to whites. *This is*

*a racist attitude and it permeates the society, on both the individual and institu-
tional level, covertly and overtly.*[24]

Although Ture and Hamilton argue that the racism is an outgrowth of colonial
domination and suggest that its contemporary expression has been institutionalized or embedded in the fabric of all institutions, they do not develop an
analysis of how this happens or how this colonial relationship operates in
practice, nor do they identify the mechanisms whereby racism is produced
and reproduced. Thus, they are left with a mysterious all-mighty notion of
racism as "a racist attitude" that "permeates the society, on both the individual
and institutional level."

Robert Miles has pointed out other limitations of this approach. First, this
perspective is intrinsically linked to a naive view of social stratification
wherein race is the sole basis of social division. Second, its definition of racism
is so inclusive that it loses its theoretical usefulness.[25] Third, its basic black-
white division excludes "white" groups (e.g., Irish[26] and Jews) as plausible
racial actors who have shared racialized experiences. Furthermore, this simplistic binary view minimizes the racialized experiences endured by racial
minority groups notably Native Americans, Puerto Ricans, and Chicanos. In
this vein, the cry for "black power," although understandable in the struggle
for civil rights, is an unnecessarily restrictive political concept that excludes
the most likely political allies of blacks in the struggle for full racial citizenship.
Fourth, and as in the case of the dominant perspective on racism, this perspective is ensnared in circularity. Racism, which is or can be almost everything, is proven by anything done (or not done) by whites. The analyst
identifies the existence of racism because any action done by whites is labeled
as racist. Finally, for institutionalists such as Ture and Hamilton, all whites are
"racist" and thus there is little room for coalition building with white progres-
sives.[27] If they truly believe this to be the case, then the logical political
options for blacks are (1) waiting until racial minorities become the numerical
majority in the United States or (2) emigrating back to Africa. The nationalist
uprisings or electoral politics they advocate, given the demography and the
nature of social power in this country, would then be untenable and unwise.[28]

The Internal Colonialism Perspective

Another group of analysts, inspired by the civil rights movement, postulate
that racism is structured by the colonial status of racial minorities in the United
States.[29] As in the case of the institutionalist perspective, proponents of the
internal colonial framework argue that racism[30] is institutionalized and based
upon a system in which the white majority "raises its social position by
exploiting, controlling, and keeping down others who are categorized in

racial or ethnic terms."[31] Blauner, the foremost exponent of this perspective, explained the emergence of modern racism in the following way:

> The association of race consciousness with social relations based on the oppression of one group by another is the logical prerequisite for the emergence of racism. The conquest of people of color by white Westerners, the establishment of slavery as an institution along color lines, and the consolidation of the racial principle of economic exploitation in colonial societies led to the elaboration and solidification of the racist potential of earlier modes of thought.[32]

After different Third World peoples were forcefully moved to the United States, a racial order was established with its own dynamics. Central to the operation of such order is the maintenance of white privilege. Although the racial order and the particular form of racial oppression are viewed as changing throughout history, white privilege is viewed as a constant systemic fact. Blauner argues that whites receive advantages at all levels but, unlike institutionalists, he gives primacy to "the special advantage of the white population in the labor market" since in "industrial capitalism economic institutions are central, and occupational role is the major determinant of social status and life style."[33]

This framework takes head on many of the limitations of mainstream approaches to race relations. While most of the perspectives developed by social scientists are ahistorical and postulate the existence of "race cycles" or common "ethnic patterns,"[34] the internal colonial model is historically contingent (Barrera) and informed by the differences between the experiences of white ethnics and racial minorities. Moreover, the internal colonial perspective challenges the purely psychological view of racism. First and foremost, it challenges the dogma of conceiving of racism as the virulent prejudice of some individuals by suggesting that prejudiced individuals are not necessary for the existence of a racial order. Racism, in Blauner's view, has an objective reality "located in the actual existence of domination and hierarchy."[35] As with the institutionalist perspective, this tradition regards racism or racial/colonial oppression as systemic, comprehensive (all actors involved), and rational (based on the interests of whites). Furthermore, by conceiving racism as rational and material (as a social structure organized to benefit whites), this tradition challenges the simplistic assertion of social scientists and most whites that the cure for racism is education. Instead, Blauner and writers in this tradition believe that the abolition of racism, as is the case with other systems of exploitation, requires social mobilization.[36]

Although this perspective offers a clear improvement over the institutionalist perspective and provides new insights for the study of race relations, it still has some serious limitations. First, because it is centered on the colonial nature of racial subordination, it assumes unity among both the dominant and the subordinated "races" and thus neglects the class- and gender-based divisions among them.[37] Second, by stressing the centrality of economic oppression as the foundation for understanding white privilege, this approach misses the process of economic marginalization and exclusion that some races may experience at some historical junctures. For instance, how would an analyst in this theoretical tradition interpret the contemporary status of "underclass" African Americans or the almost complete exclusion of American Indians in reservations?[38] Finally, neither Blauner nor other writers in this tradition formulate the conceptual tools or analysis needed for a truly structural understanding of racism. Despite asserting that racism is systemic, Blauner did not develop the theoretical apparatus to study how racism is systematized and reproduced in societies. Notwithstanding these limitations, I incorporate many of the insights developed by authors in this tradition in the alternative framework that I develop in this chapter.

The Racial Formation Perspective

The recent work of Howard Winant and Michael Omi represents a theoretical breakthrough in the area of race relations. In their *Racial Formation in the United States*, these authors provide a thorough critique of previous theoretical approaches and suggest a new approach for the study of racial phenomena: the *racial formation* perspective. They define racial formation as the "process by which social, economic, and political forces determine the content and importance of racial categories, and by which they are in turn shaped by racial meanings."[39] The essence of this approach is the idea that race "is a phenomenon whose meaning is contested throughout social life."[40] The very existence of the category race is viewed as the outcome of *racialization* or "the extension of racial meaning to a previously unclassified relationship, social practice or group . . . [it] is an ideological process, an historically specific one.[41] In their view, race should be regarded as an organizing principle of social relationships which, at the micro level, shapes the identity of individual actors, and at the macro level, shapes all spheres of social life. Although racialization affects all social spheres, Omi and Winant assign a primary role to the political level,[42] particularly to the "racial state" which they regard as the factor of cohesion of any racial order. Hence, racial conflict, particularly in the post–civil rights era, is viewed as playing itself out at the state level.

Equipped with these categories, Omi and Winant review the recent history of racial formation in the United States. Of theoretical interest is their claim that racial dynamics have been reframed in recent times through the *racial project* (the active process of reorganization of racial dynamics by a fraction of the dominant race) of neoconservatives and New Right. These groups have pushed an antistatist, moral, and individual rights agenda that, in fact, suggested that the ills of America are deeply connected to liberal racial policies going awry. Thus programs such as affirmative action have been redefined as "reverse discrimination" and welfare as a system that entraps people (many of them minorities) in poverty.

Most radical writing on race in the 1990s has been inspired by Omi and Winant.[43] My own theorization in this chapter owes heavily to their work. Nonetheless, the racial formation perspective still has some significant limitations. First, Omi's and Winant's concepts of racial formation and racialization give undue emphasis to ideological processes. Although both concepts are helpful in grasping how racial meanings are formed and reorganized, they do not help analysts understand how it is that racial orders are structured. Arguing that racial classifications are permanently contested and malleable is a reaffirmation of the old idea in the social sciences that race is a socially constructed category.[44] However, this affirmation does not make clear whether or not they believe that race is or can become an independent basis of group association and action.[45] Second, although in their book there are hints of a conception of races as social collectivities with different interests (e.g., "race is a concept which signifies and symbolizes social conflicts and interests by referring to different types of human bodies"[46]), Omi and Winant stop short of making such a claim. By failing to regard races as collectivities with different interests, their analysis of political contestation over racial projects seems to be quarrels over meanings rather than positions in the racial order. Thus, it is unclear why people fight over racial matters and why they endorse or contest racial projects (see chapters 4 and 7 in 1994 edition).[47] Third, Omi's and Winant's analysis of the most recent rearticulation of racial ideology in the United States leaves out a comprehensive or systemic view of the process. The change is described as singularly carried out by the right wing and neoconservatives instead of reflecting a general change in the nature of the United States' racial structure. In order to make this claim, Omi and Winant would have to include the agency of all the members of the dominant race—rather than privileging some actors—and conceive the change as affecting all the levels of the social formation—rather than privileging the political level. Finally, although I share with them the idea that race is "a fundamental *organizing principle* of social relationships,"[48] their theoretical framework comes close to race-reductionism in many areas. For instance, their conceptualization of the state as the "racial state" leaves out the capitalist—as well as the patriarchal—character of the state.[49]

Racism as Societal Waste

The last theory I review here is that of Joe R. Feagin and Hernán Vera in their celebrated book *White Racism: The Basics*. These authors argue that racism is a *"socially organized set of attitudes, ideas, and practices that deny African*

Americans and other people of color the dignity, opportunities, freedoms, and rewards that this nation offers white Americans."[50] Feagin and Vera suggest that racism wastes human talent and energy and, hence, that broadly viewed, it can be conceived as societal waste. Feagin and Vera operationalize racism as comprised of rituals (the rites that accompany many racial practices), discrimination, mythology (i.e., ideological constructions taken on faith), a subjective component of "sincere fictions" developed by the dominant race to feel good about themselves, and an emotive component that they label as the "madness of racism."

Joe R. Feagin has recently refined this view in his *Racist America: Roots, Current Realities, and Future Reparations.* In this book Feagin concentrates in making the case that racism is systemic and rooted in real race relations. In language that fits nicely my own theorization, Feagin writes:

> Indeed, systematic racism is perpetuated by a broad social reproduction process that generates not only recurring patterns of discrimination within institutions and by individuals but also an alienating racist relationship—on the one hand, the racially oppressed, and on the other hand, the racial oppressors. These two groups are created by the racist system, and thus have different group interests. The former seeks to overthrow the system, while the latter seeks to maintain it.[51]

Feagin's and Vera's conceptualization of racism includes the core arguments of the theorization I advance here. First, they emphasize the systematic nature of racism. Second, they focus on the relational or group nature of the phenomenon. Finally, they point to the material (group interest) foundation of racism.

The only limitation I find in their theorization is their claim that racism produces "societal waste," a claim that Feagin seems to have dropped in his recent work. Although they are right in claiming that societies would be collectively better off (less wasteful) if the energy they spent to maintain racial hierarchy was used to increase the welfare of humanity, the notion of waste conveys the idea that racism is not "rational" (in the utilitarian sense of the word) for whites. In fact, in the conclusion of *White Racism*, Feagin and Vera contend that racism involves substantial material, moral, and psychological costs to whites. These claims are problematic. Materially racism provided the foundation for the expansion of the world-system and accumulation at a world scale for the West.[52] Although economists debate today whether racism increases or decreases the rate of capital accumulation and the welfare of white workers, I am persuaded by the analysis of Steven Shulman[53] who claims that racial stratification benefits both capitalists and white workers. It is precisely this material foundation which I contend helps keep racial stratification in place. Their claim that whites behave immorally when they participate in racist structures and experience a moral dilemma is important as a political tool but not as an analytical one. Whites do not experience moral dilemmas[54] precisely because they develop what Feagin and Vera label as "sincere fictions" that allow them to ignore the inhumanity of racial stratification. Finally, the psychological costs of racism to whites have not been well documented or measured. Nevertheless, social psychologist Tony R. Brown suggests in his recent work that if anything whites either benefit somewhat from racial stratification or at least do not lose from it.[55] Hence, from a world perspective racism is wasteful (the population of the world would be better off if racism did not exist), but at the micro level (whites in the world-system) it is and has been highly profitable. Despite this limitation, Feagin's and Vera's work is theoretically sophisticated, advances the core arguments of a structural or systemic understanding of racism, and provides an impressive documentation of contemporary racist practices in a variety of social spaces.

LIMITATIONS OF MAINSTREAM AND CRITICAL FRAMEWORKS ON RACISM

I list below the main limitations of the idealist conception of racism. Because not all limitations apply to the critical perspectives I review above, I point out the ones that do apply and to what extent.

1) ***Racism is excluded from the foundation or structure of the social system***. When racism is regarded as a baseless ideology ultimately dependent on other, "real" forces in society, the structure of the society itself is not classified as racist. The Marxist perspective is particularly guilty of this shortcoming. Although Marxists have addressed the question of the historical origin of racism, they explain its reproduction in an idealist fashion. Racism, in their account, is an ideology that emerged with chattel slavery and other forms of class oppression to justify the exploitation of people of color and survives as residue of the past.

Although the institutionalist, internal colonialism, and racial formation perspectives regard racism as a structural phenomenon and provide some useful ideas and concepts, none developed the theoretical apparatus necessary to describe how this structure operates.

2) ***Racism is ultimately viewed as a psychological phenomenon to be examined at the individual level***. The research agenda that follows from this conceptualization is the examination of individuals' attitudes to determine levels of racism in society.[56] Given that the constructs used to measure racism are static—that is, that there are a number of standard questions which do not change significantly over time—this research usually finds that racism is declining in society.[57]

This psychological understanding of racism is related to the limitation I cited above. If racism is not regarded as society-wide but as a property of individuals who are "racist" or "prejudiced," then (1) social institutions cannot be racist and (2) studying racism is simply a matter of clinically surveying populations to assess the proportion of "good" and "bad" individuals (those who hold racist beliefs).

Orthodox Marxists and many Neo-Marxists conceive of racism as an ideology that affects many members of the working class. Although the authors associated with the institutionalist, internal colonialist, and racial formation perspectives focus on the ideological character of racism, they all emphasize how this ideology becomes embedded or institutionalized in organizations and social practices.

3) *Racism is treated as a static phenomenon.* Racism is viewed as unchanging; that is, racism yesterday is like racism today. Thus, when a society's racial structure and its customary racial practices are rearticulated, this rearticulation is characterized as a decline in racism (Wilson), a natural process in a cycle (Park), an example of increased assimilation,[58] or effective "norm changes."[59] This limitation, which applies particularly to mainstream survey researchers on race and Marxist scholars, derives from not conceiving racism as having an independent structural foundation. If racism is merely a matter of ideas that has no material basis in contemporary society, then those ideas should be similar to their original configuration, whatever that was. The ideas may be articulated in a different context, but most analysts essentially believe that racist ideas remain the same. For this reason, with notable exceptions,[60] attitudinal research is still based on responses to questions developed in the 1940s, 1950s, and 1960s.

4) *Analysts defining racism in an idealist manner view racism as "incorrect" or "irrational thinking"; thus they label "racists" as irrational and rigid.* Because racism is conceived of as a belief with no real social basis, it follows that those who hold racist views must be irrational or stupid.[61] This view allows for a tactical distinction between individuals with the "pathology" and social actors who are "rational" and free of racism. The problem with this rationalistic view is twofold. First, it misses the rational, *material* elements on which racialized systems originally were built. Second, and more important, it neglects the possibility that contemporary racism still has a rational foundation. In this account, contemporary racists are perceived as Archie Bunkers. Among the critical frameworks reviewed here, only orthodox Marxism insists on the irrational and imposed character of racism. Neo-Marxists and authors associated with the institutionalist, internal colonialist, and racial formation perspectives insist, to varying degrees, on the rationality of racism. Neo-Marxists (e.g., Bonacich, Wolpe, Hall) and Omi and Winant acknowledge the short-term advantages that workers gain from racism; the institutionalist and internal colonial paradigms emphasize the systematic and long-term character of these advantages.

5) ***Racism is understood as overt behavior***. Because the idealist approach regards racism as "irrational" and "rigid," its manifestations should be quite evident, usually involving some degree of hostility. This does not present serious analytical problems for the study of certain periods in racialized societies when racial practices were overt (e.g., slavery and apartheid), but does for the analysis of racism in periods where racial practices are subtle, indirect, or fluid. For instance, many analysts have suggested that in contemporary America racial practices are manifested covertly[62] and racial attitudes tend to be symbolic.[63] Therefore, it is a waste of time to attempt to detect "racism" by asking questions such as "How strongly would you object if a member of your family wanted to bring a black friend home to dinner?"[64] Also, many such questions were developed to measure the extent of racist attitudes in the population during the Jim Crow era of race relations; they are not suitable for the post-1960s period.

Furthermore, this emphasis on overt behavior limits the possibility of analyzing racial phenomena in Latin American societies such as Brazil, Cuba, and Puerto Rico where race relations do not have a clear, overt character. The form of race relations—overt or covert—depends on the pattern of racialization that structured a particular society[65] and on how the process of racial contestation and other social dynamics affected that pattern.

6) ***Contemporary racism is viewed as an expression of "original sin"—as a remnant of past historical racial situations***. In the case of the United States, some analysts argue that racism preceded slavery and/or capitalism.[66] Others, such as Nathan Glazer and Moynihan, view it as the result of slavery.[67] Even promising new avenues of research, such as that presented by Roediger in *The Wages of Whiteness*, contemporary racism is viewed as one of the "*legacies* of white workerism."[68] By considering racism as a legacy all these analysts downplay the significance of its contemporary material foundation and structure.

Again the Marxist perspective shares this limitation. Marxists believe that racism developed in the fifteenth century and has been used since then by capitalists or white workers to further their own class interests. All other approaches recognize the historic significance of this "discovery" but associate contemporary racial ideology with contemporary racially based inequalities.

7) ***Racism is analyzed in a circular manner***. "If racism is defined as the behavior that results from the belief, its discovery becomes ensnared in a circularity—racism is a belief that produces behavior, which is itself racism."[69] Racism is established by racist behavior, which itself is proved by the existence of racism. This circularity results from not grounding racism in social relations among the races. If racism, viewed as an ideology, were seen as possessing a structural[70] foundation, its examination could be associated with racial practices rather than with mere ideas and the problem of circularity would be avoided.

RACIALIZED SOCIAL SYSTEM APPROACH TO RACISM

In order to capture the society-wide, organized, and institutional character of racism I build my alternative theorization around the notion of racialized social systems.[71] This term refers to societies in which economic, political, social, and ideological levels are partially structured by the placement of actors in racial categories or races. Races typically are identified by their phenotype, but (as we see later) the selection of some human traits to designate a racial group is always socially rather than biologically based.

These systems are structured *partially* by race because modern social systems incorporate two or more forms of hierarchical patterns. Although processes of racialization are always embedded in other forms of hierarchy, they acquire autonomy and have independent social effects. This implies that the phenomenon which has been conceived as a free-floating ideology in fact has its own structural foundation.

In all racialized social systems the placement of actors in racial categories involves some form of hierarchy[72] that produces definite social relations between the races. The race placed in the superior position tends to receive greater economic remuneration and access to better occupations and prospects in the labor market, occupies a primary position in the political system, is granted higher social estimation (e.g., is viewed as "smarter" or "better looking"), often has the license to draw physical (segregation) as well as social (racial etiquette) boundaries between itself and other races, and receives what DuBois called a "psychological wage."[73] The totality of these racialized social relations and practices constitutes the racial structure of a society.

Although all racialized social systems are hierarchical, the particular character of the hierarchy, and, thus, of the racial structure, is variable. For example, the domination of blacks in the United States was achieved through dictatorial means during slavery, but in the post–civil rights period this domination has been *hegemonic*.[74] Similarly, the forms of securing domination and white privilege are variable too. For instance, the racial practices and mechanisms that kept blacks subordinated changed from overt and eminently racist in the Jim Crow era to covert and indirectly racist in the contemporary period. The unchanging element of these systems is racial inequality—that the subordinated races' life chances are significantly lower than those of the dominant race. This is the feature that ultimately distinguishes this form of hierarchical social organization. Generally, the higher the level of racial inequality, the more racialized the social system, and vice versa.

Because the races receive different social rewards at all levels, they develop different interests which can be detected in their struggles to either transform or maintain a particular racial order. These interests are collective rather than individual, are based on relations between races rather than on particular group needs, and are practical; that is, they are related to concrete struggles.

Although the races' general interests may ultimately lie in the complete elimination of a society's racial structure, its array of alternatives may not include that possibility. For instance, the historical struggle against chattel slavery led not to the development of race-free societies but to the establishment of social systems with a different kind of racialization. Race-free societies were not among the available alternatives because the nonslave populations had the capacity to preserve some type of racial privilege. The historical "exceptions" occurred in racialized societies in which the nonslaves' power was almost completely superseded by that of the slave population.[75]

A simple criticism of the argument I have advanced so far is that it ignores the internal divisions of the races along class and gender lines. Such criticism, however, does not deal squarely with the issue at hand. The fact that not all members of the dominant race receive the same level of rewards and (conversely) that not all members of the subordinate race or races are at the bottom of the social order does not negate the fact that races, as social groups, are in either a superordinate or a subordinate position in a social system. Historically the racialization of social systems did not imply the exclusion of other forms of oppression. In fact, racialization occurred in social formations also structured by class and gender. Hence, in these societies, the racialization of subjects is fragmented along class and gender lines. The important question—which interests move actors to struggle?—is historically contingent and cannot be ascertained a priori.[76] Depending on the character of racialization in a social order, class interests may take precedence over racial interests as in contemporary Brazil, Cuba, and Puerto Rico. In other situations, racial interests may take precedence over class interests as in the case of blacks throughout most of the United States' history.

In general, the systemic salience of class in relation to race increases when the economic, political, and social inequality between the races decreases substantially. Yet this broad argument generates at least one warning: the narrowing of within-class differences between racial actors usually causes *more* rather than *less* racial conflict, at least in the short run, as the competition for resources increases.[77] More significantly, even when class-based conflict becomes more salient in a social order, this cannot be interpreted as prima facie evidence that race has subsided as a social factor. For instance, because of the way in which Latin American racial formations rearticulated race and racial discourse in the nineteenth century post-emancipation era,[78] these societies silenced from above the political space for public racial contestation. Yet, more than 100 years after these societies developed the myth of racial democracy they have *more* rather than *less* racial inequality than countries such as the United States.[79]

Because racial actors are also classed and gendered (belong to class and gender groups), analysts must control for class and gender to ascertain the material advantages enjoyed by a dominant race. In a racialized society such as ours, the independent effects of race are assessed by analysts who (1) compare data between whites and nonwhites in the *same* class and gender positions, (2) evaluate the proportion as well as the general character of the races' participation in some domain of life, and (3) examine racial data at all levels—social, political, economic, and ideological—to ascertain the general position of racial groups in a social system.

The first of these procedures has become standard practice in sociology. No serious sociologist would present racial statistics without controlling for gender and class (or at least the class of persons' socioeconomic status). By doing this, analysts assume they can measure the unadulterated effects of "discrimination" manifested in unexplained "residuals." Despite its usefulness, however, this technique provides only a partial account of the "race effect" because (1) a significant amount of racial data cannot be retrieved through surveys and (2) the technique of "controlling for" a variable neglects the obvious—why a group is over- or underrepresented in certain categories of the control variables in the first place.[80] Moreover, these analysts presume that it is possible to analyze the amount of discrimination in one domain (e.g., income, occupational status) "without analyzing the extent to which discrimination also affects the factors they hold constant."[81] Hence to evaluate "race effects" in any domain, analysts must attempt to make sense of their findings in relation to a race's standing on other domains.

But what is the nature of races or, more properly, of racialized social groups? Omi and Winant state that races are the outcome of the racialization process, which they define as "the extension of racial meaning to a previously racially unclassified relationship, social practice or group."[82] Historically the classification of a people in racial terms has been a highly political act associated with practices such as conquest and colonization, enslavement, peonage, indentured servitude, and, more recently, colonial and neocolonial labor immigration. Categories such as "Indians" and "Negroes" were invented in the sixteenth and seventeenth centuries to justify the conquest and exploitation of various peoples.[83] The invention of such categories entails a dialectical process of construction; that is, the creation of the category "Other" involves the creation of a category "Same." If "Indians" are depicted as "savages," Europeans are characterized as "civilized"; if "blacks" are defined as natural candidates for slavery, "whites" are defined as free subjects.[84] Yet although the racialization of peoples was socially invented and did not override previous forms of social distinction based on class or gender, it did not lead to imaginary relations but generated new forms of human association with definite status differences. After the process of attaching meaning to a "people" is instituted, race becomes a real category of group association and identity.[85]

Because racial classifications partially organize and limit actors' life chances, racial practices of opposition emerge. Regardless of the form of racial interaction (overt, covert, or inert), races can be recognized in the realm of racial relations and positions. Viewed in this light, races are the effect of racial practices of opposition ("we" versus "them") at the economic, political, social, and ideological levels.[86]

Races, as most social scientists acknowledge, are not biologically but socially determined categories of identity and group association. In this regard, they are analogous to class and gender.[87] Actors in racial positions do not occupy those positions because they are of X or Y race, but because X or Y has been socially defined as a race. Actors' phenotypical (i.e., biologically inherited) characteristics, such as skin tone and hair color and texture, are usually, although not always, used to denote racial distinctions.[88] For example, Jews in many European nations and the Irish in England have been treated as racial groups.[89] Also, Indians in the United States have been viewed as one race despite the tremendous phenotypical and cultural variation among nations. Because races are socially constructed, both the meaning and the position assigned to races in the racial structure are always contested. What and who is to be black or white or Indian reflects and affects the social, political, ideological, and economic struggles between the races. The global effects of these struggles can change the meaning of the racial categories as well as the position of a racialized group in a social formation.

This latter point is illustrated clearly by the historical struggles of several "white ethnic" groups in the United States in their efforts to become accepted as legitimate whites or "Americans."[90] Neither light-skinned—nor, for that matter, dark-skinned—immigrants necessarily came to this country as members of X or Y race. Light-skinned Europeans, after brief periods of "not-yet white," became "white" but did not lose their "ethnic" character.[91] Their struggle for inclusion had specific implications: racial inclusion as members of the white community allowed Americanization and class mobility. On the other hand, among dark-skinned immigrants from Africa, Latin America, and the Caribbean, the struggle was to avoid classification as "black." These immigrants challenged the reclassification of their identity for a simple reason: in the United States "black" signified a subordinate status in society. Hence many of these groups struggled to keep their own ethnic or cultural identity, as denoted in expressions such as "I am not black; I am Jamaican," or "I am not black; I am Senegalese."[92] Yet eventually many of these groups resolved this contradictory situation by accepting the duality of their social classification as black in the United States while retaining and nourishing their own cultural or ethnic heritage—a heritage deeply influenced by African traditions.

Although the content of racial categories changes over time through manifold processes and struggles, race is not a secondary category of group association. The meaning of black and white, the "racial formation," changes within the larger racial structure. This does not mean that the racial structure is immutable and completely independent of the action of racialized actors. It means only that the social relations between the races become institutionalized

(form a structure as well as a culture) and affect their social life whether individual members of the races want it or not. In Barth's words, "Ethnic identity
implies a series of constraints on the kinds of roles an individual is allowed to
play [and] is similar to sex and rank, in that it constrains the incumbent in all his
activities."[93] For instance, free blacks during the slavery period struggled to
change the meaning of "blackness," and specifically to dissociate it from slavery. Yet they could not escape the larger racial structure that restricted their life
chances and their freedom.[94]

The placement of a group of people in a racial category stemmed initially[95]
from the interests of powerful actors in the social system (e.g., the capitalist
class, the planter class, colonizers). After racial categories were employed to
organize social relations in societies, however, race became an independent
element of the operation of the social system. Here I depart from analysts such
as Jordan, Robinson, and Miles, who take the mere existence of a racial discourse as manifesting the presence of a racial order.[96] Such a position allows
them to speak of racism in medieval times (Jordan) and to classify the
antipeasant views of French urbanites (Miles) or the prejudices of the aristoc-
racy against peasants in the Middle Ages (Robinson) as expressions of racism.
In my view, we can speak of racialized orders only when a racial discourse
is accompanied by social relations of subordination and superordination
between the races. The available evidence suggests that the racialization of
the world-system emerged after the imperialist expansion of Europe to the
New World and Africa.[97] Furthermore, this racialization led to the development of what Charles W. Mills calls *global white supremacy* (racial orders
structured along the axis of "white"/European and "nonwhite"/non-European)
in the world-system.

What are the dynamics of racial issues in racialized systems? Most important, after a social formation is racialized, its "normal" dynamics always
include a racial component. Societal struggles based on class or gender contain a racial component because both of these social categories are also racialized; that is, both class and gender are constructed along racial lines. In 1922,
for example, white South African workers in the middle of a strike inspired by
the Russian revolution rallied under the slogan "Workers of the world unite for
a white South Africa." One of the state's "concessions" to this "class" struggle
was the passage of the Apprenticeship Act of 1922, "which prevented Black
workers acquiring apprenticeships."[98] In another example, the struggle of
women in the United States to attain their civil and human rights has always
been plagued by deep racial tensions.[99]

Nonetheless, some of the strife that exists in a racialized social formation
has a distinct racial character; I call such strife as racial contestation—the struggle of racial groups for systemic changes regarding their position at one or
more levels. Such a struggle may be social (Who can be here? Who belongs
here?), political (Who can vote? How much power should they have? Should

they be citizens?), economic (Who should work, and what should they do? They are taking our jobs!), or ideological (Black is beautiful! The term designating people of African descent in the United States has changed from Negro to black to African American).

Although much of this contestation is expressed at the individual level and is disjointed, sometimes it becomes collective and general, and can effect meaningful systemic changes in a society's racial organization. The form of contestation may be relatively passive and subtle (e.g., in situations of fundamental overt racial domination such as slavery and apartheid) or more active and more overt (e.g., in quasi-democratic situations such as the contemporary United States). As a rule, however, fundamental changes in racialized social systems are accompanied by struggles that reach the point of overt protest.[100] This does not mean that a violent racially based revolution is the only way of accomplishing effective changes in the relative position of racial groups. It is a simple extension of the argument that social systems and their supporters must be "shaken" if fundamental transformations are to take place.[101] On this structural foundation rests the phenomenon labeled racism by social scientists.

I reserve the term racial ideology for the segment of the ideological structure of a social system that crystallizes racial notions and stereotypes. Racial ideology provides the rationalizations for social, political, and economic interactions between the races. Depending on the particular character of a racialized social system and on the struggles of the subordinated races, racial ideology may be developed highly (as in apartheid) or loosely (as in slavery) and its content expressed in overt or covert terms.

Although racial ideology originates in race relations, it acquires relative autonomy in the social system and performs practical functions.[102] In Gilroy's words, racial ideology "mediates the world of agents and the structures which are created by their social praxis."[103] Racism crystallizes the changing "dogma" on which actors in the social system operate, and becomes "common sense"; it provides the rules for perceiving and dealing with the "other" in a racialized society. In the United States, for instance, because racial notions about what blacks and whites are or ought to be pervade their encounters, whites still have difficulty in dealing with black bankers, lawyers, professors, and doctors.[104] Thus, although racist ideology is ultimately false, it fulfills a practical role in racialized societies.

At this point it is possible to sketch the elements of the racialized social system framework presented here. First, racialized social systems are societies that allocate differential economic, political, social, and even psychological rewards to groups along racial lines; lines that are socially constructed. After a society becomes racialized, a set of social relations and practices based on racial distinctions develops at all societal levels. I designate the aggregate of those relations and practices as the racial structure of a society. Second, races historically are constituted according to the process of racialization; they become the effect of relations of opposition between racialized groups at all levels of a social formation. Third, on the basis of this structure, there developed a racial ideology. This ideology is not simply a "superstructural" phenomenon (a mere reflection of the racialized system) but becomes the organizational map that guides actions of racial actors in society. It becomes as real as the racial relations it organizes. Fourth, most struggles in a racialized social system contain a racial component, but sometimes they acquire and/or exhibit a distinct racial character. Racial contestation is the logical outcome of a society with a racial hierarchy. A social formation that includes some form of racialization will always exhibit some form of racial contestation. Finally, the process of racial contestation reveals the different objective interests of the races in a racialized social system.

CONCLUSION

My central argument in this chapter has been that the commonsense understanding of racism, which is not much different than the definition developed by mainstream social scientists or even by many critical analysts, does not provide an adequate theoretical foundation for understanding racial phenomena. With notable exceptions,[105] analysts in academia are still entangled in ungrounded ideological interpretations of racism. Lacking a structural view, they tend to reduce racial phenomena to a derivation of the class structure (as Marxist interpreters do) or the result of an irrational ideology (as mainstream social scientists do).

In the racialized social system framework developed here, I suggest, as Omi and Winant, that racism should be studied from the viewpoint of racialization. I contend that after a society becomes racialized, racialization develops a life of its own.[106] Although racism interacts with class and gender structurations in society, it becomes an organizing principle of social relations in itself. Race, as most analysts suggest, is a social construct, but that construct, like class and gender, has independent effects in social life. After racial stratification is established, race becomes an independent criterion for vertical hierarchy in society. Therefore different races experience positions of subordination and superordination in society and develop different interests.

The framework for studying racial orders presented here has the following advantages over traditional views of racism:

Racial phenomena are regarded as the "normal" outcome of the racial structure of a society. Thus we can account for all racial manifestations. Instead of explaining racial phenomena as deriving from other structures or from racism (conceived of as a free-floating ideology), we can trace cultural, political, economic, social, and even psychological racial phenomena to the racial organization of that society. The changing nature of what analysts label "racism" is explained as the normal outcome of racial contestation in a racialized social system. In this framework, changes in racism are explained rather than described. Changes are due to specific struggles at different levels among the races, resulting from differences in interests. Such changes may transform the nature of racialization and the global character of racial relations in the system (the racial structure). Therefore, change is viewed as a normal component of the racialized system.

The racialized social system framework allows analysts to explain overt as well as covert racial behavior. The covert or overt nature of racial contacts depends on how the process of racialization is manifested; this in turn depends on how race originally was articulated in a social formation and on the process of racial contestation. This point implies that rather than conceiving of racism as a universal and uniformly orchestrated phenomenon, analysts should study "historically specific racisms."[107] This insight is not new; Robert Park, Oliver Cox, van den Bergue, and Marvin Harris described varieties of "situations of race relations" with distinct forms of racial interaction.

Racially motivated behavior, whether or not the actors are conscious of it, is regarded as "rational"—that is, as based on the races' different interests.[108] This framework accounts for Archie Bunker–type racial behavior as well as for more "sophisticated" varieties of racial conduct. Racial phenomena are viewed as systemic; therefore all actors in the system participate in racial affairs. Some members of the dominant racial group tend to exhibit less virulence toward members of the subordinated races because they have greater control over the form and the outcome of their racial interactions. When they cannot control that interaction—as in the case of revolts, general threats to whites, blacks moving into "their" neighborhood—they behave much like other members of the dominant race.

The reproduction of racial phenomena in contemporary societies is explained in this framework not by reference to a long-distant past but in relation to its contemporary structure. Because racism is viewed as systemic (possessing a racial structure) and as organized around the races' different interests, racial aspects of social systems today are viewed as fundamentally related to hierarchical relations between the races in those systems. Elimination of the racialized character of a social system entails the end of racialization, and hence of races altogether. This argument clashes with social scientists' most popular policy prescription for "curing" racism, namely education. This "solution" is the logical outcome of defining racism as a belief. Most analysts regard racism as a matter of individuals subscribing to an irrational view, thus the cure is educating them to realize that racism is wrong. Education is also the choice "pill" prescribed by Marxists for healing workers from racism. The alternative theorization offered here implies that because the phenomenon has structural consequences for the races, the only way to "cure" society of racism is by eliminating its systemic roots. Whether this can be accomplished democratically or only through revolutionary means is an open question, and one that depends on the particular racial structure of the society in question.

A racialization framework accounts for the ways in which racial/ethnic stereotypes emerge, are transformed, and disappear. Racial stereotypes are crystallized at the ideological level of a social system. These images ultimately indicate—although in distorted ways—and justify the stereotyped group's position in a society. Stereotypes may originate out of (1) material realities or conditions endured by the group, (2) genuine ignorance about the group, or (3) rigid, distorted views on the group's physical, cultural, or moral nature. Once they emerge, however, stereotypes must relate—although not necessarily fit it perfectly—to the group's true social position in the racialized system if they are to perform their ideological function. Stereotypes that do not tend to reflect a group's situation do not work and are bound to disappear. For example, notions of the Irish as stupid or of Jews as athletically talented have all but vanished since the 1940s, as the Irish moved up the educational ladder and Jews gained access to multiple routes to social mobility. Generally, then, stereotypes are reproduced because they reflect the group's distinct position and status in society. As a corollary, racial or ethnic notions about a group disappear only when the group's status mirrors that of the dominant racial or ethnic group in the society.

The framework developed here is not a universal theory explaining racial phenomena in societies. It is intended to trigger a serious discussion of how race shapes social systems. Moreover, the important question of how race interacts and intersects with class and gender has not yet been addressed satisfactorily. Provisionally I maintain that a nonfunctionalist reading of the concept of social system may give us clues for comprehending societies "structured in dominance," to use Stuart Hall's term. If societies are viewed as systems that articulate different structures (organizing principles on which sets of social relations are systematically patterned), it is possible to claim that race—as well as gender—has both individual and combined (interaction) effects in society.

To test the usefulness of the racialized social system framework as a theoretical basis for research, we must perform comparative work on racialization in various societies. One of the main objectives of this comparative work should be to determine what are the specific mechanisms, practices, and social relations that produce and reproduce racial inequality at all levels—that is, uncover the society's racial structure. Unlike analysts who believe that "racism" has withered away, I argue that the persistent inequality experienced by blacks and other racial minorities in the United States today is due to the *continued* albeit *changed* existence of a racial structure. In contrast to race relations in the Jim Crow period, however, racial practices that reproduce racial inequality in contemporary America (1) are increasingly covert, (2) are embedded in normal operations of institutions, 3) avoid direct racial terminology, and (4) are invisible to most whites.

NOTES

1. Ruth F. Benedict, *Race and Racism* (London: Routledge & Kegan Paul, 1945), 85.

2. Pierre van den Berghe, *Race and Racism: A Comparative Perspective* (New York: John Wiley & Sons, 1967), my emphasis, 11.

3. Richard T. Schaefer, *Racial and Ethnic Minorities* (Glencoe, IL: Scott/Foresman/Little Brown Higher Education, 1990), 16.

4. A review such as this one is necessarily incomplete. I leave out the important work of European writers such as Paul Gilroy and Pierre A. Taguieff as well as the work of Latin American writers such as Florestan Fernandes, Carlos Hansenbalg, and Nelson do Valle Silva.

5. Stanley Aronowitz, *The Politics of Identity: Class, Culture, Social Movements* (New York: Routledge, 1992).

6. One of the best representatives of the orthodox Marxist view on race and racism is Victor Perlo, *Economics of Racism U.S.A.: Roots of Black Inequality* (New York: International Publishers, 1975). But alongside this orthodox view, some African American Marxists like W. E. B. DuBois, C. L. R. James, and, more recently, Manning Marable and Robin G. Kelley have questioned the simplistic analysis of racism of their white counterparts. For particularly biting criticisms of the traditional Marxist view on racial matters see James Boggs, *Racism and the Class Struggle* (New York: Monthly Review Press, 1970); Robert L. Allen, *Reluctant Reformers* (Washington: Howard University Press, 1974); and Harold Cruse, *Rebellion or Revolution* (New York: William Morrow & Company, Inc., 1968).

7. Albert Szymanski, *Class Structure: A Critical Perspective* (New York: Praeger Publishers, 1983), 402.

8. Despite my multiple disagreements with Cox's approach to race, I regard his *oeuvre* as phenomenal, particularly considering that he did most of his work under Jim Crow. In his *Caste, Class, and Race* (New York: Doubleday, 1948), Cox developed a competent class analysis of post–World War II class matters in the United States and elsewhere. Although I disagree with the essence of his racial analysis in this book, I agree with much of his critique of Myrdal's work, the caste-school of race relations, and think that his analysis of lynching is brilliant. I also believe that he should receive more credit for his world-system analysis. On this latter matter, see his *The Foundations of Capitalism* (New York: Philosophical Library, 1959).

9. Cox, *Caste, Class, and Race*, 393.

10. Ibid.: 330.

11. Ibid.: 336.

12. Edna Bonacich, "A Theory of Ethnic Antagonism: The Split Labor Market Approach," *American Sociological Review* 37:547–59. See also her "Advanced Capitalism and Black/White Relations in the United States: A Split Labor Market Interpre-

tation," in *The Sociology of Race Relations: Reflection and Reform*, edited by T. Petti-grew (New York: Free Press, 1980).

13. Bonacich, "A Theory of Ethnic Antagonism," 343–44.

14. Ibid.: 347. This argument strikes me as blaming the victim in disguise. For two excellent alternative Marxist readings of why blacks did not join unions with their "brothers and sisters," see Philip Foner's excellent *Organized Labor and the Black Worker, 1619–1981* (1981); and David Roediger's *The Wages of Whiteness: Race and the Making of the American Working Class* (1991). For a more recent book showing the racialized character of working-class politics, see Michael Goldfield's *The Color of Politics: Race and the Mainsprings of American Politics* (1997).

15. Bonacich downplays interpretations of this "resistance" based on racial preju-dice against blacks. Therefore, she explains the race riots that occurred in the 1919–1940 period as expressions of class protectionism from whites facing "threats" from black workers. This interpretation naturalizes the racist white view symbolized in the statement *"they* are taking *our* jobs" and ignores the racial aspect of class for-mation (see Roediger's *The Wages of Whiteness,* 1992). On this point, black historian Carter G. Woodson, *The Negro in Our History* (Washington, DC: Associated Publish-ers, 1947), commented a long time ago that:

> As Negroes in the North and West, therefore, were pitted against the trades unions, they engendered much feeling between the races by allying themselves with the capitalists to serve as strikebreakers. In this case, however, *the trades unions themselves were to be blamed.* The only time the Negroes could work under such circumstance was when the whites were striking, and it is not sur-prising that some of them easily yielded then to the temptation. In those unions in which the Negroes were recognized, they stood with their white co-workers in every instance of making a reasonable demand of their employers. Some of these unions, however, accepted Negroes merely as a subterfuge to prevent them from engaging in strikebreaking. When the Negroes appealed for work, identifying themselves as members of the union in control, they were turned away with the subterfuge that no vacancies existed, while at the same time white men were gladly received (My emphasis, 439).

16. Bonacich, "A Theory of Ethnic Antagonism," 358. For a more nuanced Marxist analysis of race in the post-1930s, see Jill Quadagno's *The Color of Welfare: How Racism Undermined the War on Poverty* (New York: Oxford University Press, 1994).

17. A few European Marxists (e.g., John Solomos, Harold Wolpe, Robert Miles, and Paul Gilroy), following the pivotal work of Stuart Hall, have attempted to over-come the limitation of orthodox Marxism as it pertains to racial matters. Yet, despite providing some honest indictments of the class-reductionist reading of racial phe-nomena, these analysts share many of the limitations of orthodox Marxists. For example, they still give primacy to the class structure by conceiving the context of racialization as purely capitalist. They also stress a priori class as the central organiz-ing principle of societies and, hence, regard race as a secondary element that frac-tures or stratifies classes. Finally, they still interpret racism as a fundamentally ideological phenomenon.

18. On this point, see Omi's and Winant's biting critique in *Racial Formation in the United States.*

19. Some of the premier authors in this tradition are Stokely Carmichael and Charles Hamilton, *Black Power: The Politics of Liberation in America* (New York: Vintage Books, 1967); Louis Knowles and Kenneth Prewitt, *Institutional Racism in America* (Paterson, NJ: Prentice Hall, 1969); Mark Chesler, "Contemporary Sociological Theories of Racism," in *Towards the Elimination of Racism*, edited by Phyllis A. Katz, 21–71 (New York: Pergamon, 1976); David Wellman, *Portraits of White Racism* (Cambridge, England: Cambridge University Press, 1977); and Rodolfo Alvarez, Kenneth G. Lutterman, and Associates, *Discrimination in Organizations: Using Social Indicators to Manage Social Change* (San Francisco, CA: Jossey-Bass, 1979).

20. Carmichael and Hamilton, *Black Power*, 3.

21. Chesler, "Contemporary Sociological Theories of Racism," 22.

22. See, particularly, Knowles and Prewitt, *Institutional Racism in America*.

23. This point has been raised by Miles, *Racism*.

24. My emphasis. Carmichael and Hamilton, *Black Power*, 5.

25. If everything is or can be conceived as "racist," then the term has no boundaries; phenomena of clearly class, gender, or pertaining to any other form of social association are reduced to race. In political terms, the assumption that all whites are racists led to a suicidal political strategy (particularly for blacks in the United States) where coalition politics were basically dismissed (see chapter 3 in Carmichael and Hamilton, 1967). Yet, Miles goes too far here. This view did help blacks to mobilize, organize, and rally behind the (ill-defined) notion of black power.

26. For an example of the negative *racialization* experienced by the Irish in Ireland, see Theodore W. Allen, *The Invention of the White Race* (London and New York: Verso, 1994).

27. This point has been raised by Omi and Winant, *Racial Formation in the United States*.

28. Despite the radicalism of Carmichael's and Hamilton's approach, their book is written within the pluralist view of power so popular among political scientists. That is why they seem content with advocating for a power-sharing nationalist electoral strategy as if this were possible in a social formation where power is *structurally* based and organized around racial, class, and gender group—level domination. For a fascinating critique of myopic nationalist perspectives (whether Afrocentric, Islam-centered, or elite-based), see Rod Bush, *We Are Not What We Seem: Black Nationalism and Class Struggle in the American Century* (New York: New York University Press, 1999). See also Wahneema Lubiano, "Black Nationalism and Black Common Sense," in *The House That Race Built*, edited by Wahneema Lubiano, 232–52 (New York: Pantheon Books, 1997).

29. Joan W. Moore, "Colonialism: The Case of the Mexican-Americans," *Social Problems* 17 (1970), 463–72; Mario Barrera, *Race and Class in the Southwest: A Theory of Racial Inequality* (Notre Dame, IN: University of Notre Dame Press, 1979); Robert Blauner, *Racial Oppression in America*, New York: Harper & Row, 1972).

30. Blauner advanced several definitions of racism in his book. The most comprehensive regarded racism as "a principle of social domination by which a group seen as inferior in alleged biological characteristics is exploited, controlled, and oppressed socially and psychically by a superordinate group" (1972: 84).

31. Blauner, *Racial Oppression in America*, 22.

32. Ibid.: 21.

33. Ibid.: 23.

34. On race cycles, see Robert E. Park, *Race and Culture.* On ethnic patterns, see Nathan Glazer and Daniel P. Moynihan, *Beyond the Melting Pot* (Cambridge, MA: MIT Press, 1970).

35. Blauner, *Racial Oppression in America,* 10.

36. On this matter Blauner stated the following:

The liberal-humanist value that violence is the worst sin cannot be defended today if one is committed squarely against racism and for self-determination. Some violence is almost inevitable in the decolonization process; unfortunately racism in America has been so effective that the greatest power Afro-Americans wield today is the power to disrupt (1972: 104).

37. Blauner was very aware of this limitation and said so in the introduction to his book. What was needed was a "new theoretical model . . . based on the combined existence of, historical interaction, and mutual interpenetration of the colonial-racial and the capitalist class realities" given that "America is clearly a mixed society that might be termed colonial capitalist or racial capitalist" (1972: 13). Mario Barrera attempted to deal with this limitation by suggesting that there is an interactive class and race structure and that racial minorities constitute subordinated segments or fractions of all the classes in the structure (1979).

38. Omi and Winant, *Racial Formation in the United States;* Wilson, *The Truly Disadvantaged* and *When Work Disappears.*

39. Omi and Winant, *Racial Formation in the United States,* 61.

40. Ibid.: 23.

41. Ibid.: 64.

42. In Winant's recent book, *Racial Conditions,* the fundamentally political character of racialization is attributed to the fact that "elites, popular movements, state agencies, cultural and religious organizations, and intellectuals of all types develop *racial projects,* which interpret and reinterpret the meaning of race. . . . These projects are often explicitly, but always implicitly, political" (Minneapolis: University of Minnesota Press 1994), 24.

43. The other important theoretical spring of radical writings on race in this period has been Stuart Hall.

44. One of the earliest statements on the constructionist character of race, is found in Max Weber, "Ethnic Groups," in *Economy and Society,* edited by Herbert Roth and Claus Wittich (Berkeley, CA: University of California Press, 1978).

45. In Winant's *Racial Conditions* (1994) he comes close to enunciating a structural conception of race. He criticizes the purely ideological conception of race because it fails to: 1) appreciate the significance that a construct can acquire over a thousand years of existence and 2) recognize that race shapes our identity and everyday experiences (16). However, Winant eschews a truly structural reading of race because he thinks such a reading would *reify* the category. As I argue in this chapter, an *objective* understanding of race (similar to the case of class or gender) based upon the notion that these social groups have *different* interests does not necessarily entail *freezing* the content or meaning of the category itself.

46. Omi and Winant, *Racial Formation in the United States,* 55.

47. Omi and Winant define *racial projects* as "simultaneously an interpretation,

representation, or explanation of racial dynamics, and an effort to reorganize and redistribute resources along particular racial lines" (56).

48. Op. cit.: 66.

49. This problem is partially addressed in Howard Winant's *Racial Conditions* through the Gramscian concept of *hegemony* which he defines as "a form of rule that operates by constructing its subjects and incorporating contestation" (113). According to Winant, this form of rule prevails in most "modern" societies and organizes, among other things, cleavages based on class, race, and gender.

50. Their emphasis. Joe R. Feagin and Hernán Vera, *White Racism* (New York and London: Routledge, 1995), 7.

51. Joe R. Feagin, *Racist America* (London: Routledge, 2000), 6.

52. This is the argument of authors in the dependency and world-system tradition. It is also the argument of Cedric Robinson in *Black Marxism* and Charles Mills.

53. See his work in Steven Shulman and William Darity, Jr., *The Question of Discrimination: Racial Inequality in the U.S. Labor Market* (Middletown, CT: Wesleyan University Press, 1989). For the opposite argument, see Michael Reich, *Racial Inequality: A Political-Economic Analysis* (Princeton, NJ: Princeton University Press, 1981).

54. For a critique of the moral interpretation of racial matters, see Lawrence Bobo, James Kluegel, and Ryan Smith, "Laissez-Faire Racism: The Crystallization of a Kinder, Gentler, Antiblack Ideology," in *Racial Attitudes in the 1990s*, edited by Steven A. Tuch and Jack K. Martin, 15–42 (Westport, CT: Praeger, 1997).

55. See Tony Brown, "'Being Black and Feeling Blue': The Mental Health Consequences of Racial Discrimination," in *Race & Society* 2(2) (2000): 117–31.

56. Examples of this approach are Howard Schuman et al., *Racial Attitudes in America* (Cambridge, MA: Harvard University Press, 1997); Paul Sniderman and Thomas Piazza, *The Scare of Race* (Cambridge, MA: Harvard University Press, 1993).

57. This is the finding of analysts such as Sniderman in his various books as well as that of Glenn Firebaugh and Kenneth E. Davis, "Trends in Antiblack Prejudice, 1972–1984," *American Journal of Sociology* 94 (1988): 251–74.

58. See John Rex, *Race, Colonialism, and the City* (London: Routledge, 1973) and *Race Relations in Sociological Theory* (London: Weidenfeld and Nicoloson, 1986).

59. This has been Howard Schuman's argument for a long time. For statements of this argument, see any of the editions of *Racial Attitudes in America*.

60. There is now an explosion of survey-based authors fighting this individualistic tradition. See, for example, Donald R. Kinder and Lynn Sanders, *Divided by Color* (Chicago: University of Chicago Press, 1996), and most of the authors in *Racialized Politics*, edited by David O. Sears, Jim Sidanius, and Lawrence Bobo (Chicago: University of Chicago Press, 2000).

61. This tradition is very old, but was clearly stated in Theodore W. Adorno et al., *The Authoritarian Personality* (New York: Harper & Row. 1950). See also Gordon W. Allport, *The Nature of Prejudice* (New York: Doubleday, 1958). For excellent critiques, see Blauner, *Racial Oppression in America,* and David Wellman, *Portrait of White Racism.*

62. Roy Brooks, *Rethinking the American Race Problem*; Robert C. Smith, *Racism in the Post–Civil Rights Era.*

63. For early statements of this view, see David O. Sears and Donald R. Kinder, "Racial Tensions and Voting in Los Angeles," in *Los Angeles: Viability and Prospects*

for Metropolitan Leadership, edited by Werner Z. Hirsch, 51–88 (New York: Praeger, 1971). For a mature review of the symbolic racism tradition, see David O. Sears, "Symbolic Racism," in *Eliminating Racism: Profiles in Controversy,* edited by P. A. Katz and D. A. Taylor, 53–84 (New York: Plenum, 1988).

64. This question is used by NORC and has been employed by Schuman et al. (1997).

65. This point has been made by Oliver Cox, *Caste, Class, and Race*; Marvin Harris, *Patterns of Race Relations in the Americas* (New York: Walker, 1964); John Rex, *Race Relations in Sociological Theory*; and Pierre van den Berghe, *Race and Racism: A Comparative Perspective* (New York: John Wiley & Sons, 1967).

66. Winthrop Jordan, *White over Black: American Attitudes toward the Negro* (New York: W. W. Norton, 1968); Manning Marable, *How Capitalism Underdeveloped Black America* (Boston: South End Press, 2000 [1983]); Cedric J. Robinson, *Black Marxism: The Making of the Black Radical Tradition* (London: Zed, 1983).

67. Glazer and Moynihan, *Beyond the Melting Pot.*

68. Roediger, *The Wages of Whiteness,* 176.

69. This quote comes from Yehudi O. Webster's otherwise fruitless book, *The Racialization of America* (New York: St. Martin's, 1992), 84.

70. By *structure* I mean, following Joseph Whitmeyer, "the networks of (interactional) relationships among actors as well as the distributions of socially meaningful characteristics of actors and aggregates of actors": "Why Actors Are Integral to Structural Analysis," *Sociological Theory* 12:153–65, 154. For similar but more complex conceptions of the term, which are relational and that incorporate the agency of actors, see Pierre Bourdieu, *Distinction* (Cambridge, MA: Harvard University Press, 1984); and William H. Sewell, Jr., "A Theory of Structure: Duality, Agency, and Transformation," *American Journal of Sociology* 98 (1992): 1–29. I reserve the term *material* to refer to the economic, social, political, or ideological rewards or penalties received by social actors for their participation (whether willing, unwilling, or indifferent) in social structural arrangements.

71. All racialized social systems operate along white supremacist lines. See Mills, *Blackness Visible* (Ithaca, NY: Cornell University Press, 1998).

72. I make a distinction between race and ethnicity. Ethnicity has a primarily sociocultural foundation, and ethnic groups have exhibited tremendous malleability in terms of who belongs. In contrast, racial ascriptions (initially) are imposed externally to justify the collective exploitation of a people and are maintained to preserve status differences. The distinction I make was part of a debate that appeared recently in the pages of the *American Sociological Review*. For specialists interested in this matter, see my "The Essential Social Fact of Race."

73. Herbert Blumer was one of the first analysts to make this argument about systematic rewards received by the races ascribed the primary position in a racial order. See Herbert Blumer, "Reflections on Theory of Race Relations," in *Race Relations in World Perspective*, edited by A. W. Lind, 3–21 (Honolulu, HI: University of Hawaii Press, 1955). DuBois's argument about the psychological wages of whiteness has been used recently by Manning Marable, *How Capitalism Underdeveloped Black America,* and by David Roediger, *The Wages of Whiteness.*

74. This point has been made by Omi and Winant, *Racial Formation in the United States*; and Howard Winant, *Racial Conditions. Hegemonic* means that domination is achieved more through consent than by coercion.

75. I am referring to cases such as Haiti. Nonetheless, recent research has suggested that even in such places, the abolition of slavery did not end the racialized character of the social formation. See Michel-Rolph Troillot, *Haiti, State against Nation: Origins and Legacy of Duvalierism* (New York: Monthly Review Press, 1990).

76. For a similar argument, see Floya Anthias and Nira Yuval-Davis, *Racialized Boundaries: Race, Nation, Gender, Colour, and the Anti-Racist Struggle* (London, England: Tavistock, 1992).

77. For an early statement on this matter, see Hubert M. Blalock, Jr., *Toward a Theory of Minority-Majority Group Relations* (New York: John Wiley & Sons, 1967). For a more recent statement, see Susan Olzack, *The Dynamics of Ethnic Competition and Conflict* (Stanford, CA: Stanford University Press, 1992).

78. Nineteenth-century nation-building processes throughout Latin America included the myth of racial democracy and color- or race-blindness. This facilitated the struggles for independence and the maintenance of white supremacy in societies where white elites were demographically insignificant. For discussions pertinent to this argument see the excellent collection edited by Michael Hanchard, *Racial Politics in Contemporary Brazil* (Durham and London: Duke University Press, 1999).

79. See my "The Essential Social Fact of Race," *American Sociological Review* Vol. 64, No. 6 (December 1999):899–906.

80. On this point, see Warren Whatley and Gavin Wright, *Race, Human Capital, and Labor Markets in American History*, Working Paper #7 (Ann Arbor, MI: Center for Afroamerican and African Studies, University of Michigan, 1994). For an incisive discussion, see Samuel L. Myers, Jr., "Measuring and Detecting Discrimination in the Post–Civil Rights Era," in *Race and Ethnicity in Research Methods*, edited by John H. Stanfield II and Rutledge M. Dennis, 172–97 (London: Sage Publications, 1993).

81. Michael Reich 1976:224.

82. Omi and Winant, *Racial Formation in the United States*, 64.

83. On the invention of the white race, see Theodore W. Allen, *The Invention of the White Race,* Vol. I (London: Verso, 1994). On the invention of the "Indian" race, see Robert E. Berkhoffer, *The White Man's Indian* (New York: Vintage, 1978). On the invention of the black and white races, see Withrop Jordan, *White over Black.*

84. A classic book on the ideological binary construction of the races in America is Thomas Gossett, *Race: The History of an Idea in America* (Dallas, TX: Southern Methodist University Press, 1963). For an analysis of the earlier period in the Americas, see Tzevetan Todorov, *The Conquest of America: The Question of the Other* (New York: Harper Colophon, 1984).

85. On this matter, I stated in my recent debate in the pages of the *American Sociological Review* with Mara Loveman, that "'race,' like 'class' or 'gender,' is *always contingent* but is also *socially real*. Race operates 'as a shuttle between socially constructed meanings and practices, between subjective and lived, material reality' (Hanchard 1994:4)" (901). Michael G. Hanchard, *Orpheus and Power* (Princeton, NJ: Princeton University Press, 1994).

86. This last point is an extension of Poulantzas's view on class. Races—as classes—are not an "empirical thing"; they denote racialized social relations or racial practices at all levels (Poulantzas, *Power and Social Classes*, 67).

87. For a full discussion, see my "The Essential Social Fact of Race." For a similar argument, see Teresa Amott and Julie Matthaei, *Race, Gender, and Work: A Multicultural Economic History of Women in the United States* (Boston, MA: South End Press, 1996).

88. Frederick Barth, "Introduction," in *Ethnic Groups and Boundaries: The Social Organization of Culture Difference*, edited by F. Barth, 9–38 (Bergen, Norway: Universitetsforlaget, 1969).

89. For the case of the Jews, see Miles, *Racism* and *Racism after "Race Relations."* For the case of the Irish, see Allen, *The Invention of the White Race*.

90. For a recent excellent discussion on ethnicity with many examples from the United States' experience, see Stephen Cornell and Douglas Hartmann, *Ethnicity and Race: Making Identities in a Changing World* (London: Pine Forge Press, 1998).

91. Roediger, *The Wages of Whiteness*. See also Noel Ignatiev, *How the Irish Became White* (New York: Routledge, 1995).

92. For identity issues among Caribbean immigrants, see the excellent edited collection by Constance R. Sutton and E. M. Chaney, *Caribbean Life in New York City: Sociocultural Dimensions* (New York: Center for Migration Studies of New York, 1987).

93. Barth, "Introduction," 17.

94. A few notable discussions on this matter are, Ira Berlin, *Slaves without Masters: The Free Negro in Antebellum South* (New York: Pantheon, 1975); John Hope Franklin, *From Slavery to Freedom: A History of the Negro Americans* (New York: Alfred A. Knopf, 1974); August Meir and Elliot Rudwick, *From Plantation to Ghetto* (New York: Hill & Wang, 1970).

95. The motivation for racializing human relations may have originated in the interests of powerful actors, but after social systems are racialized, all members of the dominant race participate in defending and reproducing the racial structure. This is the crucial reason why Marxist analysts (e.g., Cox, Reich) have not succeeded in successfully analyzing racism. They have not been able to accept the fact that after the phenomenon originated with the expansion of European capitalism into the New World, it acquired a life of its own. The subjects who were racialized as belonging to the superior race, whether or not they were members of the dominant class, became zealous defenders of the racial order. For an interesting Marxist-inspired treatment, see Bush, *We Are Not What We Seem*.

96. Jordan, *White over Black*; Robinson, *Black Marxism*; Miles, *Racism after "Race Relations."*

97. Bernard M. Magubane, *The Political Economy of Race and Class in South America* (New York: Monthly Review Press, 1990); Williams, *Hierarchical Structures and Social Value*. For two recent valuable contributions, see Robin Blackburn, *The Making of New World Slavery: From the Baroque to the Modern 1492–1800* (London: Verso, 1997); and Ian Hannaford, *Race: The History of an Idea in the West* (Baltimore: Johns Hopkins University Press, 1996).

98. Hillel Ticktin, *The Politics of Race: Discrimination in South Africa* (London: Pluto, 1991), 26.

99. The classic book on this still is Paula Giddings, *When and Where I Enter: The Impact of Black Women on Race and Sex in America* (New York: Bantam, 1984). See also, Nancy Caraway, *Segregated Sisterhood: Racism and the Politics of American Feminism* (Knoxville, TN: University of Tennessee Press, 1991.)

100. This argument is not new. Analysts of the racial history of the United States have always pointed out that most of the significant historical changes in this country's race relations were accompanied by some degree of overt violence. See Harold Cruse, *Rebellion or Revolution* (New York: William Morrow, 1968); Franklin, *From Slavery to Freedom*; and James W. Button, *Blacks and Social Change: Impact of the Civil Rights Movement in Southern Communities* (Princeton, NJ: Princeton University Press, 1989).

101. This point is important in literature on revolutions and democracy. On the role of violence in the establishment of bourgeois democracies, see Barrington Moore, Jr., *Social Origins of Dictatorship and Democracy* (Boston, MA: Beacon Press, 1966). On the pivotal role of violence in social movements, see Frances Fox Piven and Richard A. Cloward, *Poor People's Movements: Why They Succeed, How They Fail* (New York: Vintage, 1979).

102. The notion of relative autonomy comes from the work of Poulantzas (1982) and implies that the ideological and political levels in a society are partially autonomous in relation to the economic level; that is, they are not merely expressions of the economic level.

103. Paul Gilroy, *"There Ain't No Black in the Union Jack": The Cultural Politics of Race and Nation* (Chicago, IL: University of Chicago Press, 1991), 17.

104. See Ellis Cose, *The Rage of a Privileged Class: Why Are Middle Class Blacks Angry? Why Should America Care* (New York: Harper Collins, 1993); Lawrence Otis Graham, *Member of the Club: Reflections on Life in a Racially Polarized World* (New York: Harper Collins, 1995).

105. In addition to the work by Joe R. Feagin and Hernán Vera that I already cited, see Bobo, Kluegel, and Smith, "Laissez Faire Racism," and, particularly, Mary R. Jackman, *Velvet Glove: Paternalism and Conflict in Gender, Class, and Race Relations* (Berkeley: University of California Press 1994).

106. Curiously, historian Eugene Genovese, *In Red and Black: Marxian Explorations in Southern and Afroamerican History* (New York: Pantheon, 1971: 340) made a similar argument. Although he still regarded racism as an ideology, he stated that once it "arises it alters profoundly the material reality and in fact becomes a partially autonomous feature of that reality."

107. Hall, "Race Articulation and Societies Structured by Dominance," 336.

108. Actions by the Ku Klux Klan have an unmistakably racial tone, but many other actions (choosing to live in a suburban neighborhood, sending one's children to a private school, or opposing government intervention in hiring policies) also have racial undertones.

3

The Blacker the Berry

Gender, Skin Tone, Self-Esteem, and Self-Efficacy

Maxine D. Thompson and Verna Keith

She should have been a boy, then color of skin wouldn't have mattered so much, for wasn't her mother always saying that a Black boy could get along, but that a Black girl would never know anything but sorrow and disappointment? But she wasn't a boy; she was a girl, and color did matter, mattered so much that she would rather have missed receiving her high school diploma than have to sit as she now sat, the only odd and conspicuous figure on the auditorium platform of the Boise high school.

Get a diploma?—What did it mean to her? College?—Perhaps. A job?—Perhaps again. She was going to have a high school diploma, but it would mean nothing to her whatsoever. (Thurman 1929, 4–5)

Wallace Thurman (1929), speaking through the voice of the main character, Emma Lou Morgan, in his novel, *The Blacker the Berry,* about skin color bias within the African American community, asserts that the disadvantages and emotional pain of being "dark skinned" are greater for women than men and that skin color, not achievement, determines identity and attitudes about the self. Thurman's work describes social relationships among African Americans that were shaped by their experiences in the white community during slavery and its aftermath. In the African American community, skin color, an ascribed status attribute, played an integral role in determining class distinctions. Mulattoes, African Americans with white progenitors, led a more privileged existence when compared with their black counterparts, and in areas of the Deep South (i.e., most notably Louisiana and South Carolina), mulattoes served as a buffer class between whites and blacks (Russell, Wilson, and Hall

This chapter was originally published in *Gender & Society* 15(3): 336–57, 2001.

1992). In the *Black Bourgeoisie,* Frazier (1957) describes affluent organized clubs within the black community called "blue vein" societies. To be accepted into *these clubs,* skin tone was required to be lighter than a "paper bag" or light enough for visibility of "blue veins" (Okazawa Rey, Robinson, and Ward 1987). Preferential treatment, given by both black and white cultures to African Americans with light skin has conveyed to many blacks that if they conformed to the white, majority standard of beauty, their lives would be more rewarding (Bond and Cash 1992; Gatewood 1988).

Although Thurman's novel was written in 1929, the issue of colorism (Okazawa Rey, Robinson, and Ward 1987), intraracial discrimination based on skin color, continues to divide and shape life experiences within the African American community. The status advantages afforded to persons of light complexion continue despite the political preference for dark skin tones in the black awareness movement during the 1960s. No longer an unspoken taboo, color prejudice within the African American community has been a "hot" topic of talk shows, novels, and movies and an issue in a court case on discrimination in the workplace (Russell, Wilson, and Hall 1992). In addition to discussions within lay communities, research scholars have had considerable interest in the importance of skin color. At the structural level, studies have noted that skin color is an important determinant of educational and occupational attainment: Lighter skinned blacks complete more years of schooling, have more prestigious jobs, and earn more than darker skinned blacks (Hughes and Hertel 1990; Keith and Herring 1991). In fact, one study notes that the effect of skin color on earnings of "lighter" and "darker" blacks is as great as the effect of race on the earnings of whites and all blacks (Hughes and Hertel 1990). The most impressive research on skin tone effects is studies on skin tone and blood pressure. Using a reflectometer to measure skin color, research has shown that dark skin tone is associated with high blood pressure in African Americans with low socioeconomic status (Klag et al. 1991; Tryoler and James 1978). And at the social-psychological level, studies find that skin color is related to feelings of self-worth and attractiveness, self-control, satisfaction, and quality of life (Bond and Cash 1992; Boyd Franklin 1991; Cash and Duncan 1984; Chambers et al. 1994; Neal and Wilson 1989; Okazawa Rey, Robinson, and Ward 1987).

It is important to note that skin color is highly correlated with other phenotypic features—eye color, hair texture, broadness of nose, and fullness of lips. Along with light skin, blue and green eyes, European-shaped noses, straight as opposed to "kinky" hair are all accorded higher status both within and beyond the African American community. Colorism embodies preference and desire for both light skin as well as these other attendant features. Hair, eye color, and facial features function along with color in complex ways to shape opportunities, norms regarding attractiveness, self-concept, and overall body image. Yet, it is color that has received the most attention in research on

African Americans. The reasons for this emphasis are not clear, although one can speculate that it is due to the fact that color is the most visible physical feature and is also the feature that is most enduring and difficult to change. As Russell, Wilson, and Hall (1992) pointed out, hair can be straightened with chemicals, eye color can be changed with contact lenses, and a broad nose can be altered with cosmetic surgery. Bleaching skin to a lighter tone, however, seldom meets with success (Okazawa Rey, Robinson, and Ward 1987). Ethnographic research also suggests that the research focus on skin color is somewhat justified. For example, it played the central role in determining membership in the affluent African American clubs.

Although colorism affects attitudes about the self for both men and women, it appears that these effects are stronger for women than men. In early studies, dark-skinned women were seen as occupying the bottom rungs of the social ladder, least marriageable, having the fewest options for higher education and career advancement, and as more color conscious than their male counterparts (Parrish 1944; Warner, Junker, and Adams 1941). There is very little empirical research on the relationship between gender, skin color, and self-concept development. In this chapter, we evaluate the relative importance of skin color to feelings about the self for men and women within the African American community.

The literature that relates skin tone to self-images has several methodological limitations. First, with the exception of doll preference studies, there is an absence of a systematic body of research on self-concept development. This is particularly true for studies on adults. Inferences about the relationship between skin tone and attitudes about the self are drawn from findings of studies on attitudes about body image, mate or dating preferences, physical attractiveness, and skin tone satisfaction. Second, much of this literature is based on data from descriptive anecdotes of personal accounts, clinical studies, and laboratory studies that use small purposive samples of respondents. Studies using generalizable survey research methodology with nationally representative samples of respondents to examine the relationship between skin tone and self-concept development are rare. Third, the use of limited databases is often joined with a lack of adequate controls for socioeconomic status variables such as education and income. Despite the strong empirical literature that shows that skin tone is an important determinant of socioeconomic status as well as studies that argue that socioeconomic status is an important determinant of self-concept development, researchers have failed to take socioeconomic status into account. Fourth, not all studies employ an objective measure of skin tone. The use of self-reported skin tone may possibly contaminate the observed relationship between skin tone and self-concept outcomes.

Our study addresses several of these limitations. Using an adult sample of respondents who are representative of the national population, we examine the relationship of skin tone to self-concept development. Our analyses employ objective and reliable measures of skin tone, self-concept, and adequate control variables for socioeconomic status. More important, we examine the way in which gender socially constructs the impact of skin tone on self-concept development. The following sections consider the gendered relationships between skin tone and self-concept development and outline the conceptual argument and prior empirical evidence.

SKIN TONE AND GENDER

Issues of skin color and physical attractiveness are closely linked and because expectations of physical attractiveness are applied more heavily to women across all cultures, stereotypes of attractiveness and color preference are more profound for black women (Warner, Junker, and Adams 1941). In the clinical literature (Boyd Franklin 1991; Grier and Cobbs 1968; Neal and Wilson 1989; Okazawa Rey, Robinson, and Ward 1987), issues of racial identity, skin color, and attractiveness were central concerns of women. The "what is beautiful is good" stereotype creates a "halo" effect for light-skinned persons. The positive glow generated by physical attractiveness includes a host of desirable personality traits. Included in these positive judgments are beliefs that attractive people would be significantly more intelligent, kind, confident, interesting, sexy, assertive, poised, modest, and successful, and they appear to have higher self-esteem and self-worth (Dion, Berscheid, and Walster 1972). When complexion is the indicator of attractiveness, similar stereotypic attributes are found. There is evidence that gender difference in response to the importance of skin color to attractiveness appears during childhood. Girls as young as six are twice as likely as boys to be sensitive to the social importance of skin color (Porter 1971; Russell, Wilson, and Hall 1992, 68). In a study of facial features, skin color, and attractiveness, Neal (cited in Neal and Wilson 1989, 328) found that

> unattractive women were perceived as having darker skin tones than attractive women and that women with more Caucasoid features were perceived as more attractive to the opposite sex, more successful in their love lives and their careers than women with Negroid features.

Frequent exposure to negative evaluations can undermine a woman's sense of self. "A dark skinned black woman who feels herself unattractive, however, may think that she has nothing to offer society no matter how intelligent or inventive she is" (Russell, Wilson, and Hall 1992, 42).

Several explanations are proffered for gender differences in self-esteem among blacks. One is that women are socialized to attend to evaluations of others and are vulnerable to negative appraisals. Women seek to validate their selves through appraisal from others more than men. And the media has encouraged greater negative self-appraisals for dark-skinned women. A second explanation is that colorism and its associated stressors are not the same for dark-skinned men and women. For men, stereotypes associated with perceived dangerousness, criminality, and competence are associated with dark skin tone, while for women the issue is attractiveness (Russell, Wilson, and Hall 1992, 38). Educational attainment is a vehicle by which men might overcome skin color bias, but changes in physical features are difficult to accomplish. Third, women may react more strongly to skin color bias because they feel less control of their lives. Research studies show that women and persons of low status tend to feel fatalistic (Pearlin and Schooler 1978; Turner and Noh 1983) and to react more intensely than comparable others to stressors (Kessler and McLeod 1984; Pearlin and Johnson 1977; Thoits 1982, 1984; Turner and Noh 1983). This suggests a triple jeopardy situation: black women face problems of racism and sexism, and when these two negative status positions—being black and being female—combine with colorism, a triple threat lowers self-esteem and feelings of competence among dark black women.

CONCEPTUAL ARGUMENT

Skin Tone and Self-Evaluation

William James (1890) conceived of the self as an integrating social product consisting of various constituent parts (i.e., the physical, social, and spiritual selves). Body image, the aspect of the self that we recognize first, is one of the major components of the self and remains important throughout life. One can assume that if one's bodily attributes are judged positively, the impact on oneself is positive. Likewise, if society devalues certain physical attributes, negative feelings about the self are likely to ensue. Body image is influenced by a number of factors including skin color, size, and shape. In our society, dark-skinned men and women are raised to believe that "light" skin is preferred. They see very light-skinned blacks having successful experiences, in advertisements, in magazines, in professional positions, and so forth. They are led to believe that "light" skin is the key to popularity, professional status, and a desirable marriage. Russell, Wilson, and Hall (1992) argue that the African American gay and lesbian community is also affected by colorism because a light-skinned or even white mate confers status. Whether heterosexual, gay, or lesbian, colorism may lead to negative self-evaluations among African Americans with dark skin.

Self-evaluations are seen as having two dimensions, one reflecting the person's moral worth and the other reflecting the individual's competency or agency (Gecas 1989). The former refers to self-esteem and indicates how we feel about ourselves. The latter refers to self-efficacy and indicates our belief in the ability to control our own fate. These are two different dimensions in that a person can feel that they are good and useful, but also feel that what happens to them is due to luck or forces outside themselves.

Self-Esteem and Skin Tone   Self-esteem consists of feeling good, liking yourself, and being liked and treated well. Self-esteem is influenced by both the social comparisons we make of ourselves with others and by the reactions that other people have toward us (i.e., reflected appraisals). The self-concept depends also on the attributes of others who are available for comparison. Self-evaluation theory emphasizes the importance of consonant environmental context for personal comparisons; that is, blacks will compare themselves with other blacks in their community. Consonant environmental context assumes that significant others will provide affirmation of one's identity and that similarity between oneself and others shapes the self. Thus, a sense of personal connectedness to other African Americans is most important for fostering and reinforcing positive self-evaluations. This explains why the personal self-esteem of blacks, despite their lower status position, was as high as that of whites (Porter and Washington 1989, 345; Rosenberg and Simmons 1971). It does not explain the possible influence of colorism on self-esteem within the African American community. Evidence suggests that conflictual and dissonant racial environments have negative effects on self-esteem, especially within the working class (Porter and Washington 1989, 346; Verna and Runion 1985). The heterogeneity of skin tone hues and colorism create a dissonant racial environment and become a source of negative self-evaluation.

Self-Efficacy and Skin Tone   Self-efficacy, as defined by Bandura (1977, 1982), is the belief that one can master situations and control events. Performance influences self-efficacy such that when faced with a failure, individuals with high self-efficacy generally believe that extra effort or persistence will lead to success (Bandura 1982). However, if failure is related to some stable personal characteristic such as "dark skin color" or social constraints such as blocked opportunities resulting from mainstreaming practices in the workplace, then one is likely to be discouraged by failure and to feel less efficacious than his or her lighter counterparts. In fact, Pearlin and colleagues (1981) argue that stressors that seem to be associated with inadequacy of one's efforts or lack of success are implicated in a diminished sense of self. Problems or hardships "to which people can see no end, those that seem to become fixtures of their existence" pose the most sustained affront to a sense of mastery and self-worth (Pearlin et al. 1981, 345). For Bandura, however, individual agency plays a role in sustaining the self. Individuals actively engage in activities that are congenial with a positive sense of self. Self-efficacy results not primarily from beliefs or attitudes about performance but from undertaking challenges and succeeding. Thus, darker skinned blacks who experience success in their everyday world (e.g., work, education, etc.) will feel more confident and empowered.

Following the literature, we predict a strong relationship between skin tone and self-esteem and self-efficacy, but the mechanisms are different for the two dimensions. The effect of skin tone on self-efficacy will be partially mediated by occupation and income. The effect will be direct for self-esteem. That is, the direct effect will be stronger for self-esteem than for self-efficacy. Furthermore, we expect a stronger relationship between skin tone and self-esteem for women than men because women's self-esteem is conditioned by the appraisals of others, and the media has encouraged negative appraisals for dark-skinned women.

DATA AND METHOD

The Sample

Data for this study come from the National Survey of Black Americans (NSBA) (Jackson and Gurin 1987). The sample for the survey was drawn according to a multistage-area probability procedure that was designed to ensure that every black household in the United States had an equal probability of being selected for the study. Within each household in the sample, one person aged 18 or older was randomly selected to be interviewed from among those eligible for the study. Only self-identified black American citizens were eligible for the study. Face-to-face interviews were carried out by trained black interviewers, yielding a sample of 2,107 respondents. The response rate was approximately 69 percent. For the most part, the NSBA is representative of the national black population enumerated in the 1980 Census, with the exception of a slight overrepresentation of women and older blacks and a small underrepresentation of southerners (Jackson, Tucker, and Gurin 1987).

Measures

Dependent Variables There are two indicators of self-evaluation: *self-esteem* and *self-efficacy*. The NSBA included six items that measure self-esteem. Two items are from Rosenberg's (1979) Self-Esteem Scale: "I feel that I am a person of worth" and "I feel I do not have much to be proud of." Two items are from the Monitoring the Future Project (Bachman and Johnson 1978): "I feel that I can't do anything right" and "I feel that my life is not very useful." Two items measure the worth dimension of self-esteem: "I am a useful person to have around" and "As a person, I do a good job these days." Respondents were asked to indicate whether the statements are almost *always true* (4), *often true* (3), *not often true* (2), and *never true* (1). Negatively worded items were reverse coded so that high values represent positive self-esteem. Items were summed to form a self-esteem scale (a = .66). Self-efficacy measures the respondents' feelings of control and confidence in managing their own lives. The four questions asked in the NSBA are the most highly correlated (Wright 1976, 107) in a commonly used scale of personal efficacy (for validity of the scale, see J. P. Robinson and Shaver 1969, 102). Each of the four items was followed by two responses:

1. "Do you think it's better *to plan your life a good ways ahead,* or would you say life is *too much a matter of luck to plan ahead very far?"*
2. "When you do make plans ahead, do you usually *get to carry out things the way you expected or do things come up to make you change your plans?"*
3. "Have you usually *felt pretty sure* your life would work out the way you want it to, or have there been times when you *haven't been sure about it?"*
4. "Some people feel they *can run their lives* pretty much the way they want to, others feel the *problems of life are sometimes too much for* them. Which one are you most like?"

The items were summed to form a scale where high values represent a high sense of personal efficacy (a = .57). The positive responses were coded 2 and negative responses were coded 1. Hughes and Demo's (1989, 140) analysis of these data shows that the measure of self-efficacy is empirically distinct from the measure of self-esteem. *Independent variables.* Skin tone is the independent variable of primary interest in this study. Values of skin tone were based on interviewers' observations of respondents' complexions and recorded after the interview. The interviewer was asked to respond to the following: "The [respondent's] skin color is (1) *very dark brown,* (2) *dark brown,* (3) *medium brown,* (4) *light brown* (light skinned), and (5) *very light brown* (very light skinned)." Ninety-eight percent of the respondents were classified according to this scheme. Of those assigned a color rating, 8.5 percent (175) were classified as being very dark brown, 29.9 percent (617) as dark brown, 44.6 percent (922) as medium brown, 14.4 percent (298) as light brown, and 2.6 percent (54) as very light brown. This measurement scheme is similar to other studies that used objective ratings of skin color (Freeman et al. 1966; Udry, Bauman, and Chase 1969). Three sets of independent variables are used in these analyses: sociodemographic, socioeconomic status, and body image. The sociodemographic variables include age, marital status, region of current residence, and urban area. Age of the respondent is self-reported and measured in years. Marital status is a dummy variable coded 1 for currently married, with those who are not married as the comparison category (0). Region of current residence is collapsed into two categories: South is coded 1 and non-South is coded 0. For the urban city variable, respondents were coded 1 if they lived in an urban area and 0 elsewhere.

The second set of variables consists of socioeconomic status variables and includes education, employment, and income. Education of respondents is measured as years of completed schooling, with 18 categories ranging from 0 to 18 years or more of educational attainment. A dummy variable for employment status is coded 1 for working with pay and 0 for laid off or not working for pay. Personal income was initially coded using 17 categories ranging from 1 for *no income* to 17 for *income of $30,000 or more*. Each respondent was assigned scores that correspond to the midpoint of his or her income category for personal income. A Pareto curve estimate was used to derive a midpoint for the open-ended categories (see Miller 1964).

Three measures of body image are physical attractiveness, weight, and disabled health status. Interviewers were asked to indicate where the respondent fell on a semantic scale from 1 = *unattractive* to 7 = *attractive*. We recognize that interviewer perceptions of skin tone are likely to affect interviewer perceptions of attractiveness. That is, interviewers probably evaluated lighter skinned African Americans, especially women, as being more attractive. However, this was the only measure in the NSBA. The correlations between skin tone and attractiveness, however, are modest (r = .13, p< .01 for men and r = .20, p < .01 for women), suggesting that they operate somewhat independently. On this basis, we concluded that omitting this information would introduce more bias than the bias produced by their correlation. Respondent's weight is also assessed by interviewers' observations. Interviewers were asked where the respondent fell on a scale from 1 = *underweight* to 7 = *overweight*. Disabled is measured as follows: For each of 13 medical conditions, respondents were asked, "How much does this health problem keep you from working or carrying out your daily tasks?" The responses were *a great deal* (2), *only a little* (1), or *not at all* (0). High scores indicate greater disability. Table 3.1 shows the means, standard deviations, and correlations of the independent and dependent variables for male and female respondents separately.

Data Analysis

To assess the impact of gender on the relationship between skin tone and self-evaluations, we analyze the data separately for men and women. Data analysis consists of a series of ordinary least squares (OLS) regression equations that assess the effects of skin tone on indicators of self-esteem and self-efficacy. A hierarchical multiple regression strategy is used to analyze the data. Successive reduced-form equations are presented for each dependent variable. The first equation looks at the bivariate relationship between skin tone and each dependent variable. Our strategy is to determine how this relationship is altered as successive groups of independent variables are controlled.

Therefore, the second equation includes skin tone and the sociodemographic variables. Equation 3 includes skin tone, sociodemographic variables, and socioeconomic status variables. The fourth equation includes all the above plus the body image variables.

RESULTS

Table 3.2 shows the regression of self-efficacy on measures of skin tone, sociodemographic, socioeconomic, and body image variables for men and women separately. Looking at column 1, we see that skin tone has a significant positive effect on self-efficacy for both men and women. A lighter complexion is associated with higher feelings of perceived mastery. Among men, each incremental change in skin color from dark to light is associated with a .33 increment in self-efficacy; for women, changes in skin color are associated with a .18 increment in self-efficacy.

Thus, the skin tone effect on self-efficacy is much stronger for men. In fact, the coefficient for the skin tone effect in the equation predicting self-efficacy for men is almost twice that of the coefficient for women.

The pattern of skin tone effects for men and women begins to diverge when the sociodemographic variables are added in the second equation. Among African American men, the effect of skin tone and self-efficacy remains statistically significant and the coefficient is reduced by 11 percent. In contrast, among women, the skin tone effect is reduced also by a similar amount, but the significance level is reduced to borderline. Adding the socioeconomic variables to the equation (column 3), we see that the effect of skin tone on self-efficacy remains statistically significant for men. Note that men's standardized coefficient for education is almost twice as large as that of skin tone, suggesting that education has a stronger effect in determining self-efficacy for them. Body image, represented by attractiveness and weight (equation 4), does not statistically alter the effect of skin tone on self-efficacy for men. Disabled health conditions, which have a significant negative effect on self-efficacy for men, do not alter the skin tone effect. When all the independent variables are accounted for (equation 4), skin tone continues to have a moderate significant effect on self-efficacy among men. By contrast, the determinants of self-efficacy for women in this study are age, education, income, disability, and urban residence. The effect of skin tone is reduced by 80 percent and is no longer statistically significant after all variables are controlled. Note that among men, skin tone has a significant moderate effect on self-efficacy when other more robust factors such as education and age are controlled. Among women, skin tone effect on self-efficacy is largely indirect, via its consequence for income and education.

Table 3.1. Correlations, Means, and Standard Deviations by Gender

	1	2	3	4	5	6	7	8	9	10	11	x̄	SD
Men (n = 647)													
1. Skin tone												2.62	.90
2. Age	.017											41.79	17.70
3. Urban	.089*	-.131**										.77	.42
4. South	.000	.064	-.410**									.55	.50
5. Married	.035	.186**	-.106**	.041								.52	.50
6. Income	.137**	-.023	.209**	-.229**	.257**							10.89	8.74
7. Education	.106**	-.516**	.266**	-.200**	-.001	.402**						11.00	3.76
8. Employed	.021	-.279**	.063	-.009	.148	.357**	.304**					.69	.46
9. Attractiveness	.133**	-.125*	-.017	.037	.084*	.060	.127**	.130**				4.41	1.37
10. Weight	.005	.110**	.038	-.070	.052	.034	-.039	-.012	-.151**			4.02	.91
11. Disabled	-.002	.443**	-.081**	.020	.033	-.138**	-.320**	-.072	.107**	.013		1.95	2.96
12. Self-efficacy	.116**	.061	.123**	-.094	.076	.160**	.159**	.017	.055	.013	-.114**	8.26	2.50
13. Self-esteem	.054	.016	-.060	.065	.089*	.123**	.071	.151**	.098*	-.004	-.161**	21.29	2.59
Women (n = 1,036)													
1. Skin tone												2.78	.90
2. Age	-.069*											42.03	17.39
3. Urban	.086**	-.101**										.78	.42
4. South	-.051	.064*	-.407**									.56	.50
5. Married	.034	.006	-.094	.034								.36	.48
6. Income	.139**	-.082*	.226**	-.219**	.044							5.95	4.45
7. Education	.154**	-.490**	.225**	-.142**	-.074*	.434**						11.03	3.27
8. Employed	.085**	-.193**	.058	-.021	.087**	.437**	.340**					.52	.50
9. Attractiveness	.196**	-.076*	.017	.042	.037	.094**	.127**	.092**				4.38	1.47
10. Weight	-.025	.061	-.019	-.008	.006	-.021	-.060	.009	-.205**			4.31	1.13
11. Disabled	-.098**	.404**	-.083**	.049	-.044	-.222**	-.399**	-.332**	.077**	.024		2.97	3.69
12. Self-efficacy	.061*	.061*	.134**	-.103	.015	.210**	.164**	.087**	.076*	.046	-.111**	7.75	2.60
13. Self-esteem	.100**	.107**	.012	.021	.005	.135**	.078*	.131**	.095**	.046	-.159**	21.06	2.55

*$p \leq .05$ (two–tailed test). **$p \leq .01$ (two–tailed test).

Table 3.2. Regression Results for Predicting Self-Efficacy, by Gender

	Men (n = 647)				Women (n = 1,036)			
	1	2	3	4	1	2	3	4
Skin tone	.325**	.288**	.220*	.208†	.177*	.157†	.063	.029
	(.116)	(.103)	(.079)	(.074)	(.061)	(.054)	(.022)	(.010)
Age		.009	.022***	.030***		.015***	.029***	.033***
		(.063)	(.157)	(.215)		(.100)	(.191)	(.221)
Urban		.629*	.406	.406		.735***	.437*	.437*
		(.106)	(.068)	(.068)		(.117)	(.070)	(.070)
South		-.292	-.137	-.165		-.313†	-.179	-.201
		(-.058)	(-.027)	(-.033)		(-.060)	(-.034)	(-.038)
Married		.372†	.218	.206		.139	.010	-.001
		(.074)	(.044)	(.041)		(.026)	(.002)	(-.000)
Income			.015	.14			.056***	.054***
			(.052)	(.048)			(.119)	(.114)
Education			.135***	.126***			.144***	.127***
			(.196)	(.183)			(.181)	(.160)
Employed			-.163	-.378			.021	-.093
			(-.030)	(-.070)			(.004)	(-.018)
Attractiveness				.080				.084
				(.043)				(.048)
Weight				.029				-.015
				(.010)				(-.007)
Disabled				-.136***				-.072**
				(-.161)				(-.102)
Constant	8.260	7.096	6.767	6.771	7.753	6.727	6.313	6.140
R^2	.014	.040	.072	.093	.004	.034	.085	.096
Adjusted R^2	.012	.033	.061	.077	.003	.029	.079	.086

NOTE: Standardized coefficients are in parentheses.
†$p ≤ .10$. *$p ≤ .05$. **$p ≤ .01$. ***$p ≤ .001$.

A similar analysis for the self-esteem measure is displayed in table 3.3 and shows that the effect for skin tone on self-esteem is not statistically significant in the equation for black men in this study. Conversely, among black women, skin tone has a significant positive association with self-esteem, even after all other variables are controlled. These findings show that among women, a change in skin color from dark to light is associated with a .28 increment in self-esteem. The effect of skin tone on self-esteem for women is slightly enhanced when the sociodemographic controls are added to the equation (column 2) and remains constant in the face of a strong pattern of socioeconomic effects (equation 3). Education and employment have positive effects on self-esteem for African American women. Two indicators for body image have significant positive effects on self-esteem—attractiveness and weight. Disabled conditions (equation 4) have a significant negative association with self-esteem. Of these socioeconomic effects, only education remains when body image variables are controlled, but the skin tone effect remains statistically significant. The body image variables have a moderate impact on the relationship between skin tone and self-esteem, reducing it by 20 percent. Women who are rated physically attractive have higher self-esteem scores, but attractiveness is at least in part related to skin tone.

Although the overall models in the analysis for self-efficacy and self-esteem are modest, they compare favorably to sociological models predicting self-esteem and self-efficacy. It is most informative to look at the size of the coefficient for skin tone compared to other variables in the model. Skin tone effects are sizable in the models predicting self-efficacy for men and self-esteem for women.

DO ACHIEVEMENT AND BODY IMAGE CONDITION THE EFFECTS OF SKIN TONE ON SELF-CONCEPT?

The literature suggests that it is reasonable to expect that skin tone may interact with socioeconomic status and body image to affect self-concept (Ransford 1970; St. John and Feagin 1998). We expect that among women, the relationship between skin tone and self-esteem and skin tone and self-efficacy will be moderated by socioeconomic status and body image. That is, the relationships will be stronger for black women from lower social classes and for black women who are judged as unattractive. To test for these possibilities, we created interaction terms for skin color and each of the socioeconomic status variables and for skin color and each of the body image variables. As suggested by Aiken and West (1991), all variables used to compute interaction terms were centered. Each interaction term was entered into the regression equation separately. Simple slope regression analyses were then used to probe significant interactions. The results are presented in table 3.4.

Table 3.3. Regression Results for Predicting Self-Esteem, by Gender

	Men (n = 647)				Women (n = 1,036)			
	1	2	3	4	1	2	3	4
Skin tone	.157	.159	.112	.088	.283***	.303***	.235**	.187*
	(.054)	(.055)	(.039)	(.031)	(.100)	(.107)	(.083)	(.066)
Age		-.001	.010	-.019**		.017***	.027***	.034***
		(-.008)	(.068)	(.132)		(.115)	(.185)	(.235)
Urban		-.235	-.405	-.400		.167	-.020	-.015
		(-.038)	(-.066)	(-.065)		(.027)	(-.003)	(-.002)
South		.244	.328	.295		.153	.218	.196
		(.047)	(.063)	(.057)		(.030)	(.042)	(.038)
Married		.429*	.153	.126		.013	-.104	-.125
		(.083)	(.030)	(.024)		(.003)	(-.019)	(-.023)
Income			.020	0.19			.028	.025
			(.069)	(.065)			(.060)	(.053)
Education			.048	.036			.081**	.053†
			(.067)	(.051)			(.104)	(.068)
Employed			.696**	.449†			.512**	.292
			(.124)	(.080)			(.100)	(.057)
Attractiveness				.142†				.121
				(.075)				(.070)
Weight				.047				.151*
				(.017)				(.067)
Disabled				-.148***				-.130***
				(-.169)				(-.189)
Constant	21.292	21.388	21.005	20.632	21.055	20.131	19.812	19.508
R^2	.003	.016	.046	.072	.010	.024	.058	.092
Adjusted R^2	.001	.008	.034	.056	.009	.019	.051	.082

NOTE: Standardized coefficients are in parentheses.
†$p \leq .10$. *$p \leq .05$. **$p \leq .01$. ***$p \leq .001$.

Table 3.4. Significant Interaction Effects and Summary of Simple Regression Analysis for Self-Esteem and Self-Efficacy, by Gender

Gender	Interaction Effect	b^1	Value of Moderator Variable	b^2	b_0
Dependent Variable = Self-Esteem					
Women	Skin Tone*Income	-.035*	Low income	.376*	19.373
			Average income	.185*	19.552
			High income	-.005	19.732
Women	Skin Tone*Attractiveness	-.113*	Low attractiveness	.350**	19.323
			Average attractiveness	.184*	19.524
			High attractiveness	.018	19.726
Men	Skin Tone*Weight	.274*	Low weight	-1.009*	20.372
			Average weight	.092	20.621
			High weight	1.192**	20.870

Gender	Interaction Effect	b	Value of Moderator Variable	b^1	b_0
Dependent Variable = Self-Efficacy					
Men	Skin Tone*Weight	.188†	Low weight	-.545	6.603
			Average weight	.210†	6.759
			High weight	.965*	6.916

NOTE: b^1 = coefficient for the interaction effect; b^2 = coefficient represents the effects of skin tone on self-esteem/self-efficacy at low (1 SD below mean), average (at mean equals 0), and high (1 SD above mean) values of the moderator variable.
†$p \le .10$. *$p \le .05$. **$p \le .01$.

In the analyses of women's self-esteem, two significant interaction effects emerge—skin tone and personal income (b = −.035, p = .025) and skin tone and interviewer-rated attractiveness (b = −.113, p = .029). The results from the simple slopes analyses indicate that the relationship between skin tone and personal income is positive and significant among women with the lowest incomes. In other words, among women with the lowest levels of income, self-esteem increases as color lightens. The relationship is also positive and significant for women with average levels of income, although the relation-ship is not as strong. There is no relationship between skin tone and self-esteem among women with the highest incomes. Thus, women who are dark and successful evaluate themselves just as positively as women who are lighter and successful: Similar to the findings for income, skin color has a sig-nificant positive effect on self-esteem among women evaluated as having low and average levels of attractiveness, although the effect is stronger for the for-mer. Self-esteem increases as skin color becomes lighter among women judged unattractive or average. There is no relationship between skin tone and self-esteem for women who are judged highly attractive. In other words, skin tone does not have much relevance for self-esteem among women who have higher levels of income and who are attractive. Education, unlike income, has no significant effect on women's self-esteem. We are at a loss to explain this finding. Perhaps income is more important because it permits women to obtain more visible symbols of success such as clothing, cars, and living quarters. We discuss this further in the concluding section.

Skin tone and interviewer-evaluated weight combine to affect men's self-esteem (h = .274, p = .012). Results from the simple-slopes regression analyses show that skin tone has a significant impact on self-esteem for men who are either underweight or overweight, although the direction of the effects is opposite. Among underweight men, self-esteem decreases as skin tone becomes lighter. However, among overweight men, self-esteem increases as skin tone becomes lighter. We suggest that cultural definitions of weight prob-ably interact with those of skin color and health as explanations of the observed effects. In our culture, a robust athletic body is associated with mas-culinity, and a thin body frame combined with light complexion might be viewed as ill health. And a negative stigma of both weight and complexion affects self-esteem for men who are overweight and dark skinned. It seems that light skin compensates for the negative stigma of weight for large body frames but enhances the negative stigma for thin frames.

In the analyses of self-efficacy, there are no significant interaction effects among women. Among men, one interaction term emerged as marginally sig-nificant: skin tone and weight (h = .188, h = .072). The simple slopes indicate that skin tone and efficacy are negatively associated for underweight men, although the relationship is not significant. The relationship is marginally sig-nificant for men judged as average and is significant and positive for men judged overweight. Among those judged overweight, lighter men are more likely to have high self-efficacy. Note additional evidence that skin tone might compensate for the effect of a negative stigma of weight on self among larger men.

DISCUSSION

The data in this study indicate that gender—mediated by socioeconomic status variables such as education, occupation, and income—socially constructs the importance of skin color evaluations of self-esteem and self-efficacy. Self-efficacy results not primarily from beliefs or attitudes about performance but rather reflects an individual's competency or agency for undertaking challenges and succeeding at overcoming them. Self-esteem consists of feeling good about oneself and being liked and treated favorably by others. However, the effect of skin color on these two domains of self is different for women and men. Skin color is an important predictor of perceived efficacy for black men but not black women. And skin color predicts self-esteem for black women but not black men. This pattern conforms to traditional gendered expectations (Hill Collins 1990, 79–80). The traditional definitions of masculinity demand men specialize in achievement outside the home, dominate in interpersonal relationships, and remain rational and self-contained. Women, in contrast, are expected to seek affirmation from others, to be warm and nurturing. Thus, consistent with gendered characteristics of men and women, skin color is important in self-domains that are central to masculinity (i.e., competence) and femininity (i.e., affirmation of the self).

Turning our attention to the association between skin color and self-concept for black men, the association between skin color and self-efficacy increases significantly as skin color lightens. And this is independent of the strong positive contribution of education—and ultimately socioeconomic status—to feelings of competence for men. We think that the effect of skin tone on self-efficacy is the result of widespread negative stereotyping and fear associated with dark-skinned men that pervade the larger society and operates independent of social class. Correspondingly, employers view darker African American men as violent, uncooperative, dishonest, and unstable (Kirschenman and Neckerman 1998). As a consequence, employers exclude "darker" African American men from employment and thus block their access to rewards and resources.

Evidence from research on the relationship between skin tone and achievement supports our interpretation. The literature on achievement and skin tone shows that lighter skinned blacks are economically better off than darker skinned persons (Hughes and Hertel 1990; Keith and Herring 1991). Hughes and Hertel (1990), using the NSBA data, present findings that show that for every dollar a light-skinned African American earns, the darker skinned person earns 72 cents. Thus, it seems colorism is operative within the workplace. Lighter skinned persons are probably better able to predict what will happen to them and what doors will open and remain open, thus leading to a higher sense of control over their environment. Our data support this finding and add additional information on how that process might work at least in the lives of black men. Perhaps employers are looking to hire African American men who will assimilate into the work environment, who do not alienate their clients (Kirschenman and Neckerman 1998), and who are nonthreatening. One consequence of mainstreaming the workplace is that darker skinned black men have fewer opportunities to demonstrate competence in the breadwinner role. It is no accident that our inner cities, where unemployment is highest, are filled with darker skinned persons, especially men (Russell, Wilson, and Hall 1992, 38). During adolescence, lighter skinned boys discover that they have better job prospects, appear less threatening to whites, and have a clearer sense of who they are and their competency (Russell, Wilson, and Hall 1992, 67). In contrast, darker skinned African American men may feel powerless and less able to affect change through the "normal" channels available to lighter skinned African American men (who are able to achieve a more prestigious socioeconomic status).

While skin color is an important predictor of self-efficacy for African American men, it is more important as a predictor of self-esteem for African American women. These data confirm much of the anecdotal information from clinical studies of clients in psychotherapy that have found that dark-skinned black women have problems with self-worth and confidence. Our findings suggest that this pattern is not limited to experiences of women who are in therapy but that colorism is part of the everyday reality of black women. Black women expect to be judged by their skin tone. No doubt messages from peers, the media, and family show a preference for lighter skin tones. Several studies cited in the literature review point out that black women of all ages tend to prefer lighter skin tones and believe that lighter hues are perceived as most attractive by their black male counterparts (Bond and Cash 1992; Chambers et al. 1994; Porter 1971; T. L. Robinson and Ward 1995).

Evidence from personal accounts reported in research on the impact of racism in the everyday lives of black women by St. John and Feagin (1998, 75) supports this interpretation. One young woman describes her father's efforts to shape her expectations about the meaning of beauty in our society and where black women entered this equation.

> Beauty, beauty standards in this country, a big thing with me. It's a big gripe, because I went through a lot of personal anguish over that, being Black and being female, it's a real big thing with me, because it took a lot for me to find a sense of self . . . in this white-male-dominated society. And just how beauty

standards are so warped because like my daddy always tell me, "white is right." The whiter you are, somehow the better you are, and if you look white, well hell, you've got your ticket, and anything you want, too.

Nevertheless, the relationship between skin color and self-esteem among African American women is moderated by socioeconomic status. For example, there is no correlation between skin color and self-esteem among women who have a more privileged socioeconomic status. Consequently, women who are darker and "successful" evaluate themselves just as positively as women of a lighter color. On the other hand, the relationship between skin color and self-esteem is stronger for African American women from the less privileged socioeconomic sectors. In other words, darker skinned women with the lowest incomes display the lowest levels of self-esteem—but self-esteem increases as their skin color lightens. Why does skin color have such importance for self-regard in the context of low income or poverty? Low income shapes self-esteem because it provides fewer opportunities for rewarding experiences or affirming relationships. In addition, there are more negative attributes associated with behaviors of individuals from less privileged socioeconomic status than with those of a more prestigious one. For example, the derisive comment "ghetto chick" is often used to describe the behaviors, dress, communication, and interaction styles of women from low-income groups. Combine stereotypes of classism and colorism, and you have a mixture that fosters an undesirable if not malignant context for self-esteem development. An important finding of this research is that skin color and income determine self-worth for black women and especially that these factors can work together. Dark skin and low income produce black women with very low self-esteem. Accordingly, these data help refine our understanding of gendered racism and of "triple oppression" involving race, gender, and class that places women of color in a subordinate social and economic position relative to men of color and the larger white population as well (Segura 1986). More important, the data suggest that darker skinned African American women actually experience a "quadruple" oppression originating in the convergence of social inequalities based on gender, class, race, and color. Earlier, we noted the absence of an interaction effect between skin tone and education, and that we can only speculate on the explanation for this finding. Perhaps education does not have the same implications for self-esteem as income because it is a less visible symbol of success. Financial success affords one the ability to purchase consumer items that tell others, even at a distance, that an individual is successful. These visible symbols include the place where we live, the kind of car we drive, and the kind of clothing that we wear. Educational attainment is not as easily grasped, especially in distant social interactions—passing on the street, walking in the park, or attending a concert event. In other words, for a dark-skinned African American woman, her M.A. or

Ph.D. may be largely unknown outside her immediate friends, family, and coworkers. Her Lexus or Mercedes, however, is visible to the world and is generally accorded a great deal of prestige.

Finally, the data indicate that self-esteem increases as skin color becomes lighter among African American women who are judged as having "low and average levels of attractiveness." There is no relationship between skin color and self-esteem for women who are judged "highly attractive," just as there is no correlation between skin color and self-esteem for women of higher socioeconomic status. That physical attractiveness influenced feelings of self-worth for black women is not surprising. Women have traditionally been concerned with appearance, regardless of ethnicity. Indeed, the pursuit and preoccupation with beauty are central features of female sex-role socialization. Our findings suggest that women who are judged "unattractive" are more vulnerable to color bias than those judged attractive.

NOTES

1. In 1990, a workplace discrimination suit was filed in Atlanta, Georgia, on the behalf of a light-skinned black female against her dark-skinned supervisor on the charge of color discrimination (for a discussion, see Russell, Wilson, and Hall 1992).

2. Skin color bias has also been investigated among Latino groups, although more emphasis has been placed on the combination of both color and European phenotype facial characteristics. Studies of Mexican Americans have documented that those with lighter skin and European features attain more schooling (Teller and Murguia 1990) and generally have higher socioeconomic status (Arce, Murguia, and Frisbie 1987) than those of darker complexion with more Indian features. Similar findings have been reported for Puerto Ricans (Rodriguez 1989), a population with African admixture.

3. Self-esteem is divided into two components: racial self-esteem and personal self-esteem. Racial self-esteem refers to group identity and personal self-esteem refers to a general evaluative view of the self (Porter and Washington 1989). In our discussion, self-esteem is conceptualized as personal self-esteem, which is defined as "feelings of intrinsic worth, competence, and self-approval rather than self-rejection and self-contempt" (Porter and Washington 1989, 344).

4. Self-concept theory argued that the experience of social inequality would foster lower self-concept of persons in lower status positions compared with their higher status counterparts. However, when comparing the self-concept of African American schoolboys and schoolgirls, Rosenberg and Simmons (1971) found that their self-feelings were as high and in some instances higher than those of white schoolchildren. This "unexpected" finding was explained by strong ties and bonds within the African American community as opposed to identifying with the larger community.

5. At the suggestion of one reviewer, we estimated all equations with respondents classified as employed part-time, employed full-time, and not employed. The results remained unchanged. The not employed group could be separated into "laid

off" and "retired," but the former category had too few cases to include as a separate group. Using occupation, as one reviewer suggested, also resulted in a substantial loss of cases as many respondents (about 40 percent) were retired.

6. The decision to conduct separate analyses for men and women is based on findings of significant higher order interaction effects, which suggested, as did the literature, that the effects of skin tone on self-esteem and self-efficacy differ for men and women in complex ways. For example, in the analysis of self-esteem, we found a significant three-way interaction effect for gender, skin tone, and income (b = −.288, p = .024). In the analysis of self-efficacy, we found a significant three-way interaction effect for gender, skin tone, and weight (b = −.832, p = .015). The two-way interactions (e.g., skin tone by gender, skin tone by income, gender by income) were not significant.

7. These findings also reflect the dual nature of colorism as it pertains to black women. Colorism is an aspect of racism that results in anti-black discrimination in the wider society and owing to historical patterns also occurs within the black community. The finding that the effects of skin tone on self-efficacy become nonsignificant when socioeconomic status variables are added suggests that the interracial discrimination aspect of colorism is more operational for black women's self-efficacy via access to jobs and income. The finding that the effect of skin tone is more central to black women's self-esteem indicates that colorism within the black community is the more central mechanism. Self-esteem is derived from family, friends, and close associates.

REFERENCES

Acre, Carlos, Edward Murguia, and W. P. Frisbie. 1987. "Phenotype and Life Chances among Chicanos." *Hispanic Journal of Behavioral Sciences* 9(1): 19–32.

Aiken, Leona S., and Stephen G. West. 1991. *Multiple Regression: Testing and Interpreting Interactions.* Newbury Park, CA: Sage.

Bachman, J. G., and L. D. Johnstone. 1978. *The Monitoring the Future Project: Design and Procedures.* Ann Arbor: University of Michigan, Institute for Social Research.

Bandura, A. 1977. "Self-Efficacy: Towards a Unifying Theory of Behavioral Change." *Psychological Review* 84: 191–215.

———. 1982. "Self-Efficacy Mechanism in Human Agency." *American Psychologist* 37:122–47.

Bond, S., and T. F. Cash. 1992. "Black Beauty: Skin Color and Body Images among African-American College Women." *Journal of Applied Social Psychology* 22(11): 874–88.

Boyd Franklin, N. 1991. "Recurrent Themes in the Treatment of African-American Women in Group Psychotherapy." *Women and Therapy* 11(2): 25–40.

Cash, T. S., and N. C. Duncan. 1984. "Physical Attractiveness Stereotyping among Black American College Students." *Journal of Social Psychology* 1:71–77.

Chambers, J. W., T. Clark, L. Dandler, and J. A. Baldwin. 1994. "Perceived Attractiveness, Facial Features, and African Self-Consciousness." *Journal of Black Psychology* 20(3): 305–24.

Dion, K., E. Berscheid, and E. Walster. 1972. "What Is Beautiful Is Good." *Journal of Personality and Social Psychology* 24:285–90.

Frazier, E. Franklin. 1957. *Black Bourgeoisie: The Rise of the New Middle Class.* New York: Free Press.

Freeman, H. E., J. M. Ross, S. Armor, and R. F. Pettigrew. 1966. "Color Gradation and Attitudes among Middle Class Income Negroes." *American Sociological Review* 31:365–74.

Gatewood, W. B. 1988. "Aristocrats of Color: South and North and the Black Elite, 1880–1920." *Journal of Southern History* 54:3–19.

Gecas, Viktor. 1989. "The Social Psychology of Self-Efficacy." *Annual Review of Sociology* 15:291–316.

Grier, W., and P. Cobbs. 1968. *Black Rage.* New York: Basic Books.

Hill Collins, Patricia. 1990. *Black Feminist Thought: Knowledge, Consciousness, and the Politics of Empowerment.* Boston: Unwin Hyman.

Hughes, M., and B. R. Hertel. 1990. "The Significance of Color Remains: A Study of Life Chances, Mate Selection, and Ethnic Consciousness among Black Americans." *Social Forces* 68(4): 1105–20.

Hughes, Michael, and David H. Demo. 1989. "Set Perceptions of Black Americans: Self-Esteem and Personal Efficacy." *American Journal of Sociology* 95:132–59.

Jackson, J., and G. Gurin. 1987. *National Survey of Black Americans, 1979–1* JRO (machine-readable codebook). Ann Arbor: University of Michigan, Inter-University Consortium for Political and Social Research.

Jackson, J., S., B. Tucker, and G. Gurin. 1987. *National Survey of Black Americans 1979–1980* (MRDF). Ann Arbor, MI: Institute for Social Research.

James, W. 1890. *The Principles of Psychology.* New York: Smith.

Keith, V. W., and C. Herring. 1991. "Skin Tone and Stratification in the Black Community." *American Journal of Sociology* 97(3): 760–78.

Kessler, R. C., and J. D. McLeod. 1984. "Sex Differences in Vulnerability to Undesirable Life Events." *American Sociological Review* 49:620–31.

Kirschenman, J., and K. M. Neckerman. 1998. "We'd love to hire them, but. . . ." In *The Meaning of Race for Employers in Working America.—Continuity, Conflict, and Change,* edited by Amy S. Wharton. Mountain View, CA: Mayfield.

Klag, Michael, Paul Whelton, Josef Coresh, Clarence Grim, and Lewis Kuller. 1991. "The Association of Skin Color with Blood Pressure in US Blacks with Low Socioeconomic Status." *Journal of the American Medical Association* 65(5): 599–602.

Miller, Herman F. 1964. *Rich Man, Poor Man.* New York: Corwell.

Neal, A., and M. Wilson. 1989. "The Role of Skin Color and Features in the Black Community: Implications for Black Women in Therapy." *Clinical Psychology Review* 9(3): 323–33.

Okacawa Rey, Margo, Tracy Robinson, and Janie V. Ward. 1987. *Black Women and the Politics of Skin Color and Hair.* New York: Haworth.

Parrish, Charles. 1944. "The Significance of Skin Color in the Negro Community." Ph.D. dissertation, University of Chicago.

Pearlin, L. L., and J. S. Johnson. 1977. "Marital Status, Life Strains, and Depression." *American Sociological Review* 42:704–15.

Pearlin, L. L., M. A. Liberman, E. G. Menaghan, and J. T. Mullan. 1981. "The Stress Process." *Journal of Health and Social Behavior* 22 (December): 337–56.

Pearlin, L. L., and C. Schooler. 1978. "The Structure of Coping." *Journal of Health and Social Behavior* 19:2–21.

Porter, J. 1971. *Black Child, White Child: The Development of Racial Attitudes.* Cambridge, MA: Harvard University Press.

Porter, J. R., and R. E. Washington. 1989. "Developments in Research in Black Identity and Self-Esteem: 1979–1988." *Review of International Psychology and Sociology* 2:341–53.

Ransford, E. H. 1970. "Skin Color, Life Chances and Anti-White Attitudes." *Social Problems* 18:164–78.

Robinson, J. P., and P. R. Shaver. 1969. *Measures of Social Psychological Attitudes.* Ann Arbor: University of Michigan, Institute of Social Research.

Robinson, T. L., and J. V. Ward. 1995. "African American Adolescents and Skin Color." *Journal of Black Psychology* 21(3): 256–74.

Rodriguez, Clara. 1989. *Puerto Ricans: Born in the USA.* Boston: Unwin Hyman.

Rosenberg, M. 1979. *Conceiving the Self.* New York: Basic Books.

Rosenberg. M., and R. Simmons. 1971. *Black and White Self-Esteem: The Urban School Child.* Washington, DC: American Sociological Association.

Russell, Kathy, Midge Wilson, and Ronald Hall. 1992. *The Color Complex: The Politics of Skin Color among African Americans.* New York: Harcourt Brace Jovanovich.

Segura, Denise. 1986. "Chicanas and Triple Oppression in the Labor Force." In *Chicana Voices: Intersections of Class, Race and Gender,* edited by Teresa Cordova and the National Association of Chicana Studies Editorial Committee. Austin, TX: Center for Mexican American Studies.

St. John, Y., and J. R. Feagin. 1998. *Double Burden: Black Women and Every Day Racism.* New York: M. E. Sharpe.

Teller, Edward E., and Edward Murguia. 1990. "Phenotypic Discrimination and Income Differences among Mexican Americans." *Social Science Quarterly* 71(4): 682–95.

Thoits, Peggy A. 1982. "Life Stress, Social Support, and Psychological Vulnerability: Epidemiological Considerations." *Journal of Community Psychology* 10:341–62.

———. 1984. "Explaining Distributions of Psychological Vulnerability: Lack of Social Support in the Face of Life Stress." *Social Forces* 63:452–81.

Turner, R. J., and S. Noh. 1983. "Class and Psychological Vulnerability among Women: The Significance of Social Support and Personal Control." *Journal of Health and Social Behavior* 24:2–15.

Tryoler, H. A., and S. A. James. 1978. "Blood Pressure and Skin Color." *American Journal of Public Health* 58:1170–72.

Udry, J. R., K. E. Bauman, and C. Chase. 1969. "Skin Color, Status, and Mate Selection." *American Journal of Sociology* 76:722–33.

Verna, G., and K. Runion. 1985. "The Effects of Contextual Dissonance on the Self-Concept of Youth from High vs. Low Socially Valued Group[s]." *Journal of Social Psychology* 125:449–58.

Warner, W. L., B. H. Junker, and W. A. Adams. 1941. *Color and Human Nature.* Washington, DC: American Council on Education.

Wright, B. 1976. *The Dissent of the Governed: Alienation and Democracy in America.* New York: Academic Press.

Part One:
Study Questions on
Race and Colorism

"Is Discrimination Dead?," by Cedric Herring

1. Why is it commonly assumed that blacks are no longer discriminated against?
2. Is there evidence that racial discrimination has become a thing of the past?
3. How does the author refute the claim that discrimination is behind us?
4. How does understanding discrimination help to understand the social world?

"What Is Racism? The Racialized Social System Framework," by Eduardo Bonilla-Silva

1. What does Bonilla-Silva mean when he says that most definitions of race have been based on an idealist philosophy? What problem does he see with the idealist perspective of race?
2. Explain what is meant by a materialist interpretation of racism. Why is this approach better than the idealist approach?
3. What has been the key idea of these major critical perspectives of racism: Marxism? Internal colonialism? Racial formation?
4. Race scholar Joe Feagin has often said that racism results in "societal waste." What is meant by this? Can you think of examples?
5. Explain what is meant by a "racialized social system" approach to racism. What are the advantages of this framework?

"The Blacker the Berry: Gender, Skin Tone, Self-Esteem and Self-Efficacy," by Maxine D. Thompson and Verna Keith

1. What is meant by colorism? How is colorism linked to notions of beauty or physical attractiveness in the United States?
2. How does skin color affect socioeconomic status and health?

3. The authors of this study examine two components of self-evaluation to see how they are related to skin color. What are those two components?
4. What are the major findings about the relationship between skin color and self-esteem?
5. How are the results of colorism "gendered," that is, how are they different for men and women?

II

FAILING SAFETY NETS AND FRAGILE FAMILIES

Growing class diversity and changing social policies have made poor African American families even more fragile. The success of middle-class blacks during the post–civil rights era has had a polarizing effect, separating the black population into the "haves" and "have-nots" and stripping those in the latter category of many of their traditional resources, such as assistance for extended kin. Durr and Hill lead the section with an overview of the family-work interface and problems associated with it for African American families. Hunter discusses how adapting to poverty and racism has led to a diversity of black families and relationships. Although qualitative and ethnographic studies emphasize extended family ties as important systems of support for blacks, many have begun to question the resiliency of these bonds in the past few decades. Brewster and Padavic, for example, show a significant drop in reliance on relatives for child care among working women between 1977 and 1994. At the same time, welfare reform policies sought to discipline poor black women based on the notion that generous welfare policies were an incentive for nonmarital childbearing, thus further reducing the resources of poor families. But as Moller shows, racialized patterns of benefits have meant that they were never really as liberal for blacks as for whites.

4

The Family-Work Interface in African American Households

Marlese Durr and Shirley A. Hill

Although patriarchal ideologies relegating women to a secondary status are ancient in origin, feminists have often cited the "doctrine of separate spheres" as most profoundly shaping white women's family roles during the twentieth century. Despite their low status in colonial society, the productive and reproductive work of women made them vital to the agricultural economy; indeed, marriage was often seen as an economic partnership between men and women. Emerging with industrialization, the "doctrine of separate spheres" relegated women to the private arena of the home and sanctioned the public arena of work and politics as the appropriate spheres for male participation. Thus, the so-called traditional family was born, validating breadwinner-homemaker families as best suited for the demands of the industrial economy. Not surprisingly, the first wave of feminism also evolved in the eighteenth century, with women challenging their exclusion from the public arena with demands for the right to vote. Many black people were still enslaved when feminism emerged, and the abolition of slavery became one of the moral crusades of feminism. Slavery forced black women to prioritize work over family, but even the demise of slavery did not free them from economic exploitation and forced labor. Legalized racial segregation became the law of the land and economic marginalization made dual-income black families the norm. Moreover, even before slavery ended, African American men were already vying for patriarchal authority in their families, arguing that they had the right to "own" their wives and children. Thus, black women have historically been challenged with the denial of equal rights on the basis of their race, class, and gender position. Still, racism precluded them from much participation in the early white feminist movement, and they formed their own organizations devoted to improving the lives of all African Americans.

This chapter was written for the current edition.

73

While most white women eventually accepted the ideology of full-time domesticity and the status that went with it, the massive entry of women into the labor market led to a resurgence of feminism during the 1960s and 1970s. The notion of distinct "sex roles" for men and women was challenged on several grounds, such as its tendency to conflate sex (biological traits) and gender (socially constructed traits) by erroneously characterizing men and women as having innately different characteristics. The "cult of true womanhood," for example, described women as naturally pious, pure, submissive, and domestic—all characteristics that justified their exclusion from public life. Such characteristics were never applied to social constructs of black womanhood, however, nor did their families fit the idealized family and its gender order. With the growing recognition of the class and racial diversity that exists among families, it is now commonly noted that the highly praised breadwinner-homemaker family was a reality primarily for those who were white and middle class. And although it presumes a tidy division between family-work and employment, more recent scholars have also contended that the two are inseparable; indeed, not only does the viability of family life rest on economic factors, but the very nature and structure of work shape family life.

The experiences of African American families highlight the validity of these assertions. For example, not only were most black people still enslaved when the breadwinner-homemaker ideology evolved, but even afterward cultural and economic factors made it impossible for them to conform to the dominant society's family model. Work had been a mandate for black women during slavery, and due to class and race disadvantage their survival afterward continued to rely on their labor market participation. While labor unions lobbied for and won a "family wage" for white men, or a wage adequate for them to support their families, black men were rarely able to secure the kinds of jobs that allowed them to become economic providers. Thus, they often found themselves deprived of patriarchal privileges such as authority, dominance, and respect in their families. Moreover, slavery and the historic labor force participation of black women created a cultural tradition of relying more on their own employment, their extended family, and eventually welfare to support families, leaving many black men with only marginal and/or tenuous connections to their families. Thus, white feminists have drawn on the experiences of African American women to champion the notion that women can combine family and labor market work and to refute the myth of work and family as separate arenas. The spillover effects of work and family are now well documented, especially in terms of how they affect the quality of intimate relationships. Just as family life might impose restraints or confer advantages on labor market participation, factors like joblessness and being confined to low-wage, dead-end jobs have a corrosive effect on couples and family life. In this chapter we examine feminism's gender perspective on families; we then look at the interface between economic factors and the historic and contemporary construction of African American families.

A GENDER PERSPECTIVE ON THE BLACK FAMILY

The premise that gender is socially constructed on the basis of economic factors and patriarchal traditions is the cornerstone of modern feminist thought, as is the notion that the way gender is constructed privileges men and disadvantages women. The nineteenth-century ideology of a breadwinner-homemaker family has been seen as the linchpin in perpetuating gender inequality, since it not only advocates economic dominance for men and dependence for women but also models these behaviors and passes them on to children. The feminist critique has thus sought to reenvision the family by calling for policies that, according to Barrie Thorne (1982), endorse a broader array of sexual and household arrangements as families, women's right to abortion, and egalitarian family roles for men and women. Yet while white feminists have criticized patriarchal families as oppressive, African Americans claimed that African American families had never really fully embraced those traditions. Indeed, while patriarchy was clearly the norm in West African societies, slavery had blurred work-based gender distinctions among black people, and diminished the impact of patriarchal privileges and norms. Even the construction of femininity in terms of submissiveness, dependency, and innate domesticity had excluded black women, who were seen as unusually strong and independent. Some theorists claimed that the family had historically been more a system of support for women than one of oppression. Such analyses have often impeded the development of a gender perspective on African American families by implying that they have simply not been affected by patriarchal traditions.

The extent to which slavery disrupted patriarchy among African Americans, however, has been a matter of some debate. Early theorists like the African American scholar E. Franklin Frazier (1966) claimed that slavery had essentially destroyed the African family and disrupted the gender order of strong men and weak women. From his work came the "black matriarch thesis" which, when reiterated by Moynihan in the 1960s, generated a wealth of revisionist scholarship arguing that black families were more likely to be headed by men (or at least conform to the two-parent structure) during slavery than they were a hundred years later. Their work in essence sought to legitimize enslaved African American families as "normal" by asserting that the two-parent family structure and (presumedly) patriarchy prevailed in those families. Revisionist theorists looking at contemporary black families also refuted Moynihan's depiction of it as a "tangle of pathology." They argued that black families took a diversity of forms, that female-headed families could be strong and viable, that black women had effectively combined labor market and family work, and that their marriages were based on relative equality between men and women—all characteristics that seemed to embody much of the feminist agenda for families.

Multicultural feminism posits the necessity of looking at the intersection of race, class, and gender in understanding the experiences of black people. It proffers a culturally sensitive approach to identifying the strengths and uniqueness of black families, but also focuses on how race, class, and gender oppression shaped those families. Rose Brewer, for example, asserted that poor, single-mother families could not be understood unless historically grounded in the "social construction of a racist/sexist social order." She wrote that

> gender, race, ideology, culture, state, and economy operate simultaneously and interactively in the family formation and change process. Capitalist racial patriarchy profoundly shapes male and female relations generally but is also conflated with cultural and ideological realities. I mean by capitalist racial patriarchy a structure of White male-dominated social arrangements. These institutional arrangements severely disadvantage Black women, men, and children. (Brewer 1995, 166)

Multicultural feminism enables us to understand the parallels as well as the differences between the experiences of black and white women. For example, despite virulent racial hatred, relentless labor, and the sexual assault experienced by black women in colonial America, they had in common with most white women the expectation that they would combine production and reproductive labor. And while patriarchal ideologies were firmly entrenched in both African and American societies, the value of women was heightened by their shortage (due to high rates of maternal mortality and, for black women, also lower rates of being taken into slavery) and the integral roles they played in the agricultural economy. Patriarchy aside, white marriages were often seen as economic partnerships between men and women, especially since economic work was centered in the home. Such traditions paralleled those in West Africa, where patriarchal ideologies were strong but women's status was enhanced by their important economic positions, which included the responsibility for feeding children. With industrialization the roles of black and white women diverged even further, as white women were excluded from the labor market and expected to devote their full-time energies to being housewives and mothers and black women continued to work outside the home, whether due to necessity or coercion. African American women and families also faced racial oppression due to legalized segregation and class oppression as they were denied equal education and widely discriminated against in the labor market. Thus, since slavery the work roles of

African American women and men have had, and continue to have, immense implications for the organization of gender in families and for family stability. We discuss that work-family interface during slavery, following emancipation, and after the 1970s postindustrial reorganization of the economy.

SLAVERY'S IMPACT ON THE FAMILY-WORK NEXUS·

Whatever social organization may have prevailed in their native Africa, whatever family arrangements, forms, and usages found in the mores of the preexistent cultures, these were stripped from, or eventually lost, to the Negroes brought to America. (Queen and Habenstein, 1967, p. 315)

Family sociology emerged in the early 1900s with concern over how industrialization was adversely affecting American families, and was gradually transformed by research on the new companionate marriages that had resulted from modernization. Only a handful of scholars devoted any attention to studying African American families, and most who did asserted that it had been destroyed by slavery. The central defining feature of American slavery was the extraction of unpaid labor from men and women, and by all accounts economic exploitation and brutality pervaded the lives of enslaved black people for more than 250 years. Policies of strict social control and dehumanization were enforced in efforts to strip Africans of their identity and power, and enforce subservience to white Americans. As Roberts points out:

From the moment that Africans arrived on the North American continent, their enslavers mounted a campaign of abuse, the goal of which was to convince them that slavery was their destiny and that white power was the only important one in their lives. By stripping Africans of their personal autonomy and basic human rights, the enslavers revealed that their objective was not merely to dominate Africans politically and physically, but to redefine black identity by destroying their sense of humanity. (Roberts 1989)

Thus, while Africans did not arrive on the shores of America without cultural and family systems, white enslavers clearly tried to minimize and displace those systems, at least to the extent that doing so served their purposes.

African traditions of patriarchal families and polygyny were undermined by the work systems enforced during slavery, but also by the fact that the slave trade, while it was still legal, mostly brought black men to the country. Black men outnumbered black women in the United States at least until the early 1800s, thus decreasing the prospect of marrying one woman, not to mention several. While the labor power of men based on their strength and stamina probably helps explain this, another interesting explanation exists: Black women's work roles were so important in Africa that they were simply less likely to be slated for slavery. During slavery, black men and women were seen as almost equal and independent laborers; indeed, work, as Jones (1985) has pointed out, dominated the lives of black women. Because black men and women were defined primarily as laborers, work systems played a salient role in defining gender and constructing families. The opportunity to create a breadwinner-homemaker family simply did not exist; moreover, slavery precluded the rights of blacks to legally marry, sold their spouses and other family members, usurped their parental rights, undermined patriarchal authority in families, and led to the sexual assault of black women by white slave owners. Thus, those who first took on the challenge of theorizing African American families, such as Frazier (1966), characterized them as still suffering from the effects of more than two centuries of slavery.

Frazier acknowledged that slavery had given rise to two-family structures among blacks—the two-parent family (some of whom had achieved middle-class status) and the single-mother family. Frazier characterized the latter families as "matriarchal" and saw their roots in slavery's greater repression of men than of women. He claimed that slavery infused in African American women an unusual boldness and strength, and that it often enabled them to challenge white authority in ways that black men would not have gotten away with. He explained that since neither "economic necessity nor tradition had instilled in her the spirit of subordination to masculine authority," black women felt free to dispense with men, seek sexual satisfaction outside of marriage, and head their own families. Jessie Bernard (1966), one of the founding mothers of family sociology, echoed a similar theme. Bernard argued that slavery had given black women an "unnatural superiority" over black men. Slavery, she pointed out, was more of a violation of masculinity than femininity, as "enforced subordination and subservience were not so far out of line with the Western world's definition of a 'woman's place.'"

Emancipation did little to free black women of labor, as most moved into a sharecropping system that demanded the labor of both men and women. Fearful of the loss of their labor, some southern states passed laws against black "female loaferism," and even when black families tried to conform to the breadwinner-homemaker family they were criticized for doing so. In addition to sharecropping, black women were also in demand in southern towns to work in private households. As Jones has pointed out, this "had a profound impact on black household life, for it meant that many married black women . . . rivaled their menfolk as primary breadwinners; the economic dependence that bound wife to husband no longer applied in these cases" (112). Men were more likely to be confined to agricultural jobs in the southern economy, where many were paid in goods rather than cash. Even among blacks who had seen their fortunes rise with emancipation, their gains often proved short-lived when Reconstruction ended and racial segregation became the law of the land.

The waning agricultural economy and the violence increasingly directed toward blacks helped spawn a massive northward migration around the turn of the twentieth century. Much of it was orchestrated by northern industrialists in search of cheap labor since the flow of European immigrants was waning. But black women were also highly recruited, sometimes signing domestic labor contracts in exchange for their transportation expenses and taking on jobs as cooks, laundresses, and maids. Northward migration thus increased the number and visibility of single-mother families, and as Frazier (1966) has pointed out, these maternal families came under fire as they became more visible in urban areas.

THE MATRIARCH DEBATE

> The matriarch concept, embracing the clichéd "female castrator," is, in the last instance, an open weapon of ideological warfare. —Angela Davis, 1995, p. 201

Even by the 1930s the promise of greater freedom and opportunity in the north was beginning to wane as African Americans found themselves confined to poor urban areas and discriminated against in the labor force. Black men who escaped the farming economy were still deprived of the family wage that was increasingly offered white men around the turn of the century, a wage necessary to support the breadwinner-homemaker family model. The absence of strong financial incentives to form patriarchal families, along with the cultural traditions and resources developed by black women during slavery, dampened the appeal of marriage, and single-mother families were prevalent. Prevailing racial ideologies continued to stigmatize African Americans as responsible for their own plight, even as voices demanding change and an end to racial segregation were increasing. Thus, when Moynihan (1965) reiterated the "matriarch thesis" in the mid-1960s and described the black family as a "tangle of pathology," a spate of revisionist research began to explore both the historical and contemporary nature of African American families.

Although the now-infamous Moynihan Report recognized the growing class diversity of black families, rejected genetic explanations of black poverty, and championed greater economic opportunity for black men, he clearly saw the problem facing black families as the weak structure created when they were headed by women. He revived Frazier's observation of black families as matriarchal and, at the height of the civil rights movement, suggested that blacks needed to embrace mainstream family models if they were to succeed in American society. His thesis spawned a genre of myth-dispelling research, most of it focusing on the strengths and diversity of African American families. In his 1968 book, *Black Families in White America*, Andrew Billingsley used functionalist theory to explain the adaptive nature of African American families, and argued that viability rather than structure should be the criterion used in evaluating them. Robert Hill challenged negative images of black families by delineating gender role flexibility, religiosity, a strong achievement orientation, and kinship bonds as their strengths (Hill 1972). Similarly, Carol Stack's (1974) ethnographic portrait of poor black single mothers made a lasting contribution to understanding the complex networks of exchange and reciprocity they used to ensure the survival of their families. Meanwhile, historian Herbert Gutman seemed to deal a final blow to the social deficit perspective with compelling evidence that black families were more likely to be composed of two parents during slavery than in the 1960s (Gutman 1976).

In refuting the black matriarch thesis, revisionists who rethought the black family during slavery highlighted the roles of African American men and their contributions to the families—in some cases adding a "masculinist bias" to the literature. Still, evidence suggests that even during slavery black men made symbolic and important economic contributions to their families, and claimed the most prestigious and diverse occupations available to black people. In some cases, these contributions might have been sufficient to lead to stable families after slavery ended. Often, however, black families were still more reliant on the whims of whites for their economic existence than the efforts of black men. For the most part, black males' provisions were too meager to effect the breadwinner-homemaker bargain and, with little incentive to tolerate male privilege, many African American women continued to head their own families.

Postrevisionist scholars, with access to a wider array of historical and archival resources, have now challenged many of the claims made by revisionists. The contention that blacks did their best, even during slavery, to abide by the dictates of mainstream culture fails to challenge the legitimacy of patriarchal families, and the revisionist account of black families as thriving during slavery inadvertently renders it a much more "humane" institution. Wilma Dunaway has recently argued that revisionists' accounts of slaveholders as trying to strengthen black families and the authority of the black men in them are nothing more than a "Disney script" that minimizes the impact of slavery. Her research on slavery in Appalachia found that not more than 40 percent of blacks lived in intact families, and that even after slavery ended black families were disrupted by forced labor migrations. The result was that many ended up having several spouses, making the simple legalizing of marriage after slavery problematic. In some cases, the Freedman's Bureau sought to solve the problem of multiple spouses by having men marry the one with helpless children.

Scholars today point out the tremendous variety that existed among slaves (1997) in their opportunity to get married and form stable families. Donna Franklin, for example, notes that such opportunities were tied largely to the size of the plantation they worked on and the organization of work. Large plantations—though fewer in number—had more slaves, more opportunities for marriage among slaves, and a greater chance that enslaved Africans would retain some of their cultural heritage. On smaller plantations, where white owners often worked side by side with their slaves, there were more interracial sexual liaisons, more early pregnancy, and less opportunity for blacks to marry or form stable unions. Overall, recent theorists have challenged the revisionist notion that black people rushed to marry once slavery had ended. Black women had often established reliable matrifocal families during slavery, and were not always eager to exchange them for patriarchal marriages. Despite vigorous efforts to convince blacks to marry once slavery had ended, Leslie A. Schwalm (1997) has argued that "marriage was not the only, or even most important, familial relationship" for women, as caring for children and kin took precedence.

Thus, revisionist theorists of the civil rights era challenged the matriarch thesis and the notion of family pathology, based on the existence of two-parent families during slavery and the functionality of diverse family structures. More recently, postrevisionist scholars, while embracing neither the matriarch thesis nor the notion of pathological black families, have effectively challenged the notion that two-parent families prevailed during slavery, and that black people rushed to legalize their marriages once it had been abolished. The strengths perspective on African American families eventually displaced the social deficit perspective, yet, ironically, rates of nonmarriage and single-woman childbearing escalated in the post–civil rights era, causing new concern over the stability of black families.

THE POSTINDUSTRIAL BLACK FAMILY

Even as scholars were discovering the heritage of African American families and proclaiming their strengths and resiliency, economic forces and cultural revolutions were reshaping patterns of marriage and family formation. While Moynihan had lamented the fact that nearly one-third of all black families in the 1960s were headed by black women, by the mid-1980s nearly 70 percent of African American children were being born to single mothers. Moreover, evidence that single mothers were a part of or had the support of a strong, extended network of kin waned. Indeed, poor inner-city areas were characterized as war zones plagued by an epidemic of drugs and violence, and child abandonment left black children substantially overrepresented among those in foster care. Many policy analysts noted that the link between marriage and childbearing among African Americans was completely severed, and social conservatives contended that generous welfare policies were further weakening poor families and actually perpetuating poverty. The most common stereotype of a "welfare mother" became a young African American woman who had several children, all fathered by different men. As Willa Mae Hemmons wrote,

> Ironicallly, the blame for [black families'] substantially diminished viability [was] primarily placed not upon the shoulders of the discriminatory society, but upon those of the Black women. The Black women [was] called emasculating, promiscuous, domineering, excessively fertile and lazy [and one who] fails to rear her children to avoid the lure of drugs, crime, violence, and more children in lieu of jobs, education, self-discipline, obedience, and abstinence. (Hemmons 1996)

A more liberal perspective was proffered by William J. Wilson (1987), who argued that the loss of industrial jobs was disproportionately affecting black men, thus undermining their opportunity or incentive to marry. More controversially, Wilson claimed that while the legacy of slavery and racism continued to adversely affect African Americans, class inequality had become more important than racial inequality in shaping the destinies of black people. What is evident is that the civil rights movement left African Americans more class-polarized than they had ever been before, with a larger segment of the black population achieving economic mobility and others falling more hopelessly into despair. While Wilson's thesis focuses on structural factors that have undermined family stability among blacks, it is also the case that structure impacts culture by producing new values or at least behavioral patterns. Cultural theories of poverty that blamed victims for their own poverty fell into disrepute during the civil rights era, when challenging racial discrimination made focusing on outward causes imperative. Yet theorists today recognize the link between structural and cultural forces, especially when the former produce despair and hopelessness. Massey and Denton, for example, argue that racial segregation and inequality produce an "oppositional culture that devalues work, schooling, and marriage."

The conservative thesis that generous welfare policies were undermining marriage among African Americans led to the passage in 1996 of the Personal Responsibility and Work Opportunity Act. The key features of this policy have been its limitation on the number of years one can claim welfare, its focus on placing poor mothers in the labor market, and its initiative to promote marriage among poor men and women. Welfare reform has been credited with a 56 percent reduction in the welfare rolls and with bringing child poverty to its lowest rate in 25 years but its ultimate success depends not only on whether women get jobs, but on whether they can keep them and improve the quality of life for themselves and their children. Sharon Hays describes welfare reform as a mixed bag; while it is based on a set of honorable principles, such as independence and the well-being of children, it can be punitive in the context of the massive changes families are facing (Hays 2003).

While welfare reform has sought to solve the problem of poverty among families mostly by changing the lives of women and children, it has also advocated marriage. In the past the majority of African Americans married, although their rates of separation and divorce were extremely high. Economic strains and female independence have made it especially difficult for black couples to reap the benefits of the traditional gender bargain in marriage—household authority and exemption from domestic work for men, and financial security for women. Marriage initiatives today rarely deal with the fundamental underlying problem that has made marriage less viable for whites and blacks—changing gender roles. While patterns of nonmarriage and single motherhood have particularly characterized African Americans, they have become more common in the broader society as women have entered the labor market and the ability of men to support their families has waned. Indeed, the highly idealized traditional family of American society has always been premised on the wage-earning abilities of men, and nothing better illustrates the family-work connection than the inability to sustain such families in the postindustrial era.

REFERENCES

Bernard, Jessie. 1966. *Marriage and Family Among Negroes.* Englewood Cliffs, NJ: Prentice-Hall, Inc.

Billingsley, Andrew. 1968. *Black Families in White America.* Englewood Cliffs, NJ: Prentice-Hall.

Brewer, Rose. 1995. "Gender, poverty, culture, and economy: Theorizing female-led families." Pp. 13–30 in *Theorizing Black Feminisms: The Visionary Pragmatism of Black Women,* edited by S. M. James and A. P. A. Busia. London: Routledge.

Burgess, Norma J. 1994. "Gender roles revisited: The development of the 'women's place' among African American women in the United States." *Journal of Black Studies* 24:391–401.

Collins, Patricia Hill. 1990. *Black Feminist Thought: Knowledge, Consciousness, and the Politics of Empowerment.* Boston: Unwin Hyman.

Dabel, Jane E. 2002. "African American women and household composition in New York City, 1827–1877." Pp. 60–72 in *Black Cultures and Race Relations,* edited by J. L. Conyers, Jr. Chicago: Burnham Inc., Publishers.

Davis, Angela. 1995. "Reflections on the black woman's role in the community of slaves." Pp. 200–18 in *Words of Fire: An Anthology of African-American Feminist Thought,* edited by B. Guy-Sheftall. New York: New Press.

Dill, Bonnie Thornton. 1979. "The dialectic of black womanhood." *Signs: Journal of Women in Culture and Society* 4:545–55.

———. 1988. "Our mothers' grief: Racial ethnic women and the maintenance of families." *Journal of Family History* 13:415–31.

Dunaway, Wilma A. 2003. *The African-American Family in Slavery and Emancipation.* New York: Cambridge University Press.

Franklin, Donna L. 1997. *Ensuring Inequality: The Structural Transformation of the African-American Family.* New York: Oxford University Press.

Frazier, E. Franklin. 1966. *The Negro Family in the United States.* Chicago: University of Chicago Press.

Gutman, Herbert G. 1976. *The Black Family in Slavery and Freedom, 1750–1925.* New York: Pantheon.

Hays, Sharon. 2003. *Flat Broke with Children: Women in the Age of Welfare Reform.* New York: Oxford University Press.

Hemmons, Willa Mae. 1996. *Black Women in the New World Order: Social Justice and the African American Female.* Westport, CT: Praeger.

Hill, Robert. 1972. *The Strengths of Black Families.* New York: Emerson-Hall.

Hymowitz, C., and M. Weissman. 1978. *A History of Women in America.* New York: Bantam.

Jones, Jacqueline. 1985. *Labor of Love, Labor of Sorrow: Black Women, Work, and the Family from Slavery to the Present.* New York: Basic Books.

Kiefer, Francine. 2002 [February 28]. "Fight over putting more work in workfare." *Christian Science Monitor:* 2, 3.

Lewis, D. K. 1975. "The black family: Socialization and sex roles." *Phylon* 36:221–38.

Marks, Carole. 1989. *Farewell—We're Good and Gone: The Great Black Migration.* Bloomington: Indiana University Press.

Massey, D. S., and N. A. Denton. 1993. *American Apartheid: Segregation and the Making of the Underclass.* Cambridge, MA: Harvard University Press.

Moynihan, Daniel Patrick. 1965. *The Negro Family: The Case for National Action.* Washington, DC: Office of Policy Planning and Research.

Murray, C. 1984. *Losing Ground: American Social Policy 1950–1980.* New York: Basic Books.

Queen, Stuart A., and R. W. Habenstein. 1967. *The Family in Various Cultures.* Philadelphia and New York: J. B. Lippincott Company.

Rapp, Rayna. 1982. "Family and class in contemporary America: Notes toward an understanding of ideology." Pp. 168–87 in *Rethinking the Family: Some Feminist Questions,* edited by B. Thorne and M. Yalom. New York & London: Longman.

Risman, Barbara. 1998. *Gender Vertigo: American Families in Transition.* New Haven and London: Yale University Press.

Roberts, John W. 1989. *From Trickster to Badman: The Black Folk Hero in Slavery and Freedom.* Philadelphia: University of Pennsylvania Press.

Schwalm, Leslie A. 1997. *A Hard Fight for We: Women's Transition from Slavery to Freedom in South Carolina.* Urbana and Chicago: University of Illinois Press.

Stack, Carol. 1974. *All Our Kin: Strategies for Survival in a Black Community.* New York: Harper & Row.

Terborg-Penn, Rosalyn. 1986. "Women and slavery in the African Diaspora: A cross-cultural approach to historical analysis." *Sage: A Scholarly Journal on Black Women* 3:11–15.

Thorne, Barrie. 1982. "Feminist rethinking of the family: An overview." Pp. 1–24 in *Rethinking the Family: Some Feminist Questions,* edited by B. Thorne and M. Yalom. New York & London: Longman.

Welter, Barbara. 1973. "The cult of true womanhood: 1820–1860." Pp. 224–50 in *The American Family in Social-Historical Perspective,* edited by M. Gordon. New York: St. Martin's.

Wilson, W. J. 1987. *The Truly Disadvantaged.* Chicago: University of Chicago Press.

5

(Re)Envisioning Cohabitation

A Commentary on Race, History, and Culture

Andrea G. Hunter

> To some listening to such a conversation, *gumbo ya ya* may sound like chaos. We may be better able to understand it as something other than confusion if we overlay it with jazz, for *gumbo ya ya* is the essence of a musical tradition where "the various voices in a piece of music may go their own ways but still be held together by their relationship to each other." (Brown 1991, 85)

The rate of cohabitation in the United States, like western Europe, has been another component of the noteworthy transformations in marriage and child-bearing that have taken place over the last several decades. Although the increase in cohabitation cuts across the U.S. population, there are significant variations across racial and ethnic groups that parallel the differences that have been found in cross-national comparisons of western Europe. African Americans spend more of their adult lives loving and raising children in non-marital cohabiting unions or in other nonmarital partnerships than do non-blacks (Hunter 1997; Tucker and Mitchell-Kernan 1995a). Although the rate of cohabitation among African Americans is only moderately higher than the rate of cohabitation among whites, blacks are less likely to convert cohabiting unions to marriage (Bumpass and Sweet 1989; London 1991; Manning and Smock 1995). African Americans are also more likely to have children in cohabiting unions but are less likely to marry to "legitimize" these births than are whites (Loomis and Landale 1994; Manning 1993). These patterns have spawned lively investigation of the sources of racial differences in cohabita-tion and its relationship to "traditional" patterns in marriage and childbearing. Recent studies of cohabitation among African Americans have been framed by

This chapter was originally published in *Just Living Together: Implications of Cohabitation on Families, Children, and Social Policy*, edited by Alan Booth and A. C. Crouter. Mahwah, NJ: Erl-baum Associates, 2002.

the dramatic transformations in marriage and childbearing that have taken place in this population since 1960 (Ellwood and Crane 1990; Walker 1988). Much of this work has focused on the role of economic and demographic factors (e.g., male unemployment and wages, public aid, and sex ratio) in the declining rates of marriage and subsequent rise in nonmarital births (for a review, see Tucker and Mitchell-Kernan 1995b). Although studies do find that a variety of economic and demographic factors are critical for understanding this shift, Raley (1996) noted these factors account for only about 20 percent of the differences in black-white marriage rates. To explain the source of remaining differences, researchers have suggested a closer look at African-American attitudes and expectations about marriage and family formation. Although more ambivalent about marriage than members of other racial groups, African Americans value marriage and would like to get married (Bulcroft and Bulcroft 1993; King 1999; South 1993). Indeed, there is no widespread ideological retreat from marriage among African Americans (King 1999; Tucker and Mitchell-Kernan 1995a). However, despite an endorsement of mainstream American values about marriage and the family, African Americans have long drawn on a diverse repertoire of union formation, childbearing, and parenting (Frazier 1939; Gutman 1976; Hunter and Ensminger 1992; Stevenson 1995). In this commentary, to inform the current examination of cohabitation in the United States, I offer a meditation on African-American families, history, and culture that highlights the diverse repertoire of partnering and parenting that has emerged out of the black experience.

MEDITATIONS ON FAMILIES, HISTORY, AND CULTURE: MINING THE BLACK EXPERIENCE

The explosion of literature on cohabitation in the United States, in my view, is not only an attempt to understand a significant social and demographic transition, it is also a search for a new cultural narrative about courtship, marriage, and childbearing. Indeed, much of the change in Western family life is seen as disordering, not fitting with either how the world once was or how it should be. We theorize and create new narratives about where cohabitation fits as an alternative to marriage, part of courtship and the transition to marriage, an alternative to or another type of singlehood, or a unique postmarital transition. Kiernan's (2002) suggestion that cohabitation is more of a process than an event is an example of (re)envisioning the ways we interpret cohabitation. If one is to use the stages of partnership transition reviewed by Kiernan as a guide to categorize patterns of union formation among African Americans, it could be argued that they are leading the edge of this transition in the United States. Hence, it is not surprising that the revisionist narratives that have emerged in the cohabitation literature tend to fit uneasily onto the patterns seen among African Americans.

With few racial differences in attitudes about marriage, researchers have suggested that we need to understand more about the unique history and culture of African Americans. Among family scholars in the United States, it has been difficult to address issues of history, race and culture, and difference without engaging a discourse of social pathology and cultural dysfunction (Hunter 1992; Miller 1993). However, interrogating racial differences, like the exploration of cross-national patterns, challenges us to unhinge ourselves from common understandings that are tied to an unspoken history and culture and often to our own unexamined biography. Elsa Barkley Brown (1991), in a wonderful essay on women's history, suggests jazz and *gumbo ya ya* (a Creole term meaning everything at once) as metaphors to explore the intersections and divergences of women's histories across race and ethnicity, class, and sexuality. *Gumbo* and *jazz* may also be useful metaphors for exploring racial and ethnic variations in family life within a society as well as across national boundaries. As Brown suggests, they direct our attention to the multiple rhythms that are being played simultaneously and the ways in which diverse rhythms are in dialogue with or in opposition to each other.

Let us take a step backward to E. Franklin Frazier's (1939) classic monograph *The Negro Family in the United States,* which is the single most influential work on the black family. This work was a sweeping epic and analysis of the history and the cultural transformations of African Americans from slavery to the early twentieth-century urban migration. Revisionist historians have well critiqued Frazier's conclusions about the cultural death of African slaves and the evolution of weak marital and matriarchal family systems under slavery (see, for example, Blassingame 1972; Genovese 1974; Gutman 1976). However, his deeply textured analysis reveals the duality, improvisational character, and diversity of African Americans' approach to sexuality, reproduction, and the family. Frazier described a variety of heterosexual unions, including legal marriage, quasi-marital forms (e.g., cohabitation, common-law unions), and nonmarital unions (e.g., quasi-cohabitation, extra-legal relationships) noting that across these contexts children were born and reared (see Stevenson 1995, for post-revisionist discussion). These pairings occurred within the context of an extended kinship system that bound slaves across time and space and was a source of family survival well into the twentieth century (Frazier 1939; Gutman 1976; Hunter 1993; Ruggles 1994; Stack 1974). *The Negro Family* (1939) illustrates the diverse repertoire of partnering, childbearing, and parenting among African Americans that was borne out of necessity and grounded in the rich cultural past of African slaves. Although emerging out of shared history and common culture, African-American families are perhaps most distinctive for their variety. Multiple rhythms in the timing and sequencing of family events both support and subvert dominant cultural mores and social conventions. It is a kind of *gumbo ya ya,* that is, everybody talking and doing everything at once. The rich diversity with which African Americans and others can organize their family lives challenges family scholars to find ways to understand the meaning(s) of various arrangements as well as under what conditions individuals engage in alternatives to marriage or other forms of union formation.

African Americans, located at the social, economic, and political margins of American life, have created ways of living that support survival and challenge dominant cultural narratives about marriage, childbearing, and the ideal social organization of families. African Americans have also created forms of family organization denied them by locating themselves between and beyond what was legally sanctioned in the larger society. The historical record, for example, indicates that slaves had marriages even while they were not legally sanctioned or morally required by the larger society (Gutman 1976; Will 1999). The slave community recognized these unions as committed pairings within which couples shared their limited resources and children were born and raised. The existence of slave marriage as a subversive act challenges us to suspend our notions about what is formal and informal or institutionalized or not, and to ask what is created in the spaces that are not governed by law, but nevertheless have a cultural presence. Today, in the face of formidable economic and demographic barriers to legal marriage, black couples enter into cohabiting relationships where they share their lives and love, have and raise children, share resources, and help and support each other. They also fight and argue, sometimes they stay together and perhaps more often they do not. Cohabitation may be different than marriage but these two forms of pairing have much in common; perhaps, this is most strikingly the case for African Americans. It is with a sense of irony that I suggest slave marriages and the late twentieth-century decline in black marriages have something in common. However, they both illustrate a people's ability to navigate, tolerate, and create spaces within the context of formidable barriers (be it the institution of slavery or too few marriageable men) and to exist within and outside (often simultaneously) the social and legal conventions of one's time.

(EN)GENDERING COUNTER NARRATIVES

In slavery and in freedom, African-American women would take on economic roles and transform gender relations in ways that were not equaled by white women until the latter half of the twentieth century (Hunter 1993, 1997, 2001; Jones 1985). In his discussion of the roots of black matriarchy, E. Franklin Frazier (1939) laments, "neither economic necessity nor tradition had instilled in her (the black woman) the spirit of subordination to masculine authority.

Emancipation only tended to confirm the self-sufficiency slavery had taught" (102). In Frazier's view, contested patriarchy and uncontrolled female sexuality and reproduction were the hallmarks of the trouble in black families. Ideological tensions around patriarchy, sexuality, and reproduction remain an integral part of the research being done on the emergence (and acceptance of) alternative forms of union formation and out-of-wedlock parenting. Exposing these tensions, African-American women's lives, their choices, and their bodies have often been discursive sites of family pathology as well as a cautionary tale for other women (Blum and Duessen 1996; Collins 1991).

African-American women's accounts of alternative marital and childbearing patterns have been explored in a number of early black community studies (Drake and Cayton 1945; Frazier 1939), ethnographies of urban communities (Aschenbrenner 1975; Rainwater 1970; Stack 1974), and recent qualitative studies on marriage and motherhood (e.g., Blum and Duessen 1996; Jarrett 1994). These texts reveal women's counter narratives with which they envisioned themselves and their lives within and beyond social conventions. Women (often simultaneously) expressed a value of and healthy cynicism about marriage. They spoke about a woman's independence, the ability and strength to "go it alone" without a partner, and a desire for autonomy from men's authority. The role of mother emerged as a prominent part of women's identities, sometimes eclipsing that of wife or partner. Women also spoke of their connections to other women and kin-based networks supported them as mothers. Women, whose lives had taken many turns outside the conventional script of courtship, marriage, and childbearing, suggested different types of relationships (e.g., legal marriage, cohabitation, causal liaison, and being alone) are best at different times in a woman's life. Furthermore, women tended to evaluate their lives and actions based on the circumstances and choices available rather than an unyielding abstract moral code. In doing so, they created narratives about their lives that were not only in opposition to culturally dominant (read white) American scripts, but also contested the values and ideology of the black elite who saw the adherence to patriarchy and "intact" families as necessary for black social mobility and integration into the mainstream of American life (see, for example, Drake and Cayton 1945; Frazier 1939; Wilson 1987).

Carol Stack's (1974) *All Our Kin* and Joyce Aschenbrenner's (1975) *Lifelines*, classic ethnographic studies of urban African-American families and kin networks, illustrate the diverse trajectories of union formation (or not), childbearing (marital and nonmarital), and parenting (own child or someone else's) that occur across black women's life course. They found that women simultaneously drew on conventional and counter narratives and this was no less true of the way they lived their lives. Women made their choices based on what was dealt them and the knowledge that life is not always what you want it to be, but it is what you make of it. The result is that the women studied had life course trajectories as different from each other as they were from the conventional patterns of white women. Both Stack and Aschenbrenner eschewed the discourse of family pathology and sexual promiscuity that had defined the academic literature at the time their works were published. It meant, as scholars, they had to find new ways to narrate African-American women's lives that provided not only an interpretive coherence to life choices but also took seriously how they made sense of their own lives. To do so was not simply an exercise in cultural relativism, but an attempt to respect people's lives and to treat them with dignity. It is a challenge that social researchers continue to face as they work to understand the lives of African Americans as well as the growing diversity in American family life in general.

CONCLUSION

Racial Differences in a Post World

African Americans, because their lives and families have diverged from that of white Americans, have historically been viewed as situated at the intersection of order and disorder. In the first hundred years after Emancipation, a substantial minority of African Americans lived in alternative family living arrangements, and racial differences in family structure, marriage, and nonmarital childbearing were evident (Frazier 1939; Gordon and McLanahan 1991; Gutman 1976; Miller 1993; Ruggles 1994). However, up to more than 70 percent of black children lived with two parents in either nuclear or extended family households (Billingsley 1992; Walker 1988). As we look across the twentieth century, there is little in the black historical experience of disenfranchisement, racial discrimination, segregation, and economic and social inequality to decrease the patterns that most disturb family scholars and policy makers. Today, most African-American children live in alternative family living arrangements and racial differences in several areas of family life have widened (Ellwood and Crane 1990; Heaton and Jacobson 1994; Manning and Smock 1997). It is with a sense of confusion among some scholars (and irony among others) that it is in the post world (i.e., postmodern, post-industrial, and post–civil rights) that one sees the most dramatic declines in "traditional" family arrangements among African Americans. In an era where the legal, social, and economic divide between blacks and whites has narrowed, social researchers continue to look to the past to understand the source of racial differences in contemporary family patterns and often in exasperation they concede that something cultural must be at work.

Perhaps family scholars have so often looked to the past because the examination of proximal factors leaves explanatory gaps, and to culture because so much of our political rhetoric points to values as the source of racial differences. Furthermore, Collins (1998) suggests that the vestiges of scientific racism and social researchers' emphasis on social class as an outcome rather than a cause of family organization have created a particular lens for the study of African-American families. She argues "cultural and psychological values have long been emphasized as central to understanding black family organization instead of economic and political phenomena, such as industrial and labor markets, employment patterns, migration histories, residential patterns, and governmental policies" (Collins 1998, 2). African-American family patterns, past and present, do illustrate the capacity of black cultural traditions to accommodate complex and diverse patterns in union formation and family life that reflect both choice and circumstance (Billingsley 1992). However, if social researchers are to understand the rather dramatic transformations in black marital and family patterns that have taken place over the last 40 years, it is important to view the cultural tools and adaptive strategies relied on by African Americans within the broader context of shifts in the economy, demography, and the body politic as well as the enduring influence of social stratification (race, class, and gender).

In conclusion, in this commentary, I have drawn on the African-American experience to highlight ways family scholars may (re)envision narratives of cohabitation that unhinge them from notions of how things ought to be, so they may better understand how things are. Improvisations in family organization, subversions of social and legal conventions, and the creation of counter narratives that both support and subvert "traditional" family values are not confined to black life. Indeed, the diversity of contemporary American family life is a kind of *gumbo ya ya*, everybody talking and doing everything at once. Brown (1991) reminds women's historians that when interrogating differences, be it race, class, ethnicity, or sexuality, that the aim is not only to isolate one conversation but also the "trick is then how to put that conversation in a context that makes evident its dialogue with so many others" (85). This is a formidable challenge for family scholars. However, if one is to interrogate racial differences and to make sense of the variety that is seen within and across race and ethnicity in the United States, it is a challenge that must be taken up.

REFERENCES

Aschenbrenner, J. (1975). *Lifelines: Black families in Chicago.* New York: Holt, Rinehart and Winston.

Billingsley, A. (1992). *Climbing Jacob's ladder.* New York: Simon & Schuster.

Blassingame, J. W. (1972). *The slave community: Plantation life in the antebellum South.* New York: Oxford University Press.

Blum, L. M., and Duessen, T. (1996). Negotiating independent motherhood: Working-class African American women talk about marriage and motherhood. *Gender & Society,* 10, 199–211.

Brown, E. B. (1991). Polyrhythms and improvisation: Lessons for women's history. *History Workshop Journal,* 31–32, 84–89.

Bulcroft, R. A., and Bulcroft, K. A. (1993). Race differences in attitudinal motivational factors in the decision to marry. *Journal of Marriage and the Family,* 55, 338–65.

Bumpass, L. L., and Sweet, J. A. (1989). National estimates of cohabitation. *Demography,* 26, 615–25.

Collins, P. H. (1991). *Black feminist thought.* New York: Routledge, Chapman, and Hall.

Collins, P. H. (1998). Intersections of race, class, gender, and nation: Some Comparative Family Studies, implications for Black family studies. *Journal of Comparative Family Studies,* 29, 27–37.

Drake, S. C., and Cayton, H. R. (1945). *Black metropolis. Vol. 2: A study of Negro life in a northern city.* New York: Harcourt, Brace, & World, Inc.

Ellwood, D. T., and Crane, J. (1990). Family change among Black Americans: What do we know? *Journal of Economic Perspectives,* 4, 65–84.

Frazier, F. E. (1939). *The Negro Family in the United States.* Chicago, IL: University of Chicago Press.

Genovese, E. (1974). *Roll, Jordan, roll: The world the slaves made.* New York: Vintage.

Gordon, L., and McLanahan, S. (1991). Single parenthood in 1900. *Journal of Family History,* 16, 97–116.

Gutman, H. (1976). *The Black Family in Slavery and Freedom: 1750–1925.* New York: Vintage Press, Random House.

Heaton, T. B., and Jacobson, C. K. (1994). Race differences in changing family demographics in the 1980s. *Journal of Family Issues,* 12, 290–307.

Hunter, A. G. (1992, March). African American families reconsidered: Old dilemmas, new directions. Paper presented at invited panel at the Biennial Meetings of the Society for Research on Child Development Pre-Conference of the Black Caucus of the Society for Research in Child Development, New Orleans, LA.

Hunter, A. G. (1993). Making a way: Strategies of southern urban Afro-American families, 1900 and 1936. *Journal of Family History,* 18, 231–48.

Hunter, A. G. (1997). Living arrangements of African American adults—Variations across age, gender, and family status. In R. Taylor, J. Jackson, and L. Chatters (Eds.), *Family life in Black America* (pp. 262–76). Thousand Oaks, CA: Sage Publications.

Hunter, A. G. (2001). The other breadwinners: The mobilization of secondary wage earners in early twentieth-century Black families. *History of the family: An International Quarterly,* 6, 69–94.

Hunter, A. G., and Ensminger, M. E. (1992). Diversity and fluidity in children's living arrangements: Family transitions in an urban Afro-American community. *Journal of Marriage and the Family,* 54, 418–26.

Hunter, T. W. (1997). *To 'joy my freedom: Southern Black women's lives and labors after the civil war.* Cambridge, MA: Harvard University Press.

Jarrett, R. L. (1994). Living poor: Family life among single parent, African-American women. *Social Problems,* 41, 30–49.

Jones, J. (1985). *Labor of love, labor of sorrow.* New York: Basic Books.

Kiernan, K. (2002). Cohabitation in Western Europe: Trends, issues, and implications. In Alan Booth and Ann C. Crouter (Eds.), *Just living together: Implications of cohabitation on families, children, and social policy* (pp. 3–33). Mahwah, NJ: Lawrence Erlbaum Associates, Inc.

King, A. E. O. (1999). African American females' attitudes toward marriage: An exploratory study. *Journal of Black Studies,* 29, 416–37.

London, K. (1991). *Cohabitation, marriage, and martial dissolution: United States. (Advance Data No. 194).* Hyattsville, MD: National Center for Health Statistics.

Loomis, L. S., and Landale, N. S. (1994). Nonmarital cohabitation and childbearing among Black and White American women. *Journal of Marriage and the Family* 56(4), 949–63.

Manning, W. D. (1993). Marriage and cohabitation following premarital conception. *Journal of Marriage and the Family,* 55, 839–50.

Manning, W. D., and Smock, P. J. (1995). Why marry? Race and the transition to marriage among cohabitors. *Demography,* 32, 509–20.

Manning, W. D., and Smock, P. J. (1997). Children's living arrangements in unmarried-mother families. *Journal of Family Issues,* 18, 526–45.

Miller, A. T. (1993). Social science, social policy, and the heritage of African American families. In M. B. Katz (Ed.), *The underclass debate* (pp. 254–92). Princeton, NJ: Princeton University Press.

Rainwater, L. (1970). *Behind ghetto walls: Black families in a federal slum.* Chicago, IL: Aldine Publishing Company.

Raley, K. (1996). A shortage of marriageable men? A note on the role of cohabitation in Black-White differences in marriage rates. *American Sociological Review,* 61, 973–84.

Ruggles, S. (1994). The origins of African-American family structure. *American Sociological Review,* 59, 136–51.

Stack, C. (1974). *All our kin.* New York: Harper & Row Company.

Stevenson, B. E. (1995). Black family structure in colonial antebellum Virginia: Amending the revisionist perspective. In M. B. Tucker and C. Mitchell-Kernan (Eds.), *The decline of marriage among African Americans: Causes, consequences, and policy implications* (pp. 27–56). New York: Russell Sage Foundation.

South, S. J. (1993). Racial and ethnic differences in the desire to marry. Journal of Marriage and the Family, 55, 357–70.

Tucker, M. B., and Mitchell-Kernan, C. (1995a). Marital behavior and expectations: Ethnic comparisons of attitudinal and structural correlates. In M. B. Tucker and C. Mitchell-Kernan (Eds.), *The decline of marriage among African Americans: Causes, consequences, and policy implications* (pp. 145–71). New York: Russell Sage Foundation.

Tucker, M. B., and Mitchell-Kernan, C. (1995b). Trends in African American family formation: A theoretical and statistical overview. In M. B. Tucker and C. Mitchell-Kernan (eds.), *The decline of marriage among African Americans: Causes, consequences, and policy implications,* (pp. 3–26). New York: Russell Sage Foundation.

Walker, H. (1988). Black and White differences in marriage and family patterns. In S. M. Dombusch and M. H. Strober (Eds.), *Feminism, children and the new families* (pp. 87–112). New York: Guilford Press.

Will, T. E. (1999). Weddings on contested grounds: Slave marriage in the antebellum South. *The Historian, 62*, 99–118.

Wilson, W. H. (1987). *The truly disadvantaged.* Chicago, IL: University of Chicago Press.

6

No More Kin Care?: Changes in Black Mothers' Reliance on Relatives for Child Care, 1977–1994

Karin W. Brewster and Irene Padavic

The importance of extended kin is a long-standing theme in the research literature on African American families, but one whose truth has recently been questioned. According to past research, strong feelings of obligation to extended family members and high levels of reliance on kin for material and emotional support are survival strategies formed in response to a long history of oppression and social, physical, and economic isolation. Bringing this theme to life are ethnographies documenting high rates of African American participation in family support networks (Aschenbrenner 1973; Burton 1990; Cherlin and Furstenberg 1992; Hays and Mindel 1973; Martin and Martin 1978; Mindel 1980; Newman 1999, 194–95; Stack 1974). The ethnographic record, however, contrasts sharply with recent quantitative research that has failed to find high degrees of kin-provided material assistance among African Americans, net of controls for marital status and family structure (Eggebeen 1992; Eggebeen and Hogan 1990; Hofferth 1984; Hogan, Eggebeen, and Clogg et al. 1993; Miner 1995; Miner and Uhlenberg 1997; Raley 1995; Roschelle 1997).

What accounts for this divergence? Some investigators point to the changing structural context, arguing that the social, political, and economic changes of the past several decades have created change in the need for kin networks and the nature of kin-provided support (Hogan, Eggebeen, and Clogg 1993; Roschelle 1997; Ruggles 1994). The past 20 years have brought profound changes in the economy and in labor force and migration patterns that have affected many aspects of African American family life, possibly including the reliance on kin networks for material support. As Hogan, Eggebeen, and Clogg (1993, 1454) have suggested, "The effective kin network that provided

This chapter was originally published in *Gender & Society* 16(4): 546–63, 2002.

support to multigenerational, matrifocal black families in past decades appears to be of limited relevance today." That the broader context has changed is indisputable. Less certain, however, is whether African Americans' reliance on kin networks has in fact declined over time and if so, whether the decline stems from changes in structural conditions.

This chapter aims to clarify recent trends in one significant aspect of black families' use of extended kin networks: mothers' reliance on relatives for child care. The use of kin for child care is a topic on which the divergence between ethnographic and quantitative research about kin networks is particularly pronounced. The ongoing debate about the relative benefits of kin- and non-kin-provided care further underscores the need for an understanding of recent trends (Hofferth et al. 1998; National Institute for Child Health and Human Development [NICHD] 1997). We draw on 18 years of nationally representative data on African American families to answer three interrelated questions about kin-provided child care: To what extent has African American mothers' reliance on relatives for child care changed significantly in recent years? Is such change universal across families, regardless of social or economic characteristics, or has it characterized some family types to a greater or lesser extent than others? And finally, are trends in black mothers' reliance on relative-provided child care consistent with what might be expected given broader social and economic changes?

Informing this investigation is an explicit recognition of the complex interplay of cultural and structural forces in determining the constraints and opportunities confronting African American women and their families. While the role of culture in shaping African Americans' responses to prevailing social and economic conditions has been a topic of much debate, following Cherlin (1992), we assume that cultural repertoires are valuable resources that families use—or not—depending on their economic and social circumstances. Prior research, whether ethnographic or quantitative, has captured the interplay between culture and structure in cross section, providing snapshots of African American families at particular points in time. Our use of trend data allows a more comprehensive view of African American families, one that incorporates both the influence of micro level economic and social characteristics and temporal change in the effects of these characteristics.

THE CHANGING CONTEXT FOR AMERICAN MOTHERS: SOME HYPOTHESES

The many political, economic, and social changes of the 1980s and 1990s have created a structural context far removed from that of the 1960s and 1970s, the period when the ethnographic work describing the strong, women-centered kin networks supporting African American mothers was first conducted.

Researchers understood these kin networks and the child care they provided as responses to a particular set of structurally determined constraints and opportunities. We argue that as these constraints and opportunities shifted, so did the extent to which employed black mothers either needed to or were able to rely on kin for material support. The following paragraphs discuss the elements of this changing opportunity structure that are likely to have implications for African Americans' reliance on extended kin for child care.

Perhaps the most significant contextual change of the past three decades was the restructuring of the economy that began in the mid-1970s. A key aspect of this restructuring was the growing demand for service and white-collar labor, a demand that African American women helped fill (Gardner 1995). Indeed, black women's rates of labor force participation rose rapidly, from about 43 percent in 1970 to 64 percent at the end of the twentieth century (Padavic and Reskin 2002; U.S. Bureau of the Census 1982). This increase was most pronounced for the mothers of young children (Spain and Bianchi 1996, 183–85), spurring a growing need for child care.

Ironically, the same forces underlying women's growing need for child care also led to the decreased availability of female family members for child care duty. Grandmothers may have become less willing to pay the opportunity costs of nonemployment as the cost in forgone wages of caring for one's grandchildren rose (Presser 1989, 532). Siblings and other female relatives also were more likely to be working for pay and thus less able to take on child care duties. In short, the rising labor force participation rate among African American women had two contradictory effects: It increased the demand for child care while decreasing the availability of relatives for care.

Concurrent with the rising need for care and the decreasing availability of relatives to provide this care was a marked increase in the availability of alternatives to kin-provided care. The number of incorporated child care centers doubled between 1977 and 1992 (Casper and O'Connell 1998a), and unregistered family day care providers and child care pools also proliferated (NICHD 1997). Together, these changes provide a picture consistent with the hypothesis that reliance on kin for child care has declined in recent years. At the same time, however, these long-run trends have been punctuated by periodic economic downturns that may be associated with short-term upswings in the reliance on kin networks. Recent research suggests that economic recessions motivate movement toward lower cost forms of care among black and white parents (Brewster, Padavic, and Fulton 2000; Casper and O'Connell 1998b). Relative-provided care tends to be less costly than other forms, and more than one-fourth of relatives who provide care receive no cash payment (Kontos et al. 1995, 190). Moreover, the high unemployment rates associated with recessions may mean greater availability of unemployed family members for child care. Thus far, our discussion of the changing structural context and its likely association with trends in relative-provided care has been framed in monolithic terms. Yet, how individual families experience macro level changes and their responses to these changes depend on their social and economic resources. Accordingly, our analysis of trends in African American women's reliance on relative-provided care considers the extent to which kin-care varies across black mothers in different social and economic locations and whether such differences have grown or narrowed over time.

Perhaps the most obvious differentiating factor is marital status. Research based on cross-sectional samples shows that participation in kin-support networks, including receipt of child care, is much more common among single than married women (Hogan, Eggebeen, and Clogg 1990; Roschelle 1997). Not only might single mothers have greater need for kin-provided support, they tend to have greater access to such support than their married counterparts since they are more likely to live with or near extended family members (Hill 1999; McAdoo 1997). If this difference has held over time—and we think that it has—then we would expect rates of reliance on kin-provided care to be higher among single than married mothers. Furthermore, if the circumstances of married mothers compared to single mothers have diverged over time (e.g., if the income differences between married and single women have grown), the kin-care trend-line for married women would look quite different from the trend-line for single mothers. Thus, in addition to examining differences by marital status over time, we also examine the interactions of marital status with the other predictor variables.

Prior research indicates the importance of social class as a determinant of reliance on kin care. Hill (1999, 135), for example, reported that low income is associated with greater involvement of extended kin in child rearing among African American families. She also reported that while involvement in kin networks is important to financially stable black families, such involvement more often takes the form of emotional and psychological rather than material support. These class differences, in conjunction with the increasing economic polarization of African American families (Hurst 1998), suggest a growing class divergence in the need for kin-provided child care. Thus, we anticipate an increase in the effect of income over time as the economic polarization of African American families becomes more pronounced.

Several reasons lead us to anticipate regional differences in trends in kin-provided care. First, during the 1970s, 1980s, and early 1990s, the wages of African American women who lived in the South tended to be lower and to grow more slowly than those of African American women in other regions (Corcoran 1999, figures 1.3 and 1.8). Not only does the slower wage growth in the South suggest a greater need for lower cost child care, it also suggests a divergence over time in the child care needs of southern versus nonsouthern women. Amplifying this divergence is the higher than average unmet demand for child care that characterizes several southern states (Casper and O'Connell

1998a) and the tendency among southerners, relative to residents of other regions, toward more traditional attitudes about working women, child rearing, and family ties (Franklin 1997; Rice and Coates 1995). All these factors underlie our expectation that southern women's likelihood of relying on kin for child care will undergo less change than that of their counterparts in other regions.

Studies based on cross-sectional samples also point to the importance of mothers' age as a determinant of reliance on kin for child care, with the likelihood of relative-provided care decreasing with increases in a mother's age (Hogan, Eggebeen, and Clogg 1990; Roschelle 1997; Stack 1974). Younger mothers appear to be less independent than their older counterparts and more reliant on their mothers and other mature relatives for advice and assistance. Furthermore, insofar as the mothers and aunts of older mothers are themselves older, they may be less physically able to provide care. We tested for change in the effect of age over time, but the direction of such change is difficult to anticipate. On one hand, mothers' age may become a more important factor in determining who receives assistance from extended kin if the demands on kin networks have become increasingly stretched over time (Newman 1999). On the other hand, the increasing availability of non-kin forms of child care, including Head Start and other programs targeted to young mothers, may have mitigated any tendency toward greater age effects over time.

Prior research indicates the importance of several additional factors as predictors of reliance on kin networks for child care, including mother's work schedule and the number and ages of her children. Mothers who work part-time or have flexible employment arrangements are more likely to rely on relatives for child care (Blau 1991, 136; Presser and Cox 1997, 26); we expect the same effect in our trend models. We also anticipate that having an infant or having more than one preschooler will raise the likelihood of kin-provided care. Many parents believe that infants and young children are best cared for by family members (Hofferth et al. 1998). Moreover, the cost of infant care tends to be higher, and these costs mount as the number of children needing care increases (NICHD 1997).

A critical predictor of relative-provided care that we cannot measure with these data is the geographic proximity of family members. Roschelle (1997) reported that the likelihood of receiving child care assistance from relatives is significantly higher among women with family members within a two-mile radius. Some ethnographic accounts, however, suggest that for women of color, distance from kin does not necessarily undermine their use as child care providers (Uttal 1999). Indeed, it is not uncommon for African American families to send their children to live with distant grandparents (Burton 1990; Stack 1996; Stack and Burton 1994). While we cannot measure proximity directly, its effects may operate through other variables in our models, including time period, marital status, age, and social class. We comment further in the discussion on the implications of the lack of proximity measures.

DATA

We rely on pooled cross sections from two sources of data for the civilian, noninstitutionalized population: the Current Population Surveys (CPS) and the Surveys of Income and Program Participation (SIPP). The CPS is an ongoing, nationally representative, household-based survey designed to collect monthly employment data. In addition to the core questions repeated in each survey, the questionnaire occasionally includes items about a specific employment-related topic. In June 1977 and June 1982, the CPS asked all employed mothers of children under age 12 about their child care arrangements in the previous month (i.e., in May).

The SIPP is a nationally representative, household-based survey designed to provide detailed information on the economic situation of households in the United States, beginning in 1983. The SIPP is a refreshed panel design: New households are selected every year, and household members are interviewed periodically over a two-and-one-half-year period before being dropped from the sample. While in the sample, employed mothers are asked to respond several times to a topical module describing their child care arrangements. By including information from just one topical module for each mother, we have created from the SIPP's panel data a series of cross-sectional files representing nine time points between the winter of 1984–1985 through the spring of 1994.

We combined the nine SIPP files with the two CPS files to form a set of eleven pooled cross sections spanning the period from 1977 to 1994.[1] Mothers included in these cross sections share three characteristics. First, because only employed women were asked the child care questions in the CPS and early waves of the SIPP, all the mothers in our files worked for pay in the month preceding the survey. Second, each woman's youngest child is younger than age five. Children in this age range are analytically and substantively distinct from older children because they require nearly constant supervision and their need for care does not vary with school schedules.[2] Third, because our substantive interest is in African American mothers, the files include only women who identified themselves as black or African American. Altogether, the pooled files contain data for 2,604 employed mothers of preschoolers. (See original article for table summary.)

Dependent Variable

Both the SIPP and the CPS questioned working mothers about their primary child care arrangements, defined in terms of both where and with whom the child spent the majority of her or his time while the mother worked. Using this information, we constructed a dichotomy indicating the primary care arrangement for the youngest child younger than age five. A value of 1 indicates that the primary caretaker is a family member (other than the child's father).[3]

Independent Variables

The primary independent variable in any analysis of pooled cross sections is time. Here, the time indicators capture the effects of structural change, including changes in macroeconomic conditions; women's labor force participation; and other variables that affect the availability and cost of child care alternatives. In our first set of multivariate analyses, time is represented by calendar year; 1977 is treated as the reference year. The second set of models assesses the interactions of individual characteristics with time; in these analyses, we distinguish among three time periods. This specification is discussed in greater detail in the Results section.

Prior research has identified several characteristics of the mother that influence the use of relatives as primary child care providers. Our data include two measures of mother's class status: family income and completed years of education. The latter is represented by a set of dummy variables distinguishing among four levels of attainment: less than high school (the reference category), high school diploma, some college, and college degree or higher. Income information from the various surveys was transformed into an indicator of monthly family income, expressed in 1983 dollars and logged to capture the decreasing effects of dollar increments at higher income levels.[4]

Marital status is measured as a dichotomous variable that indicates whether or not a woman is married with spouse present. Age is a continuous variable indicating the mother's age at the time child care arrangements were assessed. Work schedule is represented by a dichotomy indicating part-time (fewer than 35 hours per week) or full-time (35 hours or more per week). Region of residence is represented by a binary indicator of southern residence, coded 1 for South and 0 otherwise. Two variables capture the effects of the children's characteristics. As noted above, our analyses center on the child care arrangement for the youngest child. A binary variable indicates whether that child is younger than age 1 (coded 1) or between the ages of one and four (coded 0). A second dichotomy indicates the presence of other preschoolers in the family; a value of 1 indicates that the index child has at least one sibling younger than the age of five.

RESULTS

Reliance on kin care has declined significantly among employed African American mothers with preschool children. In 1977, more than half the women relied on relatives; by 1994, just more than one-third did. Much of this decline happened between 1982 and 1985. From that point forward, reliance on kin-provided child care fluctuated, but not significantly. Table 6.1 uses logistic regression to reveal the same pattern. The odds ratios, which are more easily interpreted than the coefficient estimates, show that the odds of using kin were not significantly different in 1982 than in 1977, the reference year. For each year after 1982, however, the odds of relying on relatives were about half the odds in 1977. In 1985, for example, employed African American mothers of preschoolers were 45 percent less likely than in 1977 to use relatives for child care $(1 - .546 = .454)$.

Model 2 adds the remaining independent variables to Model 1. The addition of these variables leads to a substantial improvement in model fit and little change in the year coefficients. Thus, the decline in relative-provided care was independent of changes (e.g., higher educational attainment) in the composition of the population of employed black mothers. Three of the eight individual-level predictors—education, marital status, and employment status—showed a significant negative association with the use of relative-provided child care, net of other factors. Women who completed high school were about 37 percent less likely to use kin care than those who did not, while college graduates were 68 percent less likely. Married mothers were nearly half as likely to use relative-provided care as single mothers, and full-time workers were about one-third less likely to use it than part-time workers.

Three variables raised the odds of reliance on kin. Mothers with more than one preschooler at home or with a child younger than age one were more than 30 percent more likely than other women to use kin care. The odds of using relative care also were greater for higher income women. While this finding seems counterintuitive, it is consistent with Uttal's (1999) report that women of color who could afford to do otherwise sometimes chose to spend their child care dollars on family members' services to provide them with economic resources and decent working conditions.

Recall that our aim is to assess temporal change in the effects of the predictors of relative care and, furthermore, that we anticipate that such change may itself be contingent on marital status. We assess the conditioning effects of time and marital status by adding interaction terms to Model 2 and evaluating the change in model fit. We created two sets of interaction models, one in which the time interactions are represented by multiplicative terms based on the full set of time dummies and one in which time is respecified as a set of three dummies, demarcating the periods of 1977 through 1982, 1984 through 1989, and 1990 through 1994.

The latter specification yielded roughly equal subsamples distributed across approximately equal time spans representing distinct macroeconomic climates.[5] The resulting coefficient estimates (not shown) indicate that the effects of most of the predictor variables were stable over time and did not

Table 6.1. Coefficients from Logistic Regression Models Predicting the Likelihood of Relative-Provided Care, Black Mothers of Preschool Children, 1977 to 1994

	Model 1		Model 2	
	b	Odds Ratio	b	Odds Ratio
Intercept	0.082	—	0.0123	—
Year				
1977 (reference category)				
1982	−0.014	0.989	−0.013	0.986
1985	−0.605***	0.546	−0.624**	0.536
1986	−0.607***	0.545	−0.618***	0.506
1987	−0.588***	0.555	−0.619***	0.539
1988	−0.598***	0.550	−0.581***	0.559
1989	−0.594***	0.551	−0.628**	0.534
1990	−0.876***	0.416	−0.916***	0.400
1991	−0.713***	0.490	−0.580*	0.560
1993	−0.652***	0.521	−0.643***	0.526
1994	−0.682***	0.506	−0.641***	0.527
Age			−0.013	0.987
Education				
Less than high school (reference category)				
High school			−0.453***	0.635
Some college			−0.848***	0.428
College or higher			−1.148***	0.317
Marital status				
Married, spouse present			−0.619***	0.539
Other (reference category)				
Monthly income, logged			0.170**	1.185
Work schedule				
Full-time			−0.245*	0.783
Part-time (reference category)				
Region of residence				
South			0.136	0.037
Non-South (reference category)				
Youngest child younger than one year			0.257**	1.316
Other preschool children			0.257*	1.293
−2 log likelihood	3,450.015		3,085.461	
df	10		20	
N	2,604		2,452	
X^2 for improvement in model fit			364.55***	

*$p < .05$. **$p < .01$. ***$p < .001$.

vary by marital status. However, the effects of two variables, age and region, varied by year and marital status. We explain these interactions in the following paragraphs and in tables 6.2 and 6.3.

Rather than presenting the coefficient estimates, which are difficult to interpret in models with multiple interaction terms, we instead present predicted probabilities. These are estimated for hypothetical women with a particular set of characteristics, using the coefficient estimates and the following formula:

$$Pi = \exp(Zi) / (1+\exp(Zi))$$

where P represents the probability of reliance on relative-provided care for an individual woman with a given set of characteristics, and Z_i represents the summed products of the coefficient estimates multiplied by the referenced characteristics (Aldrich and Nelson 1984).

Table 6.2 illustrates the interaction of age with time period. We estimate the probability of relative-provided care for nine hypothetical women, each of whom was married, had a high school education, had an infant along with at least one other preschooler, worked fewer than 35 hours per week, and lived in the South. The women differed in age and the period in which they "live": The three ages we've chosen (the mean age for the sample, and one standard deviation above and one below the mean) combined with three time periods yield estimates for nine composite women, each of whom is represented by one cell in the table.

Note first the effect of age. The estimated probabilities indicate that younger women were more likely to use kin-care in all three periods. Also apparent is the downward trend over time: In each subsequent period, the likelihood of relative-care was lower at each age. The interaction between age and period reveals itself in the relative difference in the age effect from one period to the next. Consider, for example, the difference between women at the mean age of 28 compared to women at age 22, a standard deviation below the mean. In the earliest period, the probability that the 28-year-old relied on relatives was about 15 percent lower than for the younger woman ($-.15 = (.513 - .591)/.513$); in the middle period, however, the 28-year-old's probability was about 30 percent lower ($-.30 = (.120 - .156)/.120$). In short, age became more effective over time in distinguishing between women who relied on kin for child care and those who did not.

We found a three-way interaction between region, time period, and marital status. Here, our hypothetical women were all age 28, high school graduates, mothers of an infant and at least one additional preschooler, and working under 35 hours per week. The predicted probabilities are calculated by varying their marital status, region of residence, and the time period, producing a set of 12 estimates: one for married women residing in the South between 1977 and 1982, one for single women residing in the South during that period, one for married non-Southern women at this time, and so on.

Table 6.2. Predicted Probability of Reliance on Relative-Provided Care, by Age and Period, Black Mothers of Preschool Children

	1977–1982	*1984–1989*	*1990–2004*
Age set at 1 *SD* below the mean	.591	.182	.156
Age set at sample mean	.513	.140	.120
Age set at 1 *SD* above the mean	.435	.106	.091

NOTE: Probability estimated for a married woman with a high school education, an infant plus other preschoolers, who works fewer than 35 hours per week, living in the South.

The negative effects of period are again apparent: For each marital status-region combination, the probability of relative-provided care was highest in the early period and decreased over time. For example, the predicted probability of using kin-care for a Southern married woman with the characteristics described above decreased by roughly 43 percent, from .51 to .29, while her non-Southern counterpart's probability dropped by under 20 percent, from .42 to .34. Note, too, the effects of marital status: Within each region-period combination, the probability of relative-provided care was higher for single than for married women.

The effect of region changes over time, and the extent of this change depends on marital status, producing the three-way interaction. Consider first the relationship between period and region. The decrease over time in the likelihood of relative-provided care is more pronounced for Southern than for non-Southern women. In fact, the likelihood of using kin-care reverses. In the first period, Southern women are more likely than comparable non-Southerners to rely on kin for care, but in the two later periods they are less likely. This

Table 6.3. Predicted Probability of Reliance on Relative-Provided Care by Marital Status, Religion, and Period: Black Mothers of Preschool Children

Region	South	Non-South
Married women		
Period		
1977–1982	.51	.42
1984–1989	.30	.37
1990–1994	.29	.34
Single women		
Period		
1977–1982	.66	.57
1984–1989	.44	.52
1990–1994	.43	.49

NOTE: Probability estimated for a 28-year-old woman with a high school education, an infant plus other preschoolers, who works fewer than 35 hours per week.

relationship is conditioned further by marital status. Among the married, the probability of relying on relatives for care in the third period dropped to about 43 percent of the probability in the first period $(.43 = (.51 - .29)/.51)$; among the single, it was only about one-third lower. In sum, then, the predicted probabilities show that the effect of living in the South reversed over time and that the impact of this reverse on the likelihood of using relative-provided child care was more marked among married than single women.

SUMMARY AND DISCUSSION

Reliance on kin for childcare and for other forms of material and emotional support is a prominent feature of ethnographic accounts of parenting among African Americans. Recent quantitative research, however, indicates that black families' reliance on kin networks is less widespread than ethnographic research has suggested. We have argued that the apparent divergence between these two branches of the research literature partly reflects a lack of information about trends in African American families' use of kin networks, including how these trends have varied across different types of families. We have drawn on nationally representative data spanning nearly two decades to describe trends in a cardinal aspect of kin support—reliance on relatives for the care of preschool children. Our analyses clarify the extent and nature of change in employed black women's use of kin-provided child care for preschoolers and consider the importance of the broader structural context in understanding the role of kin support in African American families. Here, we summarize our findings and discuss their implications.

Black women's reliance on relatives for the care of preschoolers clearly has declined. In 1977, over half of employed African American mothers identified family members as their primary child care providers while they were at work, but by 1994 this figure had decreased to about 35 percent. This decline was not steady. Rather, much of it occurred between 1982 and 1985; from that point on, the proportion using relative-provided care remained fairly stable. Further, the trend is evident even with controls for individual-level characteristics, indicating that it does not reflect changes in the composition of the population of employed black women. This pattern is consistent with the accounts of both the ethnographers who point to the integral involvement of extended family members in caring for African American children and the findings of quantitative researchers suggesting notable declines in black women's use of kin for child care. While family members remain an important source of childcare for African American women, reliance on kin-provided care has declined substantially.

What has taken the place of relative-provided care? Additional analyses (not shown) indicate there has been an increase in the use of organized center care that more than compensated for the decrease in kin care. The percentage of African American mothers using center care doubled over our observation period, from 15.6 to 33.1 percent. This trend was more pronounced for married than single mothers. By 1994, center care was the predominant arrangement among black married-couple families: Forty percent of married African-American women identified center care as their primary arrangement, while fewer than one-fourth relied on extended family members. Among black single mothers, however, kin-provided care remained the most common choice, albeit by a much-reduced margin compared to earlier years.

As these figures suggest, reliance on relatives for child care was not equally likely across sub-groups of black women. Supporting the notion that kin-care is a culturally prescribed resource used by some African American families but not others, we found that mothers with fewer social and economic resources of their own—those who were single, less educated, or very young—were significantly more likely than other mothers to use relatives for child care. Surprisingly, our analysis of trends revealed most of these sub-group differences to be stable over time. In other words, the downward trend in relative care occurred to a more or less equal extent across all groups of employed African American mothers.

The analyses revealed two important exceptions to this uniformity, however, both suggestive of the influence of broader contextual change on African American mothers' child care strategies. First, the effect of age has increased over time. While younger mothers were more likely than their older counterparts to identify relatives as primary child care providers in all survey years, this difference was more pronounced in later years. We suspect that this change is linked to black women's climbing employment rates over our observation period, which likely meant that female relatives had progressively less time available for child care. As their time became a more scarce family resource, it was apportioned increasingly to those who most needed it, particularly young mothers. Maternal age taps aspects of need not captured by the controls for income and marital status, such as inexperience and a lesser ability to marshal the skills needed to coordinate work and child rearing.

The changing influence of Southern residence is the second significant exception to the otherwise uniform decline in black mothers' use of kin care. In 1977, African American mothers living in the South were much more likely than those in other regions to use kin-provided care, but by 1994 they were somewhat less likely to do so. The decline in Southern women's reliance on relative-provided child care was most pronounced among married mothers, whose odds of using relative-provided care dropped by over 40 percent. This reversal in the effect of Southern residence probably reflects an important change in the population composition of Southern blacks. Starting in the mid-1970s and continuing into the 1990s, the South-to-North migration stream of earlier decades reversed. As a result, the proportion of Southern blacks who had been raised elsewhere, primarily in the large metropolitan areas of the North and West, rose dramatically (Frey 1995, 2001).

The changing migration stream could account for the shift we observed in the effect of Southern residence in either of two ways. The first explanation centers on culturally based preferences for family-based child care. African Americans moving to the South may bring with them the less traditional attitudes about family and employed women associated with a non-Southern upbringing (Rice and Coates 1995). As these northern transplants make up an ever-greater proportion of the Southern population, the overall preference for family-based care among southern African Americans would decline. A second explanation of the changing regional effect centers on the availability of care. African Americans returning to the birthplaces of their parents and grandparents (Stack 1996) may be leaving immediate family members behind, separating themselves from the most likely sources of relative-provided care. While we suspect the latter explanation plays the more important role, without data on the residential proximity of immediate family members or on migration history, we are unable to test this hypothesis.

Taken as a whole, our results both reconcile and extend the observations of earlier ethnographic and quantitative researchers. The decline in African American women's use of relatives as the primary caretakers of their preschool children is consistent with the argument of quantitative researchers that reliance on material support from extended kin networks is decreasing. At the same time, however, our results reveal that need continues to be associated with a greater likelihood of family-provided support, at least with respect to the provision of employment-based child care for preschoolers. Indeed, need was more tightly linked to the use of relatives for child care at the end than at the start of our observation period. This change indicates that, over our observation period, African American women's reliance on extended kin for material support was increasingly conditioned by their own resources. Those who needed kin-provided support received it, while those who could make do without material support from family members, did. This implies that the use of kin-provided support is responsive to shifts in broader social and economic conditions that affect the balance of resources and needs within families. While our evidence of contextual effects is indirect, it is noteworthy that the changes we observed occurred concurrently with rising rates of female labor force participation, the increasing availability of non-kin forms of child care, and the movement of an increasing number of African American families into the middle and upper classes.

What are the implications of these findings for the research literature on African American women's lives and, more specifically, their use of extended kin networks? Perhaps the most obvious implication is the importance of contextualizing women's lives and family processes. Reliance on support from extended kin is neither characteristic of all African American mothers nor static over time. Just as we expect variation across groups of women in their use of kin support at any single point in time, so we also should anticipate change over time in the proportion relying on kin for support as they seek to adapt to changing macro level conditions.

This is not to say that specifying the influence of contextual changes on African American women and their families will be easy. Our interpretations of the changing effects of age and Southern residence on child care choices emphasize the importance of broad social and economic conditions, but we note that context is made up of many forces, some unmeasurable and some countervailing. Indeed, one of our findings highlights the difficulty of unpacking the different strands that make up economic context. The timing of the drop-off in relative care ran counter to our expectations: It occurred primarily between 1982 and 1985, following swiftly on the heels of a recession. Black women's job displacement rate during this period was higher than in the 10 years that followed (Gardner 1995, Table 2) and so we had expected to see an increase in the need for and supply of relatives for care—the opposite of what we found. We cannot explain this finding, but simply note that economic context is complex, made up of many contributing and sometimes cross-cutting factors.

We end with an additional caveat that suggests some directions for future research. This analysis considers only primary child care arrangements and thus provides a bounded view of the kin support provided to African-American mothers. Relatives may be involved in other aspects of child rearing and child care; indeed, grandparents and other relatives are frequent sources of back-up care (Smith 2000). Moreover, we cannot say with these data whether African Americans' reliance on extended kin networks for other types of material—or nonmaterial—support has changed over time. While such changes would not be surprising given the results reported here, additional work is needed to determine if such changes have occurred and if they, too, are linked to shifts in the broader social and economic context.

NOTES

1. In preliminary analyses, we assessed the potentially biasing effects of cross-survey differences in sampling frames. Both rounds of the Current Population Surveys and the 1984/1985 Surveys of Income and Program Participation (SIPP) were based on one sampling frame derived from the 1970 Census; the remaining surveys were based on a second sampling frame derived from later data. Our assessment of design effects suggests that the change in sampling frame after the 1984–1985 SIPP has a negligible and nonsignificant impact on the coefficient estimates.

2. Some of the SIPP child care modules reference "summer month." Investigators using these files have reported systematic seasonal variations in child care arrangements and in the effects of predictor variables for school-age children (Raley, Harris,

and Rindfuss 2000). The age restriction in our files allows us to sidestep the biasing effects of seasonal variation.

3. Because of sample size limitations, we are unable to distinguish either the type of relative (e.g., grandparent versus older sibling) or where the care was provided (e.g., child's home versus provider's home).

4. Detailed information about the construction of the family income indicator is available from the authors on request.

5. Both sets of time indicators yielded comparable results, although the coefficient estimates were somewhat less stable with the more detailed specification, probably because of the greater degrees of freedom used in the analysis.

REFERENCES

Aldrich, John H., and Forrest D. Nelson. 1984. *Linear probability, logic, and probit models.* Sage University Paper Series on Quantitative Applications in the Social Sciences, 07–001. Beverly Hills, CA: Sage.

Anderson, Elijah. 1990. *Streetwise: Race, class, and change in an urban community.* Chicago, IL: University of Chicago Press.

Angel, Ronald, and Marta Tienda. 1982. Determinants of extended household structure: Cultural pattern or economic need. *American Journal of Sociology* 87: 1360–83.

Aschenbrenner, Joyce. 1993. Extended families among Black Americans. *Journal of Comparative Family Studies* 4:256–68.

Bennett, Claudette E. 1995. The Black population in the United States: March 1994 and 1993. *Current population reports,* population characteristics, series P20–480. Government Printing Office: U.S. Bureau of the Census.

Blau, David M. 1991. *The economics of childcare.* New York: Russell Sage Foundation.

Brewster, Karin L., Irene Padavic, and John Fulton. 2000. Fathers' involvement in childcare: Race effects and change over time. Paper presented at the Annual Meeting of the Population Association of America, Los Angeles.

Browne, Irene. 1999. *Latinas and African American women at work: Race, gender and economic inequality.* New York: Russell Sage Foundation.

Burton, Linda M. 1990. Teenage childbearing as an alternative life-course strategy in multigeneration Black families. *Human Nature* 1(2): 123–43.

Casper, Lynne M., and Martin O'Connell. 1998a. State estimates of organized childcare facilities. Population Division Working Paper No. 21. Washington, DC: U.S. Bureau of the Census.

———. 1998b. Work, income, the economy, and

Cherlin, Andrew. 1992. *Marriage, divorce, remarriage.* 2nd ed. Cambridge, MA: Harvard University Press.

Cherlin, Andrew, and Frank F. Furstenberg, Jr. 1992. *The new American grandparent: A place in the family, a life apart.* Cambridge, MA: Harvard University Press.

Collins, Patrica Hill. 1998. *Fighting words: Black women and the search for justice.* Minneapolis: University of Minnesota Press.

———. 1990. *Black feminist thought: Knowledge, consciousness, and the politics of empowerment.* New York: Routledge, Chapman & Hall.

Coltrane, Scott. 1996. *Family man: Fatherhood, housework, and gender equity.* New York: Oxford University Press.

Conley, Dalton. *Being Black, living in the red.* Berkeley: University of California Press.

Coontz, Stephanie. 1992. *The way we never were: American families and the nostalgia trap.* New York: Basic Books.

Corcoran, Mary. 1999. The economic progress of African American women. In *Latinas and African American women at work: Race, gender, and economic inequality,* edited by Irene Browne. New York: Russell Sage Foundation.

Edin, Kathryn, and Kathleen Mullan Harris. 1999. "Getting off and staying off: Racial differences in the work route off welfare." In *Latinas and African American women at work: Race, gender, and economic inequality,* edited by Irene Browne. New York: Russell Sage Foundation.

Edin, Kathryn, and Laura Lein. 1997. *Making ends meet: How single mothers survive welfare and low-wage work.* New York: Russell Sage Foundation.

Eggebeen, David J. 1992. Family structure and intergenerational exchanges. *Research on Aging* 14:427–47.

Eggebeen, David J., and Dennis P. Hogan. 1990. Giving between generations in American families. *Human Nature* 1:211–32.

Franklin, Donna. 1997. *Ensuring inequality: The structural transformation of the African-American family.* New York: Oxford University Press.

Frey, William H. 2001. Migration to the South brings US Blacks full circle. *Population Today.* http://www.prb.org/pt/2001/MayJune2001/migration.html.

Frey, William H. 1995. The New Geography of Population Shifts. In *State of the union: America in the 1990s,* edited by Reynolds Farley. New York: Russell Sage Foundation.

Furstenberg, Frank F., J. Brooks-Gunn, and S. Phillip Morgan. 1987. *Adolescent mothers in later life.* New York: Cambridge University Press.

Gardner, Jennifer M. 1995. Worker displacement: A decade of change. *Monthly Labor Review* April: 45–57.

Gerson, Kathleen. 1993. *No man's land: Men's changing commitments to family and work.* New York: Basic Books.

Hatchett, Shirley J., and James S. Jackson. 1999. African American extended kin systems: An empirical assessment in the National Survey of Black Americans. In *Family ethnicity: Strength in diversity,* 2nd ed., edited by Harriet Pipes McAdoo. Thousand Oaks, CA: Sage.

Hays, William, and Charles Mindel. 1973. Extended kinship relations in Black and white families. *Journal of Marriage and the Family* 35:51–57.

Hill, Shirley A. 1999. *African-American children: Socialization and development in families.* Thousand Oaks, CA: Sage.

Hofferth, Sandra. 1984. Kin networks, race, and family structure. *Journal of Marriage and the Family* 46:791–806.

Hofferth, Sandra, Kimberlee A. Shauman, Robin R. Henke, and Jerry West. 1998. *Characteristics of children's early care and education programs: Data from the 1995 National Household Education Survey.* Washington, DC: U.S. Department of Education.

Hogan, Dennis P., David J. Eggebeen, and Clifford C. Clogg. 1993. The structure of intergenerational exchanges in American families. *American Journal of Sociology* 98:1428–58.

Hogan, Dennis P., Ling-Xin Hao, and William L. Parish. 1990. Race, kin networks, and assistance to mother-headed families. *Social Forces* 68:797–812.

Hurst, Charles E. 1998. *Social inequality: Forms, causes, and consequences,* 3rd ed. Boston: Allyn & Bacon.

Kontos, Susan, Carollee Howes, Marybeth Shinn, and Ellen Galinsky. 1995. *Quality in family childcare and relative care.* New York: Teachers College Press.

Lamb, Michael E. 1997. Nonparental childcare: Context, quality, correlates. In *Handbook of child psychology.* Vol. 4: *Child psychology in practice,* 5th ed., edited by W. Damon, I. E. Siegel, and K. A. Renninger. New York: John Wiley & Sons.

Martin, Elmer P., and Joanne M. Martin. 1978. *The Black extended family.* Chicago: University of Chicago Press.

Massey, Douglas S., and Nancy A. Denton. 1993. *American apartheid: Segregation and the making of the underclass.* Cambridge, MA: Harvard University press.

McAdoo, Harriette Pipes. 1997. *Black families,* 3rd ed. Thousand Oaks, CA: Sage.

Mindel, Charles H. 1980. Extended familism among urban Mexican Americans, Anglos and Blacks. *Hispanic Journal of Behavioral Sciences* 2:21–34.

Miner, Sonia. 1995. Racial differences in family support and formal service utilization among older persons: a non-recursive model. *Journal of Gerontology: Social Sciences* 50(3): S143–S153.

Miner, Sonia, and Peter Uhlenberg. 1997. Intragenerational proximity and the social role of sibling neighbors after mid-life. *Family Relations* 46 (April):145–153.

National Institute for Child Health and Human Development, Early Childcare Research Network. 1997. Mother-child: Interaction and cognitive outcomes associated with early childcare. Symposium presented at the biennial meeting of the Society for Research in Child Development, Washington, DC.

Newman, Katherine S. 1999. *No shame in my game: The working poor in the inner city.* New York: Alfred A. Knopf and Russell Sage Foundation.

Padavic, Irene, and Barbara F. Reskin. 2002. *Women and men at work,* 2nd ed. Thousand Oaks, CA: Pine Forge Press.

Pagnini, Deanna L., and Ronald R. Rindfuss. 1993. The divorce of marriage and childbearing: changing attitudes and behavior in the United States. *Population and Development Review* 19:331–47.

Patterson, Orlando. 1998. *Rituals of blood: Consequences of slavery in two American centuries.* Washington, DC: Civitas/Counterpoint.

Presser, Harriet. 1999. Toward a 24-hour economy. *Science* 284 (11 June): 1778–79.

———. 1989. Can we make time for the children? The economy, work schedules, and childcare. *Demography* 26:523–43.

Presser, Harriet, and Amy Cox. 1997. The work schedules of low-educated American women and welfare reform. *Monthly Labor Review* , April: 25–34.

Raley, R. Kelly, Kathleen Harris, and Ronald R. Rindfuss. 2000. The quality and comparability of child care data in US Surveys. *Social Science Research* 29(3): 356–81.

Rice, Tom W., and Diane L. Coates. 1995. Gender role attitudes in the southern United States. *Gender & Society* 6:744–56.

Roschelle, Anne R. 1997. *No more kin: Exploring race, class, and gender in family networks*. Thousand Oaks, CA: Sage.

Ruggles, Steven. 1994. The origins of African-American family structure. *American Sociological Review* 59:136–51.

Smith, Kristin. 2000. Who's minding the kids? Childcare arrangements, Fall 1995. *Current population reports*, household economic studies, series P70–70. Government Printing Office: U.S. Census Bureau.

Spain, Daphne, and Suzanne Bianchi. 1996. *Balancing act: Motherhood, marriage, and employment among American women*. New York: Russell Sage Foundation.

Stack, Carol B. 1996. *Call to home: African Americans reclaim the rural south*. New York: Basic Books.

———. 1974. *All our kin: Strategies for survival in the Black community*. New York: Harper & Row.

Stack, Carol B., and Linda M. Burton. 1994. Kinscripts: Reflections on family, generation, and culture. In *Mothering: Ideology, experience, and aging*, edited by Evelyn N. Glenn, Grace Chang, and Linda R. Forcey. New York: Routledge.

Taylor, Robert J. 1986. Receipt of support from family among Black Americans: Demographic and familial differences. *Journal of Marriage and the Family* 48:67–77.

U.S. Bureau of the Census. 1982. *Statistical abstract of the United States,* 103rd ed. Washington, DC: U.S. Government Printing Office.

———. 1999. *Statistical abstract of the United States,* 119th ed. Washington, DC: U.S. Government Printing Office.

Uttal, Lynet. 1999. Using kin for childcare: Embedment in the socioeconomic networks of extended families. *Journal of Marriage and the Family* 61(4): 845–57.

Wilson, William J. 1996. *When work disappears: The world of the new urban poor*. New York: Alfred A. Knopf.

———. 1987. *The truly disadvantaged: The inner city, the underclass, and public policy*. Chicago, IL: University of Chicago Press.

7

Supporting Poor Single Mothers

Gender and Race in the U.S. Welfare State

Stephanie Moller

All industrialized, advanced capitalist democracies have developed welfare states or a compilation of social programs designed to support the needs of citizens. A broad range of programs can fall under the typology of the welfare state, including health care, family support, retirement support, support for the poor, and unemployment insurance. The shape of each country's welfare state is determined by the configuration of these social programs. Most advanced democracies offer families financial or in-kind resources (including child care). However, the United States' welfare state is considered exceptional because it is less comprehensive than most other welfare states as it does not offer universal family support (Abramovitz 1996; O'Connor, Orloff, and Shaver 1999). Instead of offering universal support to the majority of families, the U.S. welfare state targets assistance to vulnerable families. The U.S. welfare state has two tiers. Individuals with sufficient work history and wages qualify for the relatively generous, federally funded, top-tier social insurance programs such as Social Security and Medicare.

Individuals without consistent work history are relegated to the bottom tier, where they must prove destitution to qualify for meager amounts of assistance from locally administered and highly stigmatized programs (Abramovitz 1996; Nelson 1990). Feminists have argued that race and gender inequalities have been institutionalized in the U.S. welfare state. For example, eligibility for the top tier is "modeled on male patterns of labor force participation" (Quadagno 1990, 14). Women and underemployed workers are disadvantaged because they have lower wages and more interrupted employment patterns. Furthermore, black families are disproportionately represented in the bottom tier because they have historically been employed in lower wage, less secure jobs

This chapter was originally published in *Gender & Society* 16(4): 465–84, 2002.

and in jobs not protected by the top-tier forms of insurance, including agricultural employment (Oliver and Shapiro 1995; Quadagno 1994). Within the bottom tier, in particular programs that target single-mother families, racial politics generate additional uneven treatment of black and white families because black single mothers are often denied equal levels of assistance (Abramovitz 1996; Amott 1990).

In this chapter, I examine the uneven support accorded to black and white mothers at the end of the twentieth century. I analyze the generosity of Aid to Families with Dependent Children (AFDC) benefits in the 48 contiguous U.S. states in 1970, 1980, and 1990. This study is necessitated by the absence of quantitative research that incorporates feminist critiques of the welfare state. While most quantitative research on welfare generosity has focused on variables measuring class and state structure (Cauthen and Amenta 1996; Mink 1990; Quadagno 1987), feminists have demonstrated theoretically and historically that race and gender interactions are key (Abramovitz 1996; Gordon 1994). Feminists have used historical case studies to illustrate that welfare rules and procedures changed depending on the demographics of the clientele. These rules offered black and white families differential access to welfare because black families were often denied assistance. While feminists have generally focused on the qualitative elements of AFDC, including historical changes in rules, regulations, and key actors, I will focus on an easily quantifiable variable: *welfare generosity*. Understanding variations in generosity across states is imperative for understanding how equally states help their poor single mother families, especially because black women's access has improved since the 1960s and 1970s. I will argue, using ordinary least squares regression, that the race biased policies and procedures implemented with the inception and expansion of the welfare state remained throughout the program, resulting in uneven levels of support for black and white single-mother families.

FEMINIST THEORIES ON RACE, GENDER, AND THE U.S. WELFARE STATE

The most notable and notorious program serving single mothers prior to the 1996 welfare reforms was AFDC. AFDC, widely known as welfare, was a bottom-tier, state-run program that aided single-parent families with children younger than 18. Mothers were required to prove destitution to qualify for assistance. Furthermore, AFDC payments were lowered or terminated when mothers acquired employment of any sort. Using historical research, feminist authors have argued that the United States offers different levels of support to black and white families. Furthermore, they argue that uneven support results from race-specific conceptualizations of gender roles. Feminists posit that white women have historically been conceptualized as mothers and black women have been portrayed as workers. This distinctive conceptualization became institutionalized in the U.S. welfare state (Abramovitz 1996; Amott 1990; Bell 1965; Glenn 1985; Mink 1990; Sapiro 1990).

AFDC was originally designed during the New Deal to permit primarily white, Anglo-Saxon widows to remain home and care for their children (Abramovitz 1996; Garfinkel and McLanahan 1986; Katz 1997). "Suitable-home" rules that monitored living arrangements and cooking styles limited welfare access for immigrant and black families and for never-married mothers (Mink 1990; Oliver and Shapiro 1995). Furthermore, black women were often denied assistance because social workers defined them as employable and therefore not deserving of assistance (Abramovitz 1996). During the 1950s and 1960s, more black and never-married families were permitted onto the welfare rolls. However, states responded by expanding suitable-home rules and altering regulations that had previously protected client confidentiality. For example, some states ensured suitable homes by monitoring mothers' sexual relations (Soule and Zylan 1997). Furthermore, the state invaded women's privacy by releasing client names to law enforcement agencies and the general public (Abramovitz 1996). These regulations were altered to deter women, particularly black women, from seeking assistance (Abramovitz 1996; Zylan 2000). Three shifts occurred during the latter half of the twentieth century that could have diminished the uneven treatment of black and white women. First, the migration of black families and their concentration in northern urban areas increased black political power (Wilson 1980). Second, during the 1960s and 1970s, the welfare rights movement, composed primarily of poor black women, demanded higher benefits and successfully ended restrictive legislation that denied black women assistance (Quadagno 1990, 1994).[1] Third, increasing numbers of white women entered the full-time labor force and delayed childbearing. Seemingly then, toward the end of the century, the different balance between work and motherhood for black and white women was minimized. Both groups were expected to work while caring for their families. In response, AFDC rules and regulations increasingly emphasized stringent work requirements (Abramovitz 1996; Zylan 2000). Understanding the racial inequities of AFDC is imperative because it was the largest and longest antipoverty program serving single-mother families in the United States. The program spanned six decades and became the foundation for the 1996 welfare reforms in which its successor, Temporary Assistance to Needy Families (TANF), was developed. Many continuities exist between AFDC and TANF.

Therefore, understanding AFDC is a necessary precondition for understanding TANF. TANF, established in 1996, is similar to AFDC in its emphasis on local control and in its ideological underpinnings. First, TANF increases the local control found in AFDC. Researchers argue that local control is a primary reason that AFDC became a discriminatory program (Lieberman 1995). Local control permits subjectivity in determining who qualifies for welfare and family-specific levels of need, and it gives power to local bureaucrats (Funiciello 1993; Gooden 1997; Lieberman 1995).[2] In fact, applicants disqualified from AFDC assistance for having income or resources that are "too high" were not necessarily better off than families who entered the program (Lieberman 1995). Furthermore, Gooden (1997) found that white AFDC recipients are often encouraged to continue their education while black students are pushed into the low-wage labor force, once again exacerbating differential treatment by race. TANF also maintains many of the ideological underpinnings prevalent in AFDC (Gordon 2001; Mink 2001). First, TANF increases the work requirements already found under AFDC by requiring employable mothers to work within two years. In addition, states are required to impose a lifetime limit of five years of support, although exemptions are possible for up to 20 percent of each state's caseload. This presumably forces mothers into the labor market. Second, TANF condemns unmarried childbearing and promotes marriage (U.S. Department of Health and Human Services 2000). "As TANF's foremost objective is to restore the patriarchal family, numerous provisions promote marriage and paternal headship while frustrating childbearing and child-raising rights outside of marriage" (Mink 2001, 79). In 1999, five states were each awarded 20 million dollars for reporting the highest declines in out-of-wedlock births. Indeed, research has found that programs developed under TANF are more successful than AFDC at promoting marriage (U.S. Department of Health and Human Services 2000, 3). Hence, the key ideological underpinnings of AFDC, that is, the dichotomy of mothering versus working, remain salient in TANF. Although AFDC offered greater support to single mothers, TANF pushes some women into marriage while pushing others into the labor force. Furthermore, since a relatively large proportion of the clientele is black families (38 percent in 1999), TANF has further institutionalized race, class, and gender inequities (Gordon 2001; Mink 2001; U.S. Department of Health and Human Services 2000).

CLASS-BASED THEORIES

Quantitative researchers examining the development of welfare states often have neglected the contributions of U.S.-centered, feminist researchers. Instead, they draw on different theories that focus primarily on industrialization, class, and state structure. Some welfare state researchers contend that societies must industrialize to attain the necessary financial resources to develop welfare states (Amenta and Poulsen 1996; Dahl 1982; Flora and Alber

1981; Wilensky 1975). Looking cross-nationally, they argue that when states have greater revenues and wealthier populations, benefits are generally higher (Hicks and Misra 1993; Wilensky 1975). However, when states experience economic downturns, such as increasing unemployment, their ability to address citizen need is limited because both need is higher and state revenues are lower (Huber and Stephens 2001). This approach does not consider the effects of race.

Another explanation of welfare state development focuses on the strength of the working class within each country. These researchers identify a strong labor movement, accompanied by a strong labor party, as important forces promoting welfare state expansion (Esping-Andersen 1990; Korpi 1983; Stephens 1979). They have demonstrated that the United States has a weak working-class movement and party, but that the Democratic Party often approximates a working-class party (Misra, Moller, and Lenzo 1998; Soule and Zylan 1997). For example, between the 1930s and the 1960s, Democrats aligned themselves with the agendas of the working class and impoverished (see Katz 1997). However, the Democratic Party has historically been divided among regions, and southern Democrats have often opposed welfare state development because it threatened their agricultural labor markets and long established racial hierarchies (Quadagno 1994).

Therefore, nonsouthern states often have more generous benefits. This party-level focus does reveal regional race-based differences in welfare development. Another avenue for workers and citizens to advance welfare state development is through the electoral process. Researchers have found that widespread citizen participation is a prerequisite for the development of strong welfare states (Cauthen and Amenta 1996; Skocpol and Amenta 1986). Democratic institutions encourage social spending because they provide an avenue for citizens to lobby the state (Skocpol and Amenta 1986; Soule and Zylan 1997). Furthermore, enfranchisement is necessary for poor citizens to influence the state (Hicks and Misra 1993; Soule and Zylan 1997). However, poor citizens are not differentiated by race or gender. Each of these perspectives offers important insights into the development of the U.S. welfare state, but their neglect of gender and race render them incomplete.

Industrialization and electoral turnout help to explain why the U.S. welfare state developed, but they fail to explain why women and minorities are disadvantaged. Furthermore, the class perspective helps to explain why women and minorities are relegated to the bottom tier, but it fails to explain the differential treatment of black and white families within the bottom tier. These approaches also are inadequate because they disregard the ideological underpinnings of welfare. They neglect the dynamic interaction between race, gender, and family structure in the development of the welfare state. My research begins to overcome the inadequacies of a quantitative class-based approach by determining if race and gender interactions are important components of welfare state generosity. I will examine if the welfare state offers different levels of support to black and white single-mother families.

METHOD, VARIABLES, AND HYPOTHESES

To examine if AFDC offers different levels of support to black and white single-parent families, I ran a series of ordinary least squares regressions for the 48 contiguous U.S. states. I focus on the decades between the 1970s and 1990s because prior to the 1970s, published census statistics on race and family structure distinguished between white and nonwhite, instead of between white and black. Hence, data from the 1970s, 1980s, and 1990s are not entirely comparable with the previous decades. Furthermore, prior to this period, particularly between the 1950s and 1970s, the welfare rolls expanded dramatically due to changing eligibility requirements. One major change was the demise of suitable-home rules that had been used to exclude many destitute black families by monitoring their lifestyles and living arrangements (Abramovitz 1996; Levitan 1990). By the 1970s, most economically eligible families had acquired assistance, and the size of the rolls stabilized (Levitan 1990). Hence, prior to the 1970s, much of the discrepancy in generosity was not captured by payment levels because many poor single-parent families were completely denied access. Focusing on the 1970s, 1980s, and 1990s permits me to control for those unmeasured factors.

These time periods permit me to examine *generosity* rather than *access*. Prior to the 1960s, the uneven treatment of black and white women was more evident in policies and procedures governing *access* to AFDC. Law changes, social movements, and the implementation of workfare theoretically altered this differential treatment. Thus, demonstrating new forms of divergent treatment in the modern period contributes to understanding the shifting nature of black-white differences when problems of access presumably declined. Thus, analyzing *generosity* rather than *access* deepens our understanding of race inequality in the welfare state.

The state-level data used for these analyses were collected with Joy Misra and Christopher Lenzo from various government publications including the *Census of the Population* (U.S. Bureau of the Census 1970, 1980, 1990), the *Statistical Abstract of the United States* (U.S. Bureau of the Census 1991, 1992, 1994, 2000), the *Congressional Quarterly* (1994), and the *Social Security Bulletin: Annual Statistical Supplement* (Social Security Administration 1973, 1983, 1993; see table 7.1 for variable-specific sources).

The data are analyzed for the 48 contiguous U.S. states. State-level analyses are necessary because most welfare-state theories focus on the role of the state. State theorists contend that states generally respond to the needs and demands of groups within their states, not individuals. Hence, I measure the variables at the state level. These analyses do not translate directly to the individual level. For example, if I argue that states with greater voter participation (or higher percentages of white single mothers) offer more generous welfare, then I am arguing that states respond to this group of voting citizens (or white single mothers). I am not arguing that if a person votes (or is a white single mother), she will receive more welfare, because her benefit level actually is determined by numerous individual-level factors such as family size and income. Thus, I measure welfare generosity, the dependent variable, in 1972, 1982, and 1992 as the average AFDC payment per family in each state in 1990 dollars (Social Security Administration 1973, 1983, 1993). (See original article for table summary of data.)

Independent Variables

All independent variables are measured in 1970, 1980, and 1990. Four variables address the relationship between family structure, race, and AFDC generosity. First, *single-mother families* are measured as the percentage of all families in a state with children younger than 18 that are mother headed (see table 7.1 for variable definitions). I use this group because of their high poverty rates. In 1992, 21 percent of all children in the United States were impoverished, but the majority of these children resided in single-parent families. Fifty-four percent of children in single-mother families were impoverished in 1992, compared to 12 percent of children in families with a man present (U.S. Bureau of the Census 1992). Since AFDC was designed to support single mothers, I focus on them and expect generosity to increase as the population of single mothers increases.

The extent that single-mother families require support from the state is dependent on race. Black single-mother families have one of the highest poverty rates of any group in the United States. In 1992, 67 percent of children in black female-headed families were impoverished, compared to 45 percent of children in white female-headed families, 19 percent in black families with a man present, and 10 percent in white families with a man present (U.S. Bureau of the Census 1992). Although black single-mother families are among the poorest families, feminists have argued that the state is less supportive of their needs.

I include three measures to determine if *generosity* is associated with race. First is the *percentage of the state's population that is black.* Next, I examine two measures of race and family structure that account for their interactive effect: the percentage of all families with children younger than 18 that are headed by *black single mothers* and the percentage of all families with children younger than 18 that are headed by *white single mothers.* If states provide different benefits to white and black women, then welfare spending should be higher in states with a larger proportion of white single-mother families and lower in states with a larger proportion of black single-mother families.

Control Variables

All models include three control variables to account for the resources available to states. *Per capita revenue* is included because states with higher revenues have greater resources to increase AFDC spending. *Per capita income* is included because it estimates the level of income in a state and thus need for and ability to pay welfare benefits. AFDC and other social programs are designed to serve clients without undermining the market (Piven and Cloward 1993). Hence, states with higher wages have a higher potential maximum benefit level. The final control variable is the *unemployment rate*, averaged over a three-year period (1967–1970, 1977–1980, 1987–1990), which controls for economic downturns. Since state revenues are lower during economic downturns, I expect a negative relationship between *unemployment* and AFDC *generosity*.

Alternative Theories

The final set of models includes three variables to test class-based theories of the welfare state. Class power is measured through *unionization*, or the percentage of manufacturing workers unionized in 1970, 1980, and 1989. *Unionization* is expected to have a positive impact on AFDC generosity. Democratic Party power is measured as the *percent of the electorate voting Democratic* in nonsouthern gubernatorial elections, averaged over three elections. Since Democratic power is only theorized to be beneficial in nonsouthern states, all southern states are coded 0 (following Misra, Moller, and Lenzo 1998). Following Cauthen and Amenta (1996), *electoral participation* is measured as the log of the percentage of the voting-age population actually casting a vote in the previous presidential election. Since voting is a key source of political power for the poor, I expect states with greater participation to have more generous AFDC programs.

RESULTS

The following analyses explore the extent to which states support black and white mothers.[3] To determine if states serve the needs of these parents, I regress the percentage of families with children younger than 18 that are single mothers on average AFDC payments per family, controlling for measures of state resources, including *per capita income*, *per capita revenues*, and *unemployment*. In table 7.1, Model 1 presents the unstandardized regression coefficients for 1970, 1980, and 1990. Generally, I find that states with greater resources are more generous. In all three decades, states with wealthier populations had higher average benefit levels. Furthermore, during the 1980s and 1990s, states with greater revenues had more generous AFDC payments. However, *unemployment* is an unstable predictor of AFDC generosity. After controlling for state resources, we see that in each time period, states are less generous when they have relatively large proportions of single-mother families. This is an unexpected finding since the AFDC program was designed for this group, and researchers have found that when a segment of the population increases, the generosity of spending on that segment also increases due to their increased visibility and political power (Hicks and Misra 1993; Pampel, Williamson, and Stryker 1990).

Why are average payments lower in states with relatively larger populations of single-mother families? As historical research has demonstrated, AFDC was originally designed for white mothers. This research suggests that as more black mothers entered the clientele, AFDC deteriorated into a work program (Abramovitz 1996). To determine if the negative association between *single-mother families* and AFDC *generosity* is dependent on race, I incorporate the *percentage of the population that is black* into the model (see table 7.1, Model 2). Doing so significantly improves our models in 1980 and 1990, as states with relatively large black populations have less generous AFDC payments.[4]

Including race also eliminates the negative impact of *single-mother families*. In fact, for 1980 and 1990, *single-mother families* has a positive impact on AFDC generosity, once race is controlled. Interestingly, race does not significantly predict spending in 1970 nor does it completely extinguish the negative relationship between *single-mother families* and *welfare generosity*. This is partially explained by the welfare rights movement during the 1960s and 1970s. This movement, composed primarily of poor black women, achieved greater access to AFDC, diminishing the racialized nature of the AFDC program, at least for a short period.

Since the percentage of single-mother families either becomes insignificant or changes from a negative to a positive relationship when *percentage black* is entered into the models, it is important to examine the intersection of race and *single-mother families*. Thus, I regress the percentage of families with children younger than 18 that are headed by a black single mother (see table 7.2, Model 1) or by a white single mother (see table 7.2, Model 2) on average AFDC payments.

As expected, states with a larger percentage of black single-mother families have less generous welfare spending, while states with a larger proportion of white single-mother families offer more generous welfare spending. These findings are significant controlling for *per capita income* and *state revenues*. In the previous models (see table 7.1, Model 2), *percentage black* was not a

Table 7.1. Understandardized Coefficients for Aid to Families with Dependent Children Generosity Regressed on Single Mothers, Percentage Black, and Selected Controls, 1970, 1980, and 1990

Variable	Model 1			Model 2		
	1970	1980	1990	1970	1980	1990
Per capita income	0.060***	0.039***	0.022***	0.053***	0.026**	0.019***
	(0.010)	(0.007)	(0.004)	(0.011)	(0.007)	(0.004)
Per capita revenue	0.035	0.088*	0.081**	0.009	0.077	0.060*
	(0.081)	(0.042)	(0.026)	(0.082)	(0.039)	(0.024)
Unemployment	13.981	24.498*	6.056	4.466	13.045	−6.692
	(20.141)	(10.334)	(12.161)	(21.085)	(10.080)	(11.059)
Single mothers	−44.506***	−14.763*	−10.483*	−26.778	2.515	11.354
	(10.995)	(5.505)	(4.007)	(16.815)	(7.425)	(6.619)
Percentage Black				−4.571	−6.394**	−8.052***
				(3.306)	(2.028)	(2.076)
Constant	4.444	−372.203*	−111.585	44.211	−269.626	−280.038*
	(192.642)	(143.553)	(119.519)	(192.789)	(134.612)	(112.494)
Adjusted R^2	.505	.497	.526	.515	.584	.643
F change				1.912	9.937***	15.042**

NOTE: $N = 48$. Standard errors are in parentheses.
*$p < .05$. **$p < .01$. ***$p < .001$.

significant predictor of welfare generosity in 1970, but in these models (see table 7.2, Model 1), the interactive variable, *black single-mother families*, is significant in that year. This suggests that the race-gender nexus is key. In 1970, a 1 percent increase in black single-mother-headed families resulted in an average spending decline of $35 per family,[5] while a 1 percent increase in white single-mother-headed families yielded a $9 increase in average payments. The relationship between black single-mother families and AFDC becomes weaker in 1980 and 1990, associated with a $15 and $11 decline, respectively. However, the relationship between white single-mother families and AFDC becomes stronger in 1980 and 1990: A 1 percent increase is associated with a $22 and $18 increase, respectively. AFDC becomes weaker in 1980 and 1990, associated with a $15 and $11 decline, respectively. However, the relationship between white single-mother families and AFDC becomes stronger in 1980 and 1990: A 1 percent increase is associated with a $22 and $18 increase, respectively. These findings suggest that black and white families are granted uneven support by AFDC, or more specifically that the racial composition of single parents in a state influences that state's generosity.

Clearly, states neglect black single mothers' needs by offering only limited support in a second-tier welfare program, since welfare spending is lower in states with a larger proportion of this potentially needy group. While much of

Table 7.2. Understandardized Coefficients for Aid to Families with Dependent Children Generosity Regressed on Black and White Single-Mother Families and Selected Controls, 1970, 1980, and 1990

Variable	Model 1			Model 2		
	1970	*1980*	*1990*	*1970*	*1980*	*1990*
Per capita income	0.053***	0.033***	0.021***	0.054***	0.024**	0.021***
	(0.010)	(0.006)	(0.004)	(0.012)	(0.006)	(0.004)
Per capita revenue	−0.011	0.073	0.065*	0.044	0.117**	0.076**
	(0.085)	(0.039)	(0.024)	(0.097)	(0.039)	(0.023)
Unemployment	−6.615	18.643*	3.745	−3.588	4.403	−4.344
	(20.550)	(8.871)	(10.232)	(25.034)	(9.641)	(9.657)
Black single mother	−34.943**	−14.928***	−11.173***			
	(9.615)	(3.715)	(2.644)			
White single mother				9.636	22.611**	18.218***
				(18.923)	(6.841)	(4.017)
Constant	−11.492	−369.806**	−207.541*	−358.713	−488.976**	−433.401***
	(188.283)	(130.969)	(102.070)	(203.048)	(135.926)	(110.841)
Adjusted R^2	.477	.573	.612	.320	.532	.628

NOTE: $N = 48$. Standard errors are in parentheses.
*$p < .05$. **$p < .01$. ***$p < .001$.

the quantitative and class-based research on welfare states neglects the inter-action between race, gender, and family, I have illustrated that it is an impor-tant component of AFDC generosity.

To further demonstrate the importance of gender and race, I present analy-ses that control for variables widely used in class-based analyses to explain variations in welfare generosity. I examine the relationship between race, family structure, and average AFDC generosity, controlling for *unionization, Democratic vote*, and *electoral turnout*. I include *electoral turnout* in separate models because *Democratic vote, electoral turnout*, and *black single-mother families* are highly correlated. I find that *union density* and *Democratic vote* have little impact on our models because they do not significantly improve the models' fit and often were not statistically significant.[6] The U.S. labor movement is remarkably weak, and the Democratic Party is not truly a working-class party. As a result, the interactions between race, gender, and family structure are better determinants of AFDC spending than *class mobi-lization* and *Democratic power*, two variables long advocated by class-based, quantitative welfare state researchers as important. (See original article for table summary.)

An important avenue through which citizens can influence state policies and programs is voting. In states with low voter turnout, the electorate is less engaged in the political process and therefore less influential in policy making. I find that *voter turnout* is an important predictor of average AFDC spending, particularly in 1980. Although black and white single-mother families maintain their divergent relationship with spending, the strength of the relationship declines in the 1970s for both groups and in the 1980s for black single-mother families. Some of this effect results from the high correlation between *electoral turnout* and *black single-mother families*, while it is only moderately correlated with *white single-mother families*. So, states with a large population of black single mothers have low turnout, particularly in 1970. The effect of electoral turnout in the 1970s is partially explained by the welfare rights movement, which used many techniques, including electoral participation, to achieve their goals. In addition, there was a residual positive impact of increased black voting after the Voting Rights Act of 1974 (Soule and Zylan 1997). However, even when *electoral turnout* is controlled, states with a larger percentage of black single-mother families in 1990 had significantly lowered welfare generosity. Furthermore, states with more white single-mother families had significantly higher generosity in 1980 and 1990.

IMPLICATIONS

The support of single-mother families is an important component of welfare states. However, the United States has never offered generous benefits to mothers, who were generally granted access to the bottom tier of the welfare state (Nelson 1990). While workers are served primarily through stable, relatively higher paying social insurance programs, mothers and other underemployed individuals must prove financial destitution to acquire meager assistance through bottom-tier programs (Nelson 1990).

Importantly, feminists have argued that these minimal levels of support are dependent on race-specific conceptualizations of gender roles. Family and work norms have interacted to create policies that encouraged domesticity among white women and employment among black women (Abramovitz 1996; Amott 1990; Bell 1965; Glenn 1985; Mink 1990; Sapiro 1990). Researchers argue that policy makers initially created AFDC to encourage domesticity among its primarily white clients, but as the welfare population diversified, rules were changed to exclude the "immoral" and employable, who were often defined as immigrant and black families (Abramovitz 1996; Mink 1990).

In this chapter, I have begun to examine how the state supports different economic outcomes for black and white women. Whereas previous feminist researchers have examined access to welfare by studying rules and regulations, I have focused on the generosity of welfare. I find that states with a larger black single-mother population are less generous than those with a larger white single-mother population. Importantly, these measures of the interaction between race and family structure are better determinants of welfare generosity than well-established measures of working-class power. My findings are compatible with feminist theorizing on gender, race, and the welfare state, but future research is necessary to test fully this perspective by examining the relationship between the generosity of benefits and employment patterns for black and white women on welfare.

My initial analysis demonstrates that state policies reproduce white privilege. Racialized policies are detrimental to black families because they limit opportunities (Oliver and Shapiro 1995). Black single-mother families are among the most vulnerable in the United States because they are denied both the opportunity and the support to maintain economic stability. This vulnerability is evidenced in their poverty rates. Since the 1970s, about half of all black single-mother families have been impoverished, compared to only one-third of white single-mother families and less than one-tenth of married-couple families (U.S. Census Bureau 2000). AFDC was designed to support these families by providing economic aid, but since AFDC was a racialized program, it maintained white privilege, even in these critical economic situations (Neubeck and Cazenave 2001). The stability of my findings during the three time periods reflects the fact that social programs and benefit levels also are relatively stable over time since social programs are path dependent, meaning that their characteristics are dependent on their developmental histories (Quadagno 1987). In their description of AFDC payments from 1940 to 1995, Wexler and Engel (1999) found that state rankings in payments remained fairly constant over time. The most generous states in 1940 were typically the most generous in 1995, and the least generous remained ungenerous.

Given the history of AFDC and its conditioning of the TANF program, it is important to examine the extent to which race and gender inequalities remain institutionalized in the TANF program. Since the mid-1990s, citizen welfare has become even more localized. By increasing local control, TANF gives interest groups and bureaucrats increased power in policy planning and program implementation. This power is potentially detrimental to black single-mother families because local control permits discrimination (Lieberman 1995).

With these new policies, the size of the welfare rolls has diminished dramatically. In 1995, 4.8 million families were assisted by AFDC; by 1999, only 2.6 million families acquired assistance from TANF (U.S. Bureau of the Census 2000). Unfortunately, much of the current data on TANF does not disaggregate variables by race, making race and gender-centered research difficult (Burnham 2001). Uncovering the racial dimensions of the TANF program will prove complicated since researchers will need to consider not only benefit levels but also states' enforcement of time limits and work requirements.

NOTES

1. During this period, a large academic and political movement also emerged that condemned black women as single mothers. This movement argued that welfare undermined the black family and created dependency, and it challenged the right of black women to access the state as mothers (Fraser and Gordon 1994; Mead 1986; Moynihan 1967).

2. The methods for determining Aid to Families with Dependent Children (AFDC) eligibility and payments were extremely complicated. Each state had to define a standard of need, and these standards varied widely. Actual payments to clients were often less than this standard. Some states paid 100 percent of the need standard, while other states paid a percentage, depending on families' income and resources. In 1980, payments as a percentage of the need standard ranged from 42 percent in Louisiana to 95 percent in Maine (U.S. Department of Health and Human Services 1980, 233–34). Each state, therefore, had the discretion to determine need, allowable exemptions, and the penalty for various types of resources. This permitted discrimination to influence welfare generosity in multiple, although in discrete ways (Lieberman 1995).

3. To ensure that collinearity does not unduly influence the regression coefficients, I require that the variance inflation factor remain below 5. All reported models adhere to this strict requirement.

4. F tests of 9.937 and 15.042 are significant for 1980 and 1990, respectively. This indicates that adding *percentage black* to the models significantly reduces the unexplained variation in AFDC generosity.

5. *Percentage black single mothers* and *percentage black* are very strongly correlated, indicating that states that have the largest black population also have the largest black single-parent population. Hence, *percentage black* and *percentage black single mother* are capturing the same effect. However, *percentage white single mother* is not equally correlated with *percentage black*, ranging between .58 and .74. Hence, including these interactive effects clarifies the relationship for both black and white single-mother families. Furthermore, these interactive variables are more theoretically relevant than simply including *percentage black*.

6. The F test is significant for only Model 2, 1980.

REFERENCES

Abramovitz, Mimi. 1996. *Regulating the lives of women: Social welfare policy from colonial times to the present*. Boston: South End.

Amenta, Edwin, and Jane D. Poulsen. 1996. Social politics in context: The institutional politics theory and social spending at the end of the new deal. *Social Forces* 75:33–60.

Amott, Teresa. 1990. Black women and AFDC: Making entitlement out of necessity. In *Women, the state and welfare*, edited by Linda Gordon. Madison: University of Wisconsin Press.

Bell, Winifred. 1965. *Aid to dependent children*. New York: Columbia University Press.

Burnham, Linda. 2001.Welfare reform, family hardship, and women of color. *The Annals of the American Academy of Political and Social Science* 577:38–48.

Cauthen, Nancy, and Edwin Amenta. 1996. Not for widows only: Institutional politics and the formative years of Aid to Dependent Children. *American Sociological Review* 61:427–48.

Congressional Quarterly. 1994. Congressional Quarterly's guide to U.S. elections. Washington, DC: Congressional Quarterly.

Dahl, Robert. 1982. *Dilemmas of pluralist democracy.* New Haven, CT: Yale University Press.

Esping-Andersen, Gosta. 1990. *The three worlds of welfare capitalism.* Princeton, NJ: Princeton University Press.

Flora, Peter, and Jens Alber. 1981. Modernization, democratization, and the development of welfare states in Western Europe. In *The development of welfare states in Europe and America*, edited by Peter Flora and Arnold Heidenheimer. New Brunswick, NJ: Transaction Books.

Fraser, Nancy, and Linda Gordon. 1994. Dependency demystified: Inscriptions of power in a keyword of the welfare state. *Social Politics* 1:4–31.

Funiciello, Theresa. 1993. *Tyranny of kindness: Dismantling the welfare system to end poverty in America.* New York: Atlantic Monthly Press.

Garfinkel, Irwin, and Sara S. McLanahan. 1986. *Single mothers and their children: A new American dilemma.* Washington, DC: Urban Institute Press.

Glenn, Evelyn Nakano. 1985. Racial ethnic women's labor: The intersection of race, gender and class oppression. *Review of Radical Political Economics* 17(3): 86–108.

Gooden, Susan. 1997. Race and welfare report: Examining racial differences in employment status among welfare recipients. Oakland, CA: Grass Roots Innovative Policy Program.

Gordon, Linda. 1994. *Pitied but not entitled: Single mothers and the history of welfare.* Cambridge, MA: Harvard University Press.

———. 2001. Who must provide? *The Annals of the American Academy of Political and Social Science* 577:12–25.

Hicks, Alexander, and Joya Misra. 1993. Political resources and the growth of welfare in affluent capitalist democracies, 1960–1982. *American Journal of Sociology* 99:668–710.

Huber, Evelyn, and John Stephens. 2001. *Development and crisis of the welfare states: Parties and policies in global markets.* Chicago: University of Chicago Press.

Katz, Michael B. 1997. *In the shadow of the poorhouse: A social history of welfare in America.* New York: Basic Books.

Korpi, Walter. 1983. *The democratic class struggle.* Boston: Routledge and Kegan Paul.

Levitan, Sar A. 1990. *Programs in aid of the poor.* Baltimore: John Hopkins University Press.

Lieberman, Robert C. 1995. Race, institutions, and the administration of social policy. *Social Science History* 19:511–42.

Mead, Lawrence. 1986. *Beyond entitlement: The social obligations of citizenship.* New York: Free Press.

Mink, Gwendolyn. 1990. The lady and the tramp: Gender, race, and the origins of the American welfare state. In *Women, the state and welfare*, edited by Linda Gordon. Madison: University of Wisconsin Press.

——. 2001. Violating women: Rights abuses in the welfare police state. *The Annals of the American Academy of Political and Social Science* 577:79–93.

Misra, Joya, Stephanie Moller, and Chris Lenzo. 1998. Race, class, gender and the formation and sustenance of ADC/AFDC. Paper presented at the annual meeting of the American Sociological Association, San Francisco, 21–25 August.

Moynihan, Daniel Patrick. 1967. The Negro family: The case for national action. In *The Moynihan report and the politics of controversy*, edited by Lee Rainwater and W. L. Yancy. Cambridge, MA: MIT Press.

Nelson, Barbara J. 1990. The origins of the two-channel welfare state: Workmen's compensation and mother's aid. In *Women, the state, and welfare*, edited by Linda Gordon. Madison: University of Wisconsin Press.

Neubeck, Kenneth J., and Noel A. Cazenave. 2001. *Welfare racism: Playing the race card against America's poor*. New York: Routledge.

O'Connor, Julia S., Ann Shola Orloff, and Sheila Shaver. 1999. *States, markets, families: Gender, liberalism and social policy in Australia, Canada, Great Britain and the United States*. New York: Cambridge University Press.

Oliver, Melvin L., and Thomas M. Shapiro. 1995. *Black wealth/white wealth: A new perspective on racial inequality*. New York: Routledge.

Pampel, Fred C., John B. Williamson, and Robin Stryker. 1990. Class context and pension response to demographic structure in advanced industrial democracies. *Social Problems* 37:535–50.

Piven, Frances Fox, and Richard Cloward. 1993. *Regulating the poor: The functions of public welfare*. New York: Vintage.

Quadagno, Jill. 1987. Theories of the welfare state. *Annual Review of Sociology* 13:109–28.

——. 1990. Race, class, and gender in the U.S. welfare state: Nixon's failed Family Assistance Plan. *American Sociological Review* 55:11–28.

——. 1994. *The color of welfare: How racism undermined the war on poverty*. New York: Oxford University Press.

Sapiro, Virginia. 1990. The gender basis of American social policy. In *Women, the state and welfare*, edited by Linda Gordon. Madison: University of Wisconsin Press.

Skocpol, Theda, and Edwin Amenta. 1986. States and social policies. *Annual Review of Sociology* 12:131–57.

Social Security Administration. 1973. *Social security bulletin: Annual statistical supplement*. Washington, DC: Government Printing Office.

——. 1983. *Social security bulletin: Annual statistical supplement*. Washington, DC: Government Printing Office.

——. 1993. *Social security bulletin: Annual statistical supplement*. Washington, DC: Government Printing Office.

Soule, Sarah, and Yvonne Zylan. 1997. Runaway train? The diffusion of state-level reform in ADC/AFDC eligibility requirements, 1950–1967. *American Journal of Sociology* 103:733–62.

Stephens, John. 1979. *The transition from capitalism to socialism*.Urbana: University of Illinois Press.

U.S. Bureau of the Census. 1970. *Census of the population*. Washington, DC: Government Printing Office.

————. 1980. *Census of the population.* Washington, DC: Government Printing Office.

————. 1990. *Census of the population.* Washington, DC: Government Printing Office.

————. 1991. *Statistical abstract of the United States.* Washington, DC: Government Printing Office.

————. 1992. *Statistical abstract of the United States.* Washington, DC: Government Printing Office.

————. 1994. *Statistical abstract of the United States.* Washington, DC: Government Printing Office.

————. 2000. *Statistical abstract of the United States.* Washington, DC: Government Printing Office.

U.S. Department of Health and Human Services. 1980. *Characteristics of state plans for Aid to Families with Dependent Children.* Washington, DC: Government Printing Office.

————. 2000. *Temporary Assistance to Needy Families Program: Third annual report to Congress.* Washington, DC: Government Printing Office.

Wexler, Sandra, and Rafael J. Engel. 1999. Historical trends in state-level ADC/AFDC benefits: Living on less and less. *Journal of Sociology and Social Welfare* 26:37–61.

Wilensky, Harold. 1975. *The welfare state and equality.* Berkeley: University of California Press.

Wilson, William Julius. 1980. *The declining significance of race: Blacks and changing American institutions.* Chicago: University of Chicago Press.

Zylan, Yvonne. 2000. Maternalism redefined: Gender, the state, and the politics of day care, 1945–1962. *Gender & Society* 14:608–29.

Part Two:
Failing Safety Nets and Fragile Families

"The Family-Work Interface in American households," by Marlese Durr and Shirley A. Hill
1. Describe what Durr and Hill call the family-work interface.
2. How has the African American family-work interface differed from that found in mainstream society? What factors have been responsible for this difference?
3. What is the Black Matriarch thesis made famous by Moynihan?
4. What has been the consequence of the thesis for black family life?

"(Re)Envisioning Cohabitation: A Commentary on Race, History, and Culture," by Andrea G. Hunter

1. What is meant by Gumbo ya ya?
2. How does Hunter relate this concept to African American Families?
3. What has been the unique world of black women in families?

"No More Kin Care?: Changes in Black Mothers' Reliance on Relatives for Child Care, 1977–1994," by Karin L. Brewster and Irene Padavic

1. How do Brewster and Padavic attempt to measure the strength of family ties among African Americans? Do you think this is a good indicator of the level of family support among blacks?
2. What factors might have increased the need for African American women to rely on their families for child support? What factors have decreased the need for that kind of assistance?
3. What are the overall findings of Brewster and Padavic? Who relies most on the family for child care, and why?

"Supporting Poor Single Mothers: Gender and Race in the U.S. Welfare State," by Stephanie Moller

1. The United States has often been described as the "reluctant welfare state" because its welfare policies, compared to those in other industrialized countries, are meager. As Moller notes, our welfare policies also insure that class, race, and gender inequalities are institutionalized. Explain how this happens.
2. What measure does Moller use to explore the level of 'racism' in our welfare policies?
3. How do policies in TANF differ from those in the older welfare system, AFDC? What are the implications of those differences for families?
4. Discuss two class explanations for variance in the level of welfare benefits in different states in the United States.
5. According to Moller's findings, what factors are really responsible for that variance? How does race matter?

III

GENDERED RACISM AND LABOR MARKET EXPERIENCE

The three articles in this section examine obstacles faced by African American men and women in their efforts to find and retain employment. More often than not, the vast majority are overrepresented in low-wage, dead-end jobs. But, for those who have been employed in middle- to upper-level managerial posts, the adverse consequences of deindustrialization and down-sizing have caused a decline in wages, a return of multiple barriers toward promotions, and a revisiting of old perceptions undermining employment prospects. Harry Holzer provides an overview of multiple factors which undermine adequate employment and wages for black men. Newsome and DoDoo describe African American women's earnings decline because of their roles as mothers. Browne and Kennelly discuss how the perception of black women as mothers undermines their job prospects.

8

Racial Differences in Labor Market Outcomes among Men

Harry J. Holzer

This chapter reviews evidence of racial differences, among men, in labor-market outcomes such as wages, employment, and labor-force participation. Data are presented for trends over time and differences across racial and ethnic groups. Differences between whites and blacks are considered, as are some differences involving Hispanic and Asian men, both immigrants and U.S. born. Also considered are various explanations for the noted trends. Possible future trends are discussed, as well as implications for policy and further research.

RELATIVE WAGES AND EMPLOYMENT: TRENDS AND REMAINING DIFFERENCES

The wages of black men improved dramatically from 1940 to 1990. In 1940, the wages of black men were, on average, only 40 percent as high as those of white men; by 1990, they were roughly 75 percent as high. Within this overall trend, however, the rate of progress has been quite uneven. There were two periods of sharp improvement—1940 to 1950 and 1960 to 1975. In contrast, improvements during 1950 to 1960 were much more modest; and since 1975, the relative wages of black men have stagnated or even declined. Table 8.1 lists differences in the ratios of relative wages based on years of experience. It gives a brief list of earnings ratios, based on amounts of labor-market experience, for 1971, 1981, and 1988. Although black men with 10 or more years of labor market experience continued to gain in relative wages during the 1980s, the group with the fewest years of experience lost ground relative to whites.

This chapter was originally published in *America Becoming: Racial Trends and Their Consequences* (Volume II), edited by N. J. Smelser, W. J. Wilson, and F. Mitchell. Washington, DC: National Academy Press, 2001.

Data indicate that the deterioration in earnings relative to whites was greatest among young black men with a college degree; but the deterioration in absolute terms was much greater among the less educated (Juhn, Murphy, and Pierce, 1993; Bound and Holzer, 1996), and reflected the dramatic decline in earnings experienced by less-educated young men of all races during the past 20 years.

The deterioration in relative earnings among young black men can be observed even after one adjusts for black-white differences in education, region of residence, etc. In the mid-1970s, young black men were earning 10 percent less than white men with similar education, age, and area of residence; by the late 1980s, that gap had risen to about 20 percent (Bound and Freeman, 1992). Controlling for differences in other measures of skills, however, such as test scores, will account for at least some of the remaining racial difference (a point addressed below).

Table 8.2 shows differences, by race, in rates of employment, labor-force participation, and unemployment. The data indicate that in 1970, compared to whites, blacks' labor-force participation rate was roughly 3 percentage points lower, and their unemployment rate was roughly 3 percentage points higher. But the labor-force activity of black men deteriorated substantially during the 1970s and 1980s relative to whites, while unemployment rose. Some of this deterioration in the relative employment of black men was occurring during the early 1970s, while their relative wages were still improving (Cogan, 1982). Although part of this can be attributed to increases in school enrollment rates among young black men, the trend can be found even among the nonenrolled. The deterioration continued into the late 1970s and 1980s, during which time relative wages were also deteriorating.

Of course, employment and unemployment rates for both whites and blacks follow a strong cyclical pattern, and both groups showed strong improvement in the late 1990s. Unemployment rates during 1998 averaged roughly 4 and 9 percent for white and black men, respectively, even though the absolute decline in unemployment among blacks during the 1990s was

Table 8.1. Adjusted Black-White Earnings Ratios Based on Years of Experience, 1971, 1981, 1988

	Years of Experience		
Year	*0–9*	*10–19*	*20+*
1971	0.88	0.78	0.79
1981	0.85	0.80	0.83
1988	0.82	0.84	0.84

NOTE: Adjusted for differences in education, veteran and marital status, region, urban residence, number of children, and hours worked.
SOURCE: Blau and Beller (1992). Reprinted by permission.

Table 8.2. Employment Ratios, Labor Force Participation Rates, and Unemployment Rates (percent), by Race

Year	Employment		Labor-Force Participation		Unemployment	
	Blacks	*Whites*	*Blacks*	*Whites*	*Blacks*	*Whites*
1970	71.9	77.8	77.6	81.0	7.3	4.0
1975	62.7	73.6	72.7	79.3	13.7	7.2
1980	62.5	74.0	72.1	78.8	13.3	6.1
1985	60.0	72.3	70.8	77.0	15.3	6.1
1990	61.8	72.3	70.1	76.9	11.8	4.8
1994	60.8	71.8	69.1	75.9	12.0	5.4

SOURCE: Bureau of Labor Statistics data from *Employment and Earnings*, January 1971 through January 1998.

greater. The black/white unemployment ratio, however, remained roughly constant during this period. Recent gains are important, but how long will they last? Even while they last, they do not fully reverse the strong secular trend toward lower relative employment activity among black men.

Overall unemployment rates in 1994 were more than twice as high among black men as among white men. (See original article for table summary.) Unemployment rates were dramatically higher among teenagers than among prime-age (25 to 64 years old) males for each racial group; but the numbers for blacks were particularly striking, as almost 40 percent of black teenagers in the labor force were unemployed. In fact, labor-force activity was, in 1994, declining among all racial groups for young men with low levels of education—i.e., high school diplomas only and especially high school dropouts—apparently in response to the decline in real wages they had experienced in the 1970s and 1980s (Juhn, 1992). But, again, the decline among less-educated young black men was most dramatic.

EXPLAINING THE BLACK-WHITE TRENDS

How do we account for the improvements in relative earnings of black men from, roughly, 1940 to 1975, especially during 1940 to 1950 and 1960 to 1975? And what accounts for the deterioration in relative earnings and employment more recently?

Improvements in the relative earnings of blacks during the pre–Civil Rights period seem to be explained primarily by their immigration from the rural South to the industrial North and Midwest, and by improvements in the quantity and quality of education attained, particularly in the South (Smith and

Welch, 1989; Margo, 1990; Card and Krueger, 1992). Improvements in education, in turn, seem at least partly to reflect political and legal developments, including the Supreme Court decision in *Brown v. Board of Education of Topeka* in 1954 (Boozer, Krueger, and Wolkon, 1992; Donohue, Heckman, and Todd,1998). Improvements during the 1940s seem to reflect advances made by black men during World War II, as they moved into more skilled positions vacated by white men who went away to war.

The dramatic progress made by black men during the 1960s and early 1970s also seems to reflect rapid improvements in their quantity and quality of education and occupational status, as well as in relative earnings within education and occupation groups. Much of this improvement can be tied to social and economic changes induced by the Civil Rights Acts of 1964 and 1972 (Freeman, 1981; Heckman and Payner, 1989; Chay, 1995). Declines in discriminatory behavior seem to be particularly apparent in the South, where discrimination against blacks had historically been greatest, as black men began to be increasingly employed in professional/managerial occupations. Other administrative actions and court decisions, such as the implementation of affirmative action requirements for government contractors and the "disparate impact" cases brought in the aftermath of *Griggs v. Duke Power* in 1971, likely contributed as well (Brown, 1982; Leonard, 1990).[1]

Given the strong improvements that occurred during 1960 to 1975, what accounts for the stagnation and even deterioration in relative earnings, and employment, since then? A number of developments seem to be responsible for these reversals, on both the demand and the supply sides of the labor market, reflecting both employers/jobs and black workers. Some of these developments, such as rising employer demand for skills and declining industrialization/unionism, seem to account for the deterioration in employment rates and earnings observed among young blacks. Other factors, such as labor-market discrimination and social/spatial factors, have not necessarily worsened over time, but no doubt contribute to the persistence of racial gaps in employment and earnings noted above.

Rising Employer Demand for Skills

During the past two decades, earnings inequality has risen quite dramatically in the labor market. Earnings gaps have risen between educational groups and between those with different levels of cognitive ability, after controlling for education (Levy and Murnane, 1992; Murnane, Wilted, and Levy, 1995). Although the educational attainment and test scores of blacks improved somewhat over the past two decades (e.g., Mare, 1995; Hauser and Huang, 1996), large gaps remain relative to whites. The high school graduation rates of blacks continued to improve significantly during the 1980s, though their tendency to graduate from college improved much more slowly. Improvements in test scores among students continued until roughly the mid-1980s and have leveled off or mildly deteriorated since then.

Thus, as blacks remained more concentrated among the less-educated and less-skilled groups, they were likely disproportionately hurt when the relative earnings of men in the less-educated, less-skilled groups declined (Juhn, Murphy, and Pierce, 1993).[2] Furthermore, differences in educational attainment and test scores together may account for most of the racial difference in wages, though less so for differences in employment rates. Ferguson (1993) and Neal and Johnson (1996) provide evidence of lower test scores based on the National Longitudinal Survey of Youth (NLSY). Rodgers and Spriggs (1996) note, however, that racial differences remain in the market returns to these scores and also in their determinants. Significant racial differences in wages remain in other datasets besides the NLSY, even after controlling for education and test scores— e.g., in the High School and Beyond data (Murnane, Wilted, and Levy, 1995).

Employers continue to be reluctant to hire blacks for jobs that require significant cognitive skills and credentials, such as specific experience or previous training, even those jobs for which formal educational requirements are not high (Holzer, 1996).

Declining Industrialization and Unionism

Rising demand for skills can account for some of the increase in inequality during the past two decades, but some part of that increase also seems to reflect factors such as declining employment in manufacturing and declining levels of union membership (Levy and Murnane, 1992). Although black males were no more heavily concentrated in manufacturing jobs nationwide than were white males in the 1960s, they were more heavily concentrated in manufacturing jobs in the urban Midwest. Declines in manufacturing and union membership help account for the particularly strong declines in blacks' relative employment and earnings in the Midwest since 1970 (Bound and Freeman, 1992; Bound and Holzer, 1993, 1996). Black men have traditionally been more likely to be members of unions than white men, and enjoyed particularly large wage gains from such membership (Freeman and Medoff, 1984). The declining presence of unionism in the economy has, no doubt, hurt blacks disproportionately.

Persistent Discrimination

Although labor-market discrimination against blacks has clearly declined over time, there is evidence that it persists. The clearest evidence comes from audit studies, in which matched pairs of black and white job-seekers with comparable credentials, in terms of education and experience, apply for various advertised job openings. These studies found that blacks are less likely to receive job offers, on average, than whites (Fix and Struyk, 1994; Bendick, Jackson, and Reinoso, 1994). When comparing the likelihood of white and black applicants to be employed, clear differences can be found across various kinds of firms: black applicants are much less likely to be hired by small establishments than by large ones and are less likely to be hired for jobs that involve significant contact with white customers (Holzer, 1998; Holzer and Ihlanfeldt, 1998). The greater degree of informality and subjectivity in the hiring procedures of smaller establishments likely contributes to their more discriminatory behavior (Braddock and McPartland, 1987; Holzer, 1987). Discrimination might also be greater in establishments located in the suburbs than those located in central cities.

The greater tendencies of some of these establishments to discriminate seem to be, at least partly, related to the lower level of monitoring of smaller and/or suburban establishments by Civil Rights enforcement agencies. For instance, only firms with 100 or more employees are required to file Equal Employment Opportunity (EEO)-1 forms with the federal government, unless they have federal contracts. Suburban firms are also less likely to be monitored, and are therefore less likely to be found in violation of antidiscrimination statutes, as they receive fewer black applicants and have fewer blacks in their relevant local labor markets (Bloch, 1994).

Discrimination against blacks seems more clearly pronounced at the hiring stage, perhaps because of how EEO laws are implemented. Donohue and Siegelman (1991) show that most EEO cases involve allegations of discrimination in promotions or discharges, rather than hiring. Thus, some employers might feel they'd face a greater likelihood of being sued if they do hire young blacks than if they don't (Bloch, 1994).

The tendency of employers to discriminate in hiring seems to more clearly impact blacks than Hispanics, and black males than black females (Holzer, 1998). Kirschenman (1991) provides evidence that employers have a greater fear of black men than black women. The greater tendency to discriminate against blacks seems consistent with ethnographic evidence showing that employers prefer other ethnic groups, especially immigrants, to U.S.-born blacks, believing that other ethnic groups have a better "work ethic" (Kirschenman and Neckerman, 1991). Although the audit studies suggest that some hiring discrimination against Hispanics remains (Kenney and Wissoker, 1994), Hispanics might be able to avoid the adverse effects of this discrimination by applying for jobs primarily in sectors where it is known that employers do not discriminate against Hispanics and where they have strong networks (Holzer and Reaser, forthcoming [2000]; Waldinger, 1996).

If discrimination against black men is heavily related to employer (and perhaps customer) fear of crime or violence, it is likely more serious against less-educated than more-educated blacks. In fact, relative wage gaps are higher among less-educated blacks (Council of Economic Advisers, 1998). It is possible that such discrimination has grown more serious over the past few decades as crime rates, and their correlation with education levels, have increased in regard to black men (Freeman, 1992). The growing value that employers seem to put on "soft skills," such as social and verbal skills, might also contribute to a growing reluctance to hire less-educated black men for jobs where such skills are important (Moss and Tilly, 1995).

Social/Spatial Factors

Although residential segregation between whites and blacks has declined modestly over the past few decades, it remains high (Massey and Denton, 1992; Farley and Frey, 1993). Furthermore, economic segregation seems to be rising, especially the tendency of low-income blacks to live in predominantly black and poor neighborhoods (Jargowsky, 1997).

These facts are likely to have a number of implications for the labor market performance of blacks, especially those with lower incomes. For one thing, residential segregation seems to be associated with lower educational attainment and lower employment outcomes (Cutler and Glaeser, 1997). Economic segregation of blacks also seems to contribute to these problems (O'Regan and Quigley, 1996). Although the exact mechanisms through which these effects occur are somewhat obscure, data suggest that "social isolation" contributes to a lower quality of education and a variety of problematic behaviors among blacks.[3] The social isolation of low-income blacks might also limit their access to employment and/or higher wages because it denies them access to effective employment networks (Braddock and McPartland, 1987; Holzer, 1987).

Another mechanism through which residential segregation appears to limit labor-market opportunities for blacks is "spatial mismatch," in which inner-city blacks have difficulty gaining access to jobs located in relatively distant suburbs. Although this notion has been controversial for decades, recent evidence seems largely to bear it out (e.g., Holzer, 1991; Kain, 1992). Blacks are generally located further away from areas of strong employment growth and high job vacancy rates than are whites, and this distance seems to be associated with lower employment rates for them (Hughes and Sternberg, 1992; Raphael, 1998; Ihlanfeldt, 1998). Black employees at central-city firms are also more likely to quit their jobs when such firms relocate to suburban areas (Zax and Kain, 1996; Fernandez, 1994). Among the factors that seem to contribute to "spatial mismatch" are the lack of automobile ownership among lower-income blacks, and the distance of many suburban firms from public transportation (Holzer, Ihlanfeldt, and Sjoquist, 1994; Holzer and Ihlanfeldt, 1996). Limited information about firms and job openings in these areas seems to play some role as well (Ihlanfeldt, 1997; Raphael, Stool, and Holzer, 1998).

Expectations, Alternative Income, and Illegal Activity

Declining employment rates among young black men in the 1960s and 1970s, even while their relative wages were improving, suggest that shifts in labor supply away from the low-wage labor market might have contributed to their declining employment in this and later periods. One possible reason might be that wage expectations among young blacks appear to have risen more rapidly than did the wage offers they received; and "menial" work that was once regarded as acceptable came to be regarded as unacceptable (Anderson, 1980). These notions receive some support from an analysis of self-reported "reservation wages" (or the lowest wages considered acceptable) among young people. Although absolute levels of reservation wages reported by young blacks are generally lower than those reported by young whites, they appear to be higher relative to wages actually offered in the market (Holzer, 1986; Petterson, 1996); and this likely contributes somewhat to their longer durations of nonemployment.[4]

The issue of high-wage expectations and unwillingness to accept low-wage employment appears to be one explanation for the high rate of participation of young black men in illegal activities. These rates are particularly pronounced among black male high school dropouts (Freeman, 1992), whose earnings have declined dramatically in recent years. Indeed, perceptions that one can do better on the "street" than in a regular job gained popularity during the 1980s, regardless of the overall state of the labor market (Freeman, 1991); and participation in crime seems to be related to this perception of relative returns in the legal and illegal sectors, even after adjusting for risks of incarceration or violence (Viscusi, 1986). Survey evidence suggests that many young men involved in illegal activities would demand hourly wages of $8 to $10 before they would consider returning to legal work (Freeman, 1992).

WHAT DOES THE FUTURE HOLD?

Given these past trends in black-white employment outcomes among men, and their causes, what do we expect these trends to look like in the future? There are at least some reasons to be hopeful. For one thing, there continue to be signs of long-term progress in college-enrollment rates and educational attainment in the black community (Council of Economic Advisers, 1998). Residential segregation, at least for those in the middle class, seems to be slowly but steadily declining, especially in metropolitan areas of the South and West with more racially diverse populations (Farley and Frey, 1993). The impressive drop in urban crime rates of the past few years suggests that fewer young black men are leaving the labor force for this kind of activity, and might even lead to further declines in segregation and employment discrimination against these young men, as middle-class whites, and blacks, become less fearful of them.

Finally, if the current level of labor-market tightness can be sustained for some period of time, it might have longer-term effects on labor-market outcomes for black men, as occurred, for example, during World War II. Discriminatory behavior seems to decline in tight labor markets, as employers are willing to hire workers whom they otherwise would not consider. If their experiences with these groups, and with newer modes of recruiting and screening, are more positive than they expected, their hiring behavior over the longer term might be affected. Also, some young men might gain early labor-market experience during this time that will have positive effects on their future employability and wages.

On the other hand, there are reasons for pessimism as well. The rising costs of postsecondary education make it relatively more difficult for enrollment rates among blacks to continue to grow (Kane, 1994). Declining political and legal support for affirmative action, especially in university admissions policies, could threaten these enrollment rates as well. Furthermore, children in poor black families are growing up in more economically segregated neighborhoods, with greater threats from crime and drugs, and less income support from the welfare system, than did those of earlier generations. If family poverty and "neighborhood effects"/social isolation have important causal effects on the educational and employment outcomes of children, this does not bode well for their future. The long-term labor-market prospects of the roughly 1 million black men who have been incarcerated for illegal activity also look particularly grim.

IMPLICATIONS FOR POLICY

One important implication of the above discussion for policy is the need to maintain, for as long as possible, the labor-market tightness of the past few years. Whether current low rates of inflation can be sustained with unemployment rates lower than 5 percent is unknown, but the important benefits that accrue to disadvantaged groups such as black men from tight markets must not be lost in the evaluation of these tradeoffs.

Education and Skill Development

Over the long term, enhancing the skills and employment credentials that young black men bring to the labor market must be a top priority. Of course, there is no single policy intervention that will accomplish this, particularly for those who live in low-income neighborhoods with poor quality schools. There are, nevertheless, policy options that need to be considered.

Early Childhood Development Programs

The work of Currie and Thomas (1996) suggests that Head Start has had positive long-term effects on cognitive outcomes for poor whites and Hispanics but generally not for blacks. Their reasoning is that Head Start is not sufficient to overcome negative family and neighborhood influences that limit the performance of poor blacks; however, other, more intensive, early-childhood development programs have been more successful for young blacks—e.g., the Perry Preschool Program and the Child-Parent Centers of Chicago (Reynolds and Temple, 1998). Currie and Thomas (1996) suggest that these programs might merit strengthening and expansion.

School Reforms and Choice

Improving the performance of schools located in the inner city is a high priority, though how to achieve this is not always clear. A number of reform models exist that have shown some promise in various evaluation programs—e.g., Robert Slavin's "Success for All," or James Comer's School Development Program (Barnett, 1996). Using financial incentives to reward schools and teachers who achieve more progress is another approach (Clotfelter and Ladd, 1996). School-choice programs, if implemented in ways that provide inner-city children with real access to good schools, might improve the quality of the education the "movers" receive and also put competitive pressure on the schools they leave behind to become more effective.[5] Finally, some recent evidence suggests that black inner-city students perform much better academically when they attend Catholic schools (Evans and Schwab, 1995; Neal, 1997). At a minimum, we need to understand better why these effects exist and the extent to which the reasons for them can be emulated in the public schools.

School-to-Work Programs

Establishing more effective links between employers and high schools might overcome early "mismatch" problems, and might improve student performance incentives. Through direct contact with employers, students might more clearly perceive the link between performance and later employment opportunities.

Support for Postsecondary Education

Expansion of Pell Grants and other financial support for postsecondary options is critical for maintaining and improving enrollment rates among blacks. Combining financial aid with counseling about opportunities (Kane, 1994) might be useful as well.

Second-Chance Training for Out-of-School Youth

Far too many second-chance training programs do not appear to have worked for youth, for example, the Job Training Partnership Act or the National Supported Work Demonstration. A few have, perhaps, been more successful, such as the Job Corps (Lalonde, 1995). Successful programs may require taking young people out of their homes and neighborhood environments, offering a wide range of services and intensive interventions, and providing these over a sustained period of time. The up-front costs of these interventions might be high. Structure and communication of expectations might be critical as well (American Youth Policy Forum, 1997).

Improving Access to Housing and Transportation

Given the evidence that racial and economic segregation generate a wide range of negative outcomes among young blacks, and that "spatial mismatch" also limits their employment opportunities, improving the access of blacks to residences and jobs in suburban areas seems critical. Greater residential mobility would likely generate positive outcomes along a wide range of dimensions. Rosenbaum and Popkin (1991) provide such evidence from the well-known Gautreaux experiment, in which central-city residents who moved to suburban areas enjoyed improvements in their employment and earnings relative to those who did not move. Preliminary, and somewhat more ambiguous, evidence from the more recent Moving-to-Opportunity demonstration project is discussed by Katz, Kling, and Leibman (1997). Greater residential mobility can be encouraged through greater enforcement of open housing laws, and pressure or incentives for suburban areas to limit zoning and other exclusionary practices (Haar, 1996).

Alternatively, greater job mobility could be provided for those who remain in poorer black neighborhoods (Hughes and Sternberg, 1992; Harrison and Weiss, 1997), through the efforts of "labor-market intermediaries" who provide job-placement assistance and transportation to suburban employment. The Center for Employment and Training (CET), originally located in San Jose, California, is perhaps the best-known program that relies on a combination of these interventions, along with training that is customized to meet the needs of local employers. Evaluations have indicated positive effects on the employment and earnings of minority participants (Melendez, 1996); however, CET primarily serves disadvantaged Hispanics and their community, and it remains unclear whether this model would work for other groups, such as black males.

Local economic development assistance, which has traditionally occurred through "enterprise zones," but which more recently can involve support for a broader range of institutions and services, is not inconsistent with this approach (Giloth, 1997). Although enterprise zones have not traditionally been a cost-effective mechanism for improving employment and earnings of disadvantaged zone residents (Papke, 1993), the more recent federally funded "empowerment zones" can potentially be used to fund a much wider array of services to disadvantaged workers who reside in a zone. However, no formal evaluations of the effects of these zones have been performed to date.

EEO Laws and Affirmative Action

Recent evidence suggests that affirmative action raises the employment of minorities and women in establishments that practice it, without generating major losses of economic efficiency or productivity (Leonard, 1984, 1990; Holzer and Neumark, 1998, 1999; Conrad, 1997). Nevertheless, affirmative action remains extremely unpopular with white voters, especially when it is perceived as generating "preferential treatment." There is evidence to support the notion that employment in the affirmative action sector is redistributed from white males to other groups whose educational credentials are lower than their own, even though their productivity is generally comparable. Evidence also suggests that employment of white males in firms that practice affirmative action is about 15 percent lower than it otherwise would be, but that most of this employment is redistributed to white females rather than minorities (Holzer and Neumark, 1999). The "displaced" white males presumably gain employment in the non-affirmative action sector, though perhaps at somewhat lower wages than they otherwise would earn. Holzer and Neumark (1999) also show that firms engaging in affirmative action recruit applicants much more broadly, screen them more intensely, and invest more heavily in training new employees. This, presumably, enables them to hire minorities whose credentials on paper might be weaker but whose actual job performance compares favorably with that of white males.

A clearer public discussion of the benefits as well as costs of affirmative action is desirable, particularly while so many political and legal efforts are under way to dismantle it. Furthermore, some investigation is needed of how alternative university admission mechanisms affect educational and employment outcomes of minorities. One such mechanism is affirmative action based on family income rather than race/gender, which has been analyzed by Kane (1995). Another approach, used at the University of Texas, guarantees admission to all Texas high school students who rank within the top 10 percent of their high school class.

If political and legal restrictions to affirmative action continue to grow, these restrictions should be accompanied by a strong public embrace of EEO principles, and better enforcement of existing EEO laws. More specifically, EEO laws at the hiring stage need to be strengthened precisely in those areas where employment discrimination against blacks seems to be most serious—

i.e., at smaller and/or suburban establishments. This could be done either through more extensive use of the audit methodology, or by relying on real applicants whose access to smaller/suburban establishments is encouraged through the kinds of job mobility policies described above. Because most firms traditionally do not keep records of the race of their job applicants, the courts have generally inferred these numbers from the number of blacks who reside in the local area (Bloch, 1994). If mobility policies succeed in generating many more black applicants in areas where few currently live, there would be some need to document exactly where they apply for work and where they are—and are not—being hired.

Job Creation and Wage/Benefit Supports for Low-Wage Workers

Less-educated young black males face many barriers in the labor market, and some—especially those with poor skills, little work experience, and/or criminal records—may not be employable in the private sector, even under the best of conditions. Therefore, greater use of employer-wage subsidies or public-sector employment to improve job availability for this group is probably warranted (Gottschalk, 1998; Katz, 1998). Some promising models of public-sector employment for young men include the Youth Corps and Youth Build (American Youth Policy Forum, 1997). For young males, these programs combine skills acquisition with employment and the provision of service to communities. When used, public-sector employment should be thought of as "transitional" and providing credentials that might make participants more attractive to private-sector employers.

Ultimately, however, low-wage employment in either the private or public sector will not enable young males to support families or resist the appeals of the illegal job market. Therefore, approaches to improve their earnings and benefits need to be considered. Two methods to directly increase the wages of low-wage workers are to (1) increase the minimum wage or (2) expand the Earned Income Tax Credit, perhaps by making it more generous to adults without custody of children. There remains some controversy among economists about whether minimum-wage increases reduce employment, though relatively modest increases, such as those legislated to date, are likely to generate only small disemployment effects.

Reducing Crime/Helping Incarcerated Youth

As noted above, crime reduction could have quite positive implications for young black males in the labor market, if employers, both white and black, become less fearful of them and become willing to employ them. Of course, this assumes that crime reduction can be accomplished in fair and racially unbiased ways (Kennedy, 1997). But it also raises the potential number of incarcerated young black men, whose labor-market opportunities, once they leave prison, are severely constrained. Special training and job-creation efforts for them, perhaps undertaken with government financial support but administered by the kinds of effective labor-market intermediaries described above, would be an important complement to the kinds of "get tough" policies that have been implemented nationally.

IMPLICATIONS FOR RESEARCH

A number of issues remain unclear in the research literature about the differences in labor-market outcomes of men across racial groups. For many issues, there is a strong need for continued work.

What Are the Specific Mechanisms by Which Differential Labor Outcomes Occur?

Although there seems to be little doubt about the overall importance of factors such as skills, spatial location, and racial discrimination in the labor market for black men, the exact mechanisms by which these effects operate remain somewhat unclear. For instance, is "spatial mismatch" primarily a function of limited transportation, limited information, or some other factor such as perceived hostility among white suburbanites? Regarding skills, exactly which skills do employers find most deficient among young black men, and are the perceptions of these employers accurate? Do these deficiencies manifest themselves primarily through black men's performance during job interviews, in which case the deficient skills are more "soft" than "hard," through limited and/or unstable work experience, or through other means? And to what extent do their skill deficiencies limit their performance on the job when hired? As for discrimination against young black men, is it really driven by employer fear of poor work performance, poor attitudes, crime, lawsuits, or some other factor? Answers to these questions are critical for developing effective policy responses; yet our knowledge of these matters remains quite limited.

What Are the Effects of the Interplay between Personal, Familial, and Neighborhood Factors?

Related to the previous issue is an uncertainty about the extent to which the problems of blacks in low-income communities are the result of personal, familial, or neighborhood forces. For instance, to what extent are the weaker skills that young blacks bring to the labor market a result of underfunded schools, a poor social environment in the schools and neighborhood, or limited family educational resources? To what extent is participation in crime influenced by the same set of factors? Even when the right data are available, it is notoriously difficult to sort out neighborhood effects statistically from personal/family factors, given the problems of individual and family sorting (or self-selection) across neighborhoods (Ellen and Turner, 1997). Sorting out the exact causal patterns here is also difficult—e.g., does crime among young black men lead to residential segregation and discrimination—especially among white suburbanites—or vice versa? And to what extent are the labor-market problems the result of interactions between their skills, social networks, etc.? If that is the case, is addressing these factors separately bound to fail?

Identifying Cost-Effective Policy Responses

In this critical area, our knowledge is perhaps weakest of all. Given the many programs that have failed to generate sustained improvements for disadvantaged black youth, which ones are effective? When some programs or institutions do succeed for minority men, such as CET for Hispanics, or the Catholic schools for young blacks, do we know why they work, and can we replicate their success elsewhere? This requires effective evaluation studies, using random-assignment methodology as much as possible, as well as more qualitative analyses of the processes underlying the various interventions.

REFERENCES

American Youth Policy Forum. 1997. *Some Things Do Make a Difference for Youth.* Washington, DC: American Youth Policy Forum.

Anderson, E. 1980. "Some Observations on Black Youth Unemployment." In *Youth Employment and Public Policy*, B. Anderson and I. Sawhill, eds. Englewood Cliffs, NJ: Prentice Hall.

Barnett, S. 1996. "Economics of School Reform: Three Promising Models." Pp. 299–326 in *Holding Schools Accountable*, H. Ladd, ed. Washington, DC: The Brookings Institution.

Bendick, M., C. Jackson, and V. Reinoso. 1994. "Measuring Employment Discrimination through Controlled Experiments." *Review of Black Political Economy* 23 (Summer): 25–48.

Blau, F. D., and A. H. Beller. 1992. "Black-White Earnings over the 1970s and 1980s: Gender Differences In Trends." *Review of Economics and Statistics* 74(2): 276–86.

Bloch, F. 1994. *Antidiscrimination Law and Minority Employment*. Chicago: University of Chicago Press.

Boozer, M., A. Krueger, and S. Wolkon 1992. "Race and School Quality since *Brown v. Board of Education*." Brookings Papers on Economic Activity—Microeconomics. Washington, DC: Brookings Institution.

Borjas, G. 1992. "Ethnic Capital and Intergenerational Mobility." *Quarterly Journal of Economics* 107 (February): 123–50.

———. 1994. "The Economics of Immigration." *Journal of Economic Literature* 32 (December): 1667–717.

———. 1996. *Labor Economics.* New York: McGraw Hill.

Bound, J., and R. Freeman. 1992. "What Went Wrong? The Erosion of Relative Earnings and Employment among Young Black Men in the 1980s." *Quarterly Journal of Economics* 107 (February): 201–32.

Bound, J., and H. Holzer. 1993. "Industrial Shifts, Skill Levels and the Labor Market for Black and White Males." *Review of Economics and Statistics* 75 (November): 387–96.

———. 1996. "Demand Shifts, Population Adjustments and Labor Market Outcomes, 1980–1990." Working paper, National Bureau of Economic Research.

Braddock, J., and J. McPartland. 1987. "How Minorities Continue to Be Excluded from Equal Employment Opportunities: Research on Labor Market and Institutional Barriers." *Journal of Social Issues* 43:5–39.

Brown, C. 1982. "The Federal Attack on Labor Market Discrimination: The Mouse That Roared?" *Research in Labor Economics* 5:33–69.

Card, D., and A. Krueger. 1992. "School Quality and Black-White Relative Earnings: A Direct Assessment." *Quarterly Journal of Economics* 107 (February): 151–200.

Card, D., and T. Lemieux. 1994. "Changing Wage Structure and Black-White Wage Differentials." *American Economic Review* 84 (May): 29–32.

Carlson, L., and C. Swartz. 1988. "The Earnings of Women and Ethnic Minorities, 1959–1979." *Industrial and Labor Relations Review* 41(4): 530–46.

Case, A., and L. Katz. 1991. "The Company You Keep: The Effects of Family and Neighborhood on Disadvantaged Youth." Working paper, National Bureau of Economic Research.

Chay, K. 1995. "Evaluating the Impact of the 1964 Civil Rights Act on the Economic Status of Black Men Using Censored Longitudinal Earnings Data." Unpublished, Princeton University.

Chay, K., and D. Lee. 1997. "Changes in Relative Wages in the 1980s: Returns to Observed and Unobserved Skills and Black-White Wage Differentials." Unpublished, University of California at Berkeley.

Chiswick, B. 1986. "Is the New Immigrant Less Skilled than the Old?" *Journal of Labor Economics* (April).

Clotfelter, C., and H. Ladd. 1996. "Recognizing and Rewarding Success in Public Schools." In *Holding Schools Accountable*, H. Ladd, ed. Washington, DC: Brookings Institution.

Cogan, J. 1982 "The Decline in Black Teenage Employment." *American Economic Review* (September).

Conrad, C. 1997. "The Economic Costs of Affirmative Action." In *Economic Perspectives on Affirmative Action*, M. Simms, ed. Washington, DC: Joint Center for Political and Economic Studies.

Council of Economic Advisers. 1998. *Changing America: Indicators of Social and Economic Well-Being by Race and Hispanic Origin.* Washington, DC: U.S. Government Printing Office.

Currie, J., and D. Thomas. 1996. "Does Subsequent School Quality Affect the Long-Term Gains from Head Start?" Working paper, National Bureau of Economic Research.

Cutler, D., and E. Glaeser. 1997. "Are Ghettoes Good or Bad?" *Quarterly Journal of Economics* 112 (August): 827–87.

Donohue, J., J. Heckman, and P. Todd. 1998. "Social Action, Private Choice, and Philanthropy: Understanding the Sources of Improvements in the Black Schooling in Georgia." Working paper, National Bureau of Economic Research.

Donohue, J., and P. Siegelman. 1991. "The Changing Nature of Employment Discrimination Litigation." *Stanford Law Review* (May).

Ehrenberg, R., and R. Smith. 1997. *Modern Labor Economics*. Reading, MA: Addison Wesley.

Ellen, I., and M. Turner. 1997. "Does Neighborhood Matter? Assessing Recent Evidence." *Housing Policy Debate* 8(4).

Evans, W., and R. Schwab. 1995. "Finishing High School and Starting College: Do Catholic Schools Make a Difference?" *Quarterly Journal of Economics* (November).

Farley, R., and W. Frey. 1993. "Latino, Asian and Black Segregation in Multi-Ethnic Metro Areas: Findings from the 1990 Census." Working paper, Population Studies Center, University of Michigan.

Ferguson, R. 1993. "New Evidence on the Growing Value of Cognitive Skills and Consequences for Racial Disparity and Returns to Schooling." Mimeograph, Kennedy School of Government, Harvard University.

Fernandez, R. 1994. "Race, Space, and Job Accessibility: Evidence from a Plant Relocation." *Economic Geography* 70 (October): 390–416.

Filer, R., D. Hamermesh, and A. Rees. 1996. *The Economics of Work and Pay*. New York: Harper Collins.

Fix, M., and R. Struyk. 1994. *Clear and Convincing Evidence*. Washington, DC: Urban Institute Press.

Freeman, R. 1981. "Black Economic Progress since 1964: Who Has Gained and Why?" In *Studies in Labor Markets*, S. Rosen, ed. Chicago: University of Chicago Press.

———. 1991. "The Employment and Earnings of Disadvantaged Young Workers in a Labor Shortage Economy." Pp. 103–121 in *The Urban Underclass*, C. Jencks and P. Peterson, eds. Washington, DC: Brookings Institution.

———. 1992. "Crime and the Employment of Disadvantaged Youth." Pp. 201–233 in *Urban Labor Markets and Job Opportunities*, G. Peterson and W. Vroman, eds. Washington, DC: Urban Institute.

Freeman, R., and J. Medoff. 1984. *What Do Unions Do?* New York: Basic Books.

Giloth, R. 1997. *Jobs and Economic Development*. New York: Sage Publications.

Gottschalk, P. 1998. "The Impact of Changes in Public Employment on Low-Wage Labor Markets." In *Generating Jobs*, R. Freeman and P. Gottschalk, eds. New York: Russell Sage Foundation.

Haar, C. 1996. *Suburbs under Siege: Race, Space and Audacious Judges*. Princeton, NJ: Princeton University Press.

Harrison, B., and M. Weiss. 1997. *Workforce Development Networks*. New York: Sage Publications.

Hauser, R., and M. Huang. 1996. "Trends in Black-White Test Score Differentials." Discussion paper, Institute for Research on Poverty.

Heckman, J., and B. Payner. 1989. "Determining the Impact of Federal Antidiscrimination Policy on the Economic Status of Blacks." *American Economic Review* 79 (March): 138–77.

Holzer, H. 1986. "Reservation Wages and Their Labor Market Effects for White and Black Male Youth." *Journal of Human Resources* 21 (Spring): 157–77.

———. 1987. "Informal Job Search and Black Youth Unemployment." *American Economic Review* 77 (June): 446–52.

———. 1991. "The Spatial Mismatch Hypothesis: What Has the Evidence Shown?" *Urban Studies* 28 (February): 105–22.

———. 1996. *What Employers Want: Job Prospects for Less-Educated Workers.* New York: Russell Sage Foundation.

———. 1998. "Why Do Small Firms Hire Fewer Blacks Than Larger Ones?" *Journal of Human Resources* 33(4): 896–914.

Holzer, H., and K. Ihlanfeldt. 1996. "Spatial Factors and the Employment of Blacks at the Firm Level." *New England Economic Review* (May/June):65–82.

———. 1998. "Customer Discrimination and Employment Outcomes for Minority Workers." *Quarterly Journal of Economics* 113:835–67.

Holzer, H., K. Ihlanfeldt, and D. Sjoquist. 1994. "Work, Search and Travel for White and Minority Youth." *Journal of Urban Economics* 35 (May): 320–45.

Holzer, H., and D. Neumark. 1998. "What Does Affirmative Action Do?" National Bureau of Economic Research working paper.

———. 1999. "Are Affirmative Action Hires Less Qualified?" *Journal of Labor Economics* 167 (July):534–69.

Holzer, H., and J. Reaser. 2000. "Black Applicants, Black Employees, and Urban Labor Market Policy." *Journal of Urban Economics* 48(3): 365–87.

Hoxby, C. 1996. "The Effects of Private School Vouchers on Schools and Students." In *Holding Schools Accountable,* H. Ladd, ed. Washington, DC: Brookings Institution.

Hughes, M., and J. Sternberg. 1992. *The New Metropolitan Reality: Where the Rubber Meets the Road in Antipoverty Policy.* Washington, DC: Urban Institute.

Ihlanfeldt, K. 1997. "Information on the Spatial Distribution of Job Opportunities." *Journal of Urban Economics* 41:218–42.

———. 1998. "Is the Labor Market Tighter Outside of the Ghetto?" Unpublished manuscript, Georgia State University.

Jargowsky, P. 1997. *Poverty and Place.* New York: Russell Sage Foundation.

Juhn, C. 1992. "Declines in Male Labor Force Participation: The Role of Declining Opportunities." *Quarterly Journal of Economics* 107 (February): 79–122.

Juhn, C., K. Murphy, and B. Pierce. 1993. "Wage Inequality and the Rise in Returns to Skills." *Journal of Political Economy* 101 (June): 410–42.

Kain, J. 1992. "The Spatial Mismatch Hypothesis Three Decades Later. *Housing Policy Debate* 3(2): 371–460.

Kane, T. 1994. "College Entry by Blacks since 1970: The Role of College Costs, Family Background and the Returns to Education." *Journal of Political Economy* 102 (October): 878–911.

———. 1995. "Racial Preferences in College Admissions." Unpublished, Harvard University.

————. 1996. "Comments on Chapters 5 and 6." In *Holding Schools Accountable,* H. Ladd, ed. Washington, DC: Brookings Institution.

Katz, L. 1998. "Wage Subsidies for Disadvantaged Workers." In *Generating Jobs,* R. Freeman and P. Gottschalk, eds. New York: Russell Sage Foundation.

Katz, L., J. Kling, and J. Leibman. 1997. "Moving to Opportunity in Boston: Early Impacts of a Housing Mobility Study." Unpublished paper, Harvard University.

Kennedy, R. 1997, *Race, Crime and the Law*. New York: Pantheon.

Kenney, G., and D. Wissoker. 1994. "An Analysis of the Correlates of Discrimination Facing Young Hispanic Job Seekers." *American Economic Review* 84 (June): 674–683.

Kirschenman, J. 1991. "Gender within Race." Unpublished manuscript, University of Chicago.

Kirschenman, J., and K. Neckerman. 1991. "We'd Love to Hire Them but. . . ." Pp. 203–34 in *Urban Underclass,* C. Jencks and P. Peterson, eds. Washington, DC: Brookings Institution.

Lalonde, R. 1995. "The Promise of Public Sector-sponsored Training." *Journal of Economic Perspectives* 9(2): 149–68.

Leonard, J. 1984. "Antidiscrimination or Reverse Discrimination: The Impact of Changing Demographics, Title VII and Affirmative Action on Productivity." *Journal of Human Resources* 19 (Spring): 145–74.

————. 1990. "The Impact of Affirmative Action and Equal Employment Opportunity Law on Black Employment." *Journal of Economic Perspectives* 4 (Fall): 47–63.

Levy, F., and R. Murnane. 1992. "U.S. Earnings Levels and Earnings Inequality: A Review of Recent Trends and Proposed Explanations." *Journal of Economic Literature* 30 (December):1332–81.

Mare, R. 1995. "Changes in Educational Attainment and School Enrollment." In *State of the Union,* R. Farley, ed. New York: Russell Sage Foundation.

Margo, R. 1990. *Race and Schooling in the South: 1880–1950*. Chicago: University of Chicago Press.

Massey, D., and N. Denton. 1992. *American Apartheid*. Cambridge, MA: Harvard University Press.

Melendez, E. 1996. *Working On Jobs: The Center for Employment and Training*. Boston: Mauricio Gastonia Institute.

Moss, P., and C. Tilly. 1995. "Soft Skills and Race. Working paper, Russell Sage Foundation.

Murnane, R., J. Wilted, and F. Levy. 1995. "The Growing Importance of Cognitive Skills in Wage Determination." *Review of Economics and Statistics* 77 (May): 251–66.

Neal, D. 1997. "The Effects of Catholic Secondary Schooling on Educational Attainment." *Journal of Labor Economics* 15 (January): 98–123.

Neal, D., and W. Johnson 1996. "Black-White Differences in Wages: The Role of Premarket Factors." *Journal of Political Economy* 104 (October): 869–95.

O'Regan, K., and J. Quigley. 1996. "Spatial Effects upon Employment Outcomes: The Case of New Jersey Teenagers." *New England Economic Review* (May/June):41–57.

Papke, L. 1993. "What do we know about enterprise zones?" Working paper, National Bureau of Economic Research.

Petterson, S. 1996. "Are Young Black Men Really Less Willing to Work?" *American Journal of Sociology.*

Raphael, S. 1998. "The Spatial Mismatch Hypothesis of Black Youth Unemployment: Evidence from the San Francisco Bay Area." *Journal of Urban Economics* 43 (Spring): 79–111.

Raphael, S., M. Stool, and H. Holzer. 1998. "Are sUburban Firms More Likely to Discriminate against African-Americans?" Discussion paper, Institute for Research on Poverty.

Reimers, C. 1983. "Labor Market Discrimination against Hispanic and Black Men." *Review of Economics and Statistics* 65:570–79.

Reynolds, A., and J. Temple. 1998. "Extended Early Childhood Development and School Achievement: Age Thirteen Findings from the Chicago Longitudinal Study." Discussion paper, Institute for Research on Poverty.

Rodgers, W., and W. Spriggs. 1996. "What Does the AFQT Really Measure? Race, Wages, Schooling and the AFQT Score." *Review of Black Political Economy* 24 (Spring): 13–46.

Rosenbaum, J., and S. Popkin. 1991. "Employment and Earnings of Low-income Blacks Who Move to the Suburbs." Pp. 342–56. In *Urban Underclass,* C. Jencks and P. Peterson, eds. Washington, DC: Brookings Institution.

Rouse, C. 1997. "Private School Vouchers and Student Achievement: An Evaluation of the Milwaukee Parental Choice Program." Working paper, National Bureau of Economic Research.

Smith, J., and F. Welch. 1989. "Black Economic Progress since Myrdal." *Journal of Economic Literature* 27 (June): 519–64.

Trejo, S. 1997. "Relative Earnings of Mexican-Americans." *Journal of Political Economy* 105(December): 1235–68.

Viscusi, W. 1986. "Market Incentives for Criminal Behavior." In *The Black Youth Employment Crisis,* R. Freeman and H. Holzer, eds. Chicago: University of Chicago Press.

Waldinger, R. 1996. *Still the Promised City? African-Americans and Immigrants in Post-Industrial New York.* Cambridge, MA: Harvard University Press.

Zax, J., and J. Kain. 1996. "Relocating to the Suburbs: Do Firms Leave Their Black Employees Behind?" *Journal of Labor Economics* 14 (July): 472–504.

9

Reversal of Fortune

Explaining the Decline in Black Women's Earnings

Yvonne D. Newsome and F. Nii-Amoo DoDoo

The 1980s brought reversals in the gains that African American women had seen in their earnings over the prior decades. This development is puzzling, because there is a positive link between human capital and wages and, over the period, black women continued to make marked gains in their human capital (Blau and Beller 1992; Bound and Dresser 1999; Cotton 1989). Although recent studies have tried to explain this anomalous concurrence (Bound and Dresser 1999; Corcoran 1999; Fosu 1995), they have generally come up short. We believe this is largely because they emphasize human capital and deindustrialization approaches that originate in research focused on whites and males and which fail to capture some factors (e.g., family structure and public sector concentration) that may be pertinent to explaining black women's earnings.

There is evidence that African American women's labor market experiences differ significantly from those of other race-gender groups (Bernhardt, Morris, and Handcock 1995; King 1988; Simms and Malveaux 1986). Indeed, the decline in black women's earnings in the face of human capital gains is further evidence of a need to focus analyses on African American women (Corcoran 1999) and highlights the importance of developing theories that centrally consider structural factors specifically pertaining to black women's lives.

In this paper, we ask what accounts for the 1980s declines in black women's earnings given that their human capital improved over this period. We examine family-related characteristics and structural factors that are typically missing from studies on black women's earnings (i.e., the effects of marriage, parenting, and public sector employment) in addition to variables obtained

This chapter was originally published in *Gender & Society* 16(4): 465–84, 2002.

from human capital, restructuring, underclass, and occupational segregation approaches.

WHY STUDY THE 1980S AND 1990S?

The 1980s are interesting because of the conflicting influences on African American women's circumstances. Between 1980 and 1990, the high school completion rate among black women aged 25 to 64 rose from 51.3 percent to 66.5 percent and the proportion with four or more years of college increased from 8.1 percent to 10.8 percent (U.S. Census Bureau 2000). According to human capital theory, black women's higher educational attainment should have been associated with earnings gains. Yet, the 1980s recessions and other societal changes seemed to have worsened black women's economic circumstances. The 1980s also brought major transformations in all American family structures, many of which are theorized to relate to the recessions, shrinking manufacturing jobs, falling male wages, and corporate "down-sizing." Underclass theorists link these transitions to declining marriage rates and steep rises in divorce rates, female headship, and out-of-wedlock childbearing, especially among blacks (Kasarda 1989; Wilson 1987). These trends developed among all racial groups, but the rates were highest among blacks partly because the recession and other aspects of the changing economy and society most adversely affected them. By the mid-1980s, black families maintained by single mothers were nearly as common as those maintained by two parents (U.S. Department of Labor 1997).

Moreover, the 1980s brought two policy changes that may have negatively affected African American women's earnings. First, the Reagan and Bush administrations reduced Federal subsidies for the social programs that provided a safety net to the low income and unemployed. Second, these administrations eliminated many grant-funded public jobs, including those mainly held by middle-class blacks to administer social services to low-income African Americans and others (Collins 1997). Paradoxically, therefore, both the demand for black women's labor and their access to public jobs may have declined during a time of great progress in their human capital.

It is possible, however, that affirmative action worked to improve African American women's earnings during the 1980s despite the reductions in certain public jobs. From one standpoint, increasing conservatism may have yielded a situation in which hiring black women allowed employers to meet affirmative action goals on both gender and race fronts. Widely implemented, such practices could have counteracted some of the hardships imposed by the recessions and changing economy. Alternatively, being both female and black may have doubly disadvantaged black women during a time when employers experienced less government pressure to hire from amongst these groups (Collins 1997; Xu and Leffler 1992). In the context of the conservative labor policies of the time, the paradox of black women's declining earnings in the face of improved human capital necessitates explanations that are more complex than they heretofore have been.

PREVIOUS RESEARCH ON EMPLOYMENT EARNINGS

There is a small but growing literature on how and why black women's earnings have changed over time. Few studies, however, have African American women as their sole focus. Instead, they typically aim to explain black women's earnings relative to those of men and women of various racial groups (Bernhardt, Morris, and Handcock 1995; Blau and Beller 1992; Bound and Dresser 1999; Browne 1999; Cunningham and Zalokar 1992; Fosu 1992, 1995; Glass, Tienda, and Smith, 1988; Gwartney-Gibbs and Taylor 1986; Kilbourne, England, and Heron, 1994; King 1993, 1995). These studies tend to investigate those factors that have been theorized or found to explain earnings gaps between groups. Cross-group comparisons have produced valuable findings, some of which guide our investigation. Yet, focusing only on the cross-group literature might preclude consideration of causal factors more specific to black women's experiences. It is not yet clear, for instance, how changes in occupational and industrial distributions, geographic location, family structure, and the availability of public-sector jobs have uniquely, or in combination, affected African American women's earnings. Furthermore, the existing evidence suggests that the earnings reversals of the 1980s are not readily explained by the individual-level changes in black women's characteristics suggested by human capital models (Blau and Beller 1992; Bound and Dresser 1999; Cotton 1989).

What we know about African American women's earnings comes primarily from studies that try to explain race and gender gaps in pay. These generally analyze structural and/or individual-level variables to explain the earnings differentials between groups. Although we limit our analysis to black women, the literature that exclusively speaks to their economic circumstances is small enough that we must expand our review to incorporate cross-sectional and trend studies on black women's earnings, on gender and earnings, and on race and earnings. We review literature that contributes useful concepts and measures for pursuing our research question and discuss the theoretical basis for those constructs included in our research. The study draws on theories of employment and earnings framed around human capital, industrial restructuring and the underclass, occupational segregation, affirmative action, and family structure.

Human Capital

Much of the research on earnings is guided by human capital theory. The theory assumes that labor markets are race and gender neutral and that earnings are based on individual endowments or investments in productivity characteristics, including schooling and work experience. In addition, human capital theorists believe that women's productivity, and therefore their wages, are compromised by childbirth and other "female" traits associated with primary child care responsibilities, low job attachment, and "preferences" for fewer working hours (Budig and England 2001). Past studies have shown that, regardless of race or gender, years of schooling, college completion, and work experience predict earnings. We therefore include each of these variables to test if they predict black women's earnings although previous studies suggest that these may not predict black women's 1980s earnings decline (Bound and Dresser 1999).

Critics of human capital theory contend that structural processes influence the remuneration for and acquisition of human capital. These critics assert that black women suffer earnings penalties based on the devaluation of their labor, the organization of work, and racial and gender discrimination in hiring, pay, and promotions. Next, we consider several structural perspectives.

Industrial Restructuring and the Underclass

Another literature that is pertinent to the study of black women's earnings centers on the labor market consequences of industrial restructuring. Most of this literature, however, focuses on African American men rather than women (Browne 1999). This literature contends that the decline of manufacturing, growth of the lower-paying service sector, and movement of manufacturing jobs out of the Rustbelt and central cities cause industrial and occupational shifts that may affect workers' employment and earnings.

Wilson (1980) argues that blacks moved North in the early 1900s to seek new employment opportunities in the burgeoning manufacturing sector. Likewise, affirmative action, particularly in the public sector, facilitated black progress from the 1960s to 1980s. Moreover, African Americans' education and other human capital skills improved throughout the century thereby making it possible for them to access higher paying jobs. However, by the 1980s underclass theorists were highlighting the plight of a disadvantaged segment of the black population. These mainly central-city blacks suffered increased joblessness due to industrial restructuring and the shrinkage of manufacturing jobs in the Northeast and Midwest. The result was a worsening hypersegregation (or spatial-mismatch) that isolated central-city blacks in poor neighborhoods and blocked their access to decent schooling, job skills, and meaningful employment (Wilson 1987).

Most studies of industrial restructuring's impact on African Americans compare the effects of living in different regions and in the central city versus the suburbs. Less studied is the impact of restructuring on the earnings of metropolitan versus small town and rural blacks.[1] However, the 1980 and 1981–1982 recessions led to greater job losses in nonmetropolitan than in urban areas (USDA 1996). Moreover, between 1979 and 1987 nearly half of all manufacturing job losses occurred in nonmetropolitan areas (USDA 2000). Not only were rural areas slower to recover from the recessions, but most of their job growth in the 1980s occurred in the lower paying services-producing industry while manufacturing increased only slightly (USDA 1999).[2] Furthermore, nonmetropolitan areas had higher unemployment rates and lower wages than the metropolises and the wage gap between the two grew by 47.8 percent between 1979 and 1993 (USDA 1996). These nonmetropolitan transitions were an important part of the 1980s restructuring, thus making it important to consider the differential effects of metropolitan versus nonmetropolitan residence on black women's earnings. Because we know that restructuring has geographic effects at the level of region and central-city versus suburban residence, and because we are confident that geography affects black women's earnings, we control for region and nonmetropolitan/ metropolitan residence to capture some of the effects of restructuring. These geographic controls will reduce the likelihood that any family structure effects we observe are spurious.

Moreover, a weakness of the industrial restructuring and underclass literatures is that they usually mention black women only within the context of how black male joblessness leads to women's welfare dependency and single motherhood (Browne 1999; Corcoran 1999). Consequently, it is not clear how restructuring has impacted black women's labor market experiences. A few studies find that industrial down-sizing and job displacement caused black women to lose considerable ground in their earnings relative to other groups (Kletzer 1991; Spalter-Roth and Deitch 1999), while other literature indicates that restructuring has no significant impact on their earnings (Browne 2000). These findings contrast with Glass, Tienda, and Smith's (1988) conclusion that occupational upgrading and services-producing industrial growth benefited minority women.

Restructuring effects may also be indicated by transitions in black women's occupational and industrial locations. We know that in 1980 black women were overrepresented in the unskilled and semi-skilled jobs that were at the greatest risk of displacement (Kletzer 1991). Large-scale displacement could directly affect their earnings by redistributing them into higher or lower paying occupations and industries. Also, displacement—

and prolonged unemployment—might indirectly affect earnings by reducing the amount of work experience. We next consider how labor market segmentation may affect African American women's earnings.

Occupational Segregation

Occupational segregation theory postulates systemic inequities in the labor market which relegate racial, gender, or other groups to specific occupations and industrial sectors. Women of every race suffer the effects of a sex-segregated labor market that segments them into jobs with lower pay rates than jobs for men (Reskin 1993). Black women are concentrated in low wage, semi- and unskilled, female-intensive jobs (such as domestics, factory operatives, and services) and are underrepresented in better-paying white collar jobs like retail sales, clerical work, and professional, managerial, and technical work (Burbridge 1994; Cunningham and Zalokar 1992). Significantly, Kilbourne, England, and Beron (1994) found that black women suffer a higher wage penalty for being in predominantly female jobs than do white women.

In recent decades, however, women have experienced earnings gains linked to occupational mobility. Still, the breadth and depth of this mobility vary by race. Black and white women are segregated into different occupations even within the same industries (Cunningham and Zalokar 1992; Dodoo and Kasari 1995; King 1993; Reid 1998). Thus, for white women occupational mobility has resulted from their improved educational and skill levels, as well as from some movement into male-dominated occupations (Reskin and Roos 1990). In contrast, most of black women's earnings gains have resulted from their moving out of domestic and agricultural work into traditionally white female occupations such as clerical work (Cunningham and Zalokar 1992; King 1993).[3] Moreover, race and sex differences in earnings and occupational segregation remain and labor queues continue to reflect employer preferences for males and whites (Cotton 1988; England, Reid, and Kilbourne 1996; Kennelly 1999; Moss and Tilly 2001; Neckerman and Kirschenman 1991; Reskin 1993; Reskin and Roos 1990; Tienda, Smith, and Ortiz 1987).

The occupational mobility that African American women (and men) did experience led to reduced levels of racial occupational segregation and considerable wage gains throughout the 1960s and 1970s. For example, Smith (1979) found that among full-time employed black and white women, earnings parity was nearly approached by 1975, when blacks had earnings that were 98.6 percent those of white women. The U.S. Census Bureau (1978) mapped a more conservative progress for full-time, black female workers: An improvement in wages from 82 percent of white women's in 1970 to 93 percent in 1977. However, a trend toward wage stagnation and reversal among black women surfaced in the 1980s (Blau and Beller 1992; Browne 1999). In order to factor in the effects of occupational segregation on the changes in black women's earnings between 1980 and 1990, we include measures of respondents' occupations and industrial sectors.

Affirmative Action

Most research on affirmative action explores its impact on occupational attainment rather than on earnings per se. The few studies that do look at affirmative action's effects on African Americans' earnings offer mixed results (King 1993). Smith (1993) found that between the late 1960s and early 1970s, affirmative action significantly decreased the black-white wage gap, particularly among male college graduates. However, these gains vanished by the mid-1970s. Fosu (1992, 1995) found that affirmative action was likely responsible for black women's post-1964 occupational mobility and resulting earnings gains. Leonard (1996) found no consistent evidence that affirmative action worked to improve blacks' earnings in the private sector in the 1980s. However, Cancio, Evans, and Maume (1996) showed that the Federal government's 1980s retreat from affirmative action increased the racial wage penalty for young African Americans.

Like most other studies, our data do not include affirmative action policy measures, however we can speculate on the impact of affirmative action retrenchment by comparing changes in earnings among African American women in public- and private-sector jobs (Boyd 1993; Collins 1997). The Federal government was among the earliest and largest employers to adopt nondiscriminatory hiring policies (Boyd 1993; King 1995). Collins (1997) finds that the improved earnings and job attainment that occurred among African Americans after the mid-1960s were directly stimulated by government intervention to enact and enforce antidiscrimination, affirmative action, and social welfare laws and policies. She also found that relative to whites, black beneficiaries of affirmative action disproportionately occupy public sector jobs (Collins 1997). As for black women more specifically, their overrepresentation in the public sector makes them highly vulnerable to related policy shifts (Burbridge 1994; Collins 1997).

There is much less race and sex segregation in public- than in private-sector occupations. In the 1960s, many African Americans sought public-sector jobs to circumvent the greater hiring discrimination and earnings-attainment barriers in the private sector (Boyd 1993; Collins 1983). By 1980, African Americans were nearly twice as likely (27 percent) as whites (16 percent) to hold public-sector jobs. That same year, fully 31 percent of the black female labor force worked in the public sector (King 1993). This over-representation means that there is a strong likelihood that the Federal government's 1980s paring of grant-funded, public jobs and its visible retreat from affirmative action adversely affected black women. Hence, we include a public-sector dummy variable to determine what impact if any these cutbacks had on black women's earnings.

Family Characteristics

Other studies have explored earnings penalties associated with family characteristics, such as marriage and parenting. Most of these studies focus on women, since the evidence is that men, in general, experience no earnings penalties associated with their parental or marital statuses (Budig and England 2001; Korenman and Neumark 1991; Lundberg and Rose 2000; Waldfogel 1998). For women, the findings on marital status and earnings are mixed. Although the differences are not statistically significant Hill (1979) finds that, among whites, married women earned more than never-married women, but less than divorced, widowed, and separated women. For black women, however, she finds a positive correlation between marriage and earnings, as well as between motherhood and earnings. By comparison, Goldin and Polachek (1987) find higher earnings for all never-married compared to all married women.

Studies on the effects of motherhood on earnings also yield mixed results, however most find that mothers earn less than childless women (Goldin 1997; Korenman and Neumark 1991; Lundberg and Rose 2000; Waldfogel 1998). In general, mothers of any race experience a 10 to 15 percent earnings penalty compared to childless women (Waldfogel 1998). Also, the earnings penalty accrues to youthful motherhood and first childbirth (Budig and England 2001; Lundberg and Rose 2000), and it may vary according to the number of children (Waldfogel 1998).

Several studies document that parental and marital status interact to affect women's earnings. Hill (1979) finds that, after controlling for marital status, the negative relationship between earnings and motherhood becomes insignificant after measures of work interruptions and labor force attachment are included in the analysis. Similarly, Korenman and Neumark (1991) provide evidence that the marriage and motherhood penalties are attenuated—although still significant—when work experience and job tenure are added to regression analyses. In contrast, beyond the indication that the motherhood penalty varies significantly by marital status (Budig and England 2001; Waldfogel 1998), Waldfogel (1998) also finds that from 1978 to 1994, the earnings of formerly married and never-married mothers fared much worse than those of married mothers. By 1991, the earnings gap between non-mothers and mothers had become larger than the sex gap. Mothers aged 30 and under fared worst of all. Marriage apparently increases the motherhood penalty yet reduces the marriage premium for women with more than two children (Budig and England 2001).

Unfortunately, most studies on the effects of family characteristics on earnings do not distinguish their findings by race. Therefore, the extent to which marital or parental status affected African American women's earnings in the 1980s is unclear. Although Hill (1979) finds that marital and parental statuses impact black and white women's earnings differently, Budig and England (2001) find that motherhood penalties do not vary for black and white women except for women with three or more children. Among these mothers, black women suffer smaller earnings penalties than do white women. These differences were not explained by the fact that black women bear more children outside marriage. Budig and England (2001, 204) also consider that the lower earnings that accrue with childbearing, rather than primarily being employer driven (i.e., discrimination) may actually be a result of diminished productivity caused by women being "exhausted or distracted at work," or by their taking "mother-friendly" jobs that pay less. In short, the mixed findings of prior studies indicate a need to clarify the effects of marital and parental status on black women's earnings and on how these family structure effects influenced their earnings decline. This study uses marital status and the number of children to tap into these effects.

Summary

Past studies have explored how human capital, restructuring, occupational segregation, affirmative action, and family structure affect earnings, but none of these explore the combined effects of all these factors. Moreover, unlike previous studies our objective is to see how family structure contributes to the decline in black women's earnings net of these other effects. Against the backdrop of the 1980s' earnings decline, our review of the literature inclines us to hypothesize that the improvements in black women's human capital may have likely been offset by less favorable industrial and occupational distributions resulting from restructuring. We expected that the depreciating effect of marriage would decline as marital disintegration led to greater numbers of female-headed homes, but that this would increase the effects of parenting, given the competing claim on time by work and children. Finally, we expected that the cuts in public-sector jobs would contribute adversely to black women's earnings. Although we are not able to explore the isolated effects of socialization, aspirations, work motivation, or employer discrimination, we have no reason to believe that these changed much in the 10-year span observed.

DATA AND METHODS

The data for this study come from the 1980 and 1990 U.S. population censuses. In each of these, the data comprise a 10 percent sample of native-born black women selected from the 5 percent Public Use Microsample (PUMS). We focus on full-time, employed black women and restrict the analysis to 25- to 64-year-old, noninstitutionalized respondents who are neither in school nor in the military, and who are in the labor force and report positive earnings in the year leading up to the respective census.[4] In 1980 and 1990 respectively, 15,670 and 17,382 African American women remain in the sample.

The dependent variable is the logged hourly wage, obtained by dividing the number of hours worked in the year preceding the census into the total annual wage and salary income. Hours worked is calculated as the product of weeks worked and the usual hours worked per week. To reduce the effect of outliers, hourly wages exceeding $100 are coded to this amount. The selected explanatory variables include four human capital measures: years of schooling, a dummy variable distinguishing college graduates, imputed years of work experience (age – years of schooling – 6), and experience squared. Family structure variables include a three-category measure of marital status that distinguishes never married, currently married, and formerly married women. There is also a continuous measure of the number of children each respondent has given birth to.

The effects of affirmative action are indirectly judged with a binary measure that differentiates public-sector workers (coded 1) from all others (coded 0). The effects of restructuring are tapped by including geographic controls to create a metropolitan versus nonmetropolitan dichotomy and a four-category regional measure: Northeast, Midwest, West, and South. South is the excluded category. The effects of occupational segregation are tapped by including occupational and industrial measures. A six-category measure of occupation reflects work in the following areas: managerial and professional (MPS); technical, sales, and administrative (TSA); services (SVC); farming, forestry, and fishing (FFF); precision production, crafts, and repairs (PRP); and operators, fabricators, and laborers (OPR). Likewise, a 13-category measure includes workers in the following industries: agriculture, forestry, and fisheries (AFF); mining industries (MIN); construction industries (CNS); manufacturing (MFG); transportation, communications, and utilities (TCP); wholesale trade (WHL); retail trade (RET); finance, insurance, and real estate (FIR); business and repair services (BRS); personal services (PER); professional and related services (PRS); entertainment and recreational services (ERS); and public administration (PUB). In the regression analysis, MPS is the excluded occupational category and PRS is the excluded industrial category.

The analysis begins with the means for explanatory measures. We then separately assess wage determination in 1980 and 1990. Subsequently, a regression analysis explores the contribution of these variables representing each theoretical approach to the determination of mean hourly wage.[5] Finally, we use decomposition analysis to explore the extent to which change in earnings over the period can be attributed to these explanatory factors. At this stage of the analysis, the difference in real (rather than nominal) wages is assessed using an average consumer price index from the period 1982–1984 as the base for standardizing wages.

ANALYSIS AND RESULTS

Table 9.1 presents descriptive statistics for our dependent and independent variables for the 1980 and 1990 samples of black women. The measures of central tendency indicate that African American women did not fare well economically in the 1980s. Although from 1980 to 1990 there was an increase in mean nominal wages from $6.30 to $9.98 an hour, in real terms mean wages actually declined by 7.3 percent from $8.69 to $8.06 per hour. This amounts to an average loss of over $22 for a 35-hour work week or $25 for a 40-hour week. A change of this magnitude can be costly for working-class women, especially if they are single parents with no other sources of income. Theoretically, this could derive from a variety of factors. The findings in table 9.1 immediately rule out the possibility that a reduction in human capital led to the increase in low-wage black women. To the contrary, there was a marked improvement in the educational attainment of black women, although there was a slightly lower level of work experience in 1990 (21.2 years) than in 1980 (21.9 years).

Table 9.1 also reveals substantial change in the marital status of full-time employed African American women. There was a drop of 6.6 percent in the proportion of married women. Moreover, there was a 7 percent gain in single women between 1980 and 1990. This was largely due to a 7.7 percent rise in the never-married. The proportion of formerly married women (i.e., widowed and divorced) fell from 33.9 to 32.9 percent. Meanwhile, black women had fewer children in 1990 (3.2) than in 1980 (3.5). Thus, the reduction in their years of work experience is likely not attributable to an increased burden of child care. Each of these developments may have consequences for African American women's earnings, and we will explore the possibility of an interaction effect between marital status and fertility in the ensuing regression analyses. The regional distribution of full-time, African American women workers also changed during the decade (see table 9.1). The percentage of these dropped by 5.5 percent in the Northeast and by 1.6 percent in the Midwest, while the rate rose by 4.6 percent in the South and by 2.4 percent in the West. It is no coincidence that the drop in the numbers of full-time black women workers occurred precisely in those regions that suffered the largest decline in factory jobs in the 1980s. Similarly, the increases occurred in the Sunbelt regions to which many Northern companies relocated in search of lower operating costs and higher profits. Thus, the apparent regional redistribution of full-time, black women workers may reflect migration to the Sunbelt; disproportionate increases in the numbers of part-time, unemployed, or discouraged workers in the Northeast and Midwest; or a combination of these and other factors (Adelman, Moretti, and Tolnay 2000; U.S. Department of Labor 1997; Frey 1987; Kletzer 1991; USDA 1996; Wilson 1987).

There were several notable occupational shifts between 1980 and 1990. In both years, most black women were in TSA and SVC. Nevertheless, the share of MPS jobs increased by almost 25 percent. There were also increases of 9 percent in TSA jobs, and of 15 percent in PRP occupations. These changes may reflect black women's movement out of domestic service and blue-collar jobs and into lower-level clerical work (King 1993). In contrast, declines of about 16 to 17 percent occurred in the proportions found in SVC; FFF; and in OPR occupations. Kletzer (1991) finds that black women who lost jobs between 1979 and 1986 were slower to be reemployed compared to other groups. This was especially true for black women in OPR occupations, of whom more than 95 percent became reemployed in other occupations. It is thus possible that job displacement and low reemployment rates contributed to the reduction in black women's years of work experience that was observed in table 9.1.

The declines in SVC (–4.8 percent) and OPR (–2.9 percent) occupations are striking because they involved a large number of women. The exodus of black women from hotel and private household service jobs cannot account entirely for this change. One possible explanation for the decline is employers' growing preference for hiring individuals with "soft skills" such as interaction skills and certain cultural and personality traits (Moss and Tilly 2001). Although some scholars argue that women benefit from this trend, others find that the racial stereotyping and cultural biases that accompany it shut out many African American women (Kennelly 1999; Moss and Tilly 2001). Also, the reduced proportion of African American women in semi-skilled and unskilled OPR work suggests again that many lost factory jobs as a result of industrial restructuring. This conforms with Kletzer's (1991) finding that between 1979 and 1986 OPR-related occupations accounted for 44.7 percent of African American women's job losses.

Comparisons of public- versus private-sector occupations are revealing. Since the 1960s, African Americans have pursued public-sector jobs as a way to expand their employment opportunities and earnings (Boyd 1993; Collins 1997). Yet, Table 9.1 reveals that the proportion of black women working in public jobs declined slightly from 31.8 to 28.3 percent over the period.

Meanwhile, considerable change is also apparent in the industrial distribution. While the modal categories were those associated with PRS and MFG, the greatest percentage increases were among workers in CNS, WHL, and BRS, while the largest declines were in MIN and PER. The increases in the CNS, WHL, and BRS industries seem less impressive, however, when one considers that the numbers of African American women in them were so low in 1980 that even a small increase in absolute terms translates into a dramatic proportionate rise. In substantive terms, the 3.3 percent drop in the number of black women in manufacturing is important, since traditionally this industry had provided them with higher wages than most other industries.

Table 9.1. Selected Characteristics of Full-Time, African American Women Workers Aged 25 to 64

Variable	1980	1990
Mean years of schooling	11.9	12.9
College graduate (%)	12.6	16.0
Mean years of experience	21.9	21.2
Marital status (%)		
Never-married	16.5	24.2
Currently married	49.6	43.0
Formerly married	33.9	32.9
Mean number of children	3.5	3.2
Employed in public sector (%)	31.8	28.3
Region of residence (%)		
Northeast	17.4	11.9
South	58.2	62.8
Midwest	17.9	16.3
West	6.6	9.0
Nonmetropolitan residence (%)	14.1	15.1
Occupational category (%)		
Managerial and professional	17.2	21.8
Technical, sales, and administrative	31.0	33.8
Services	29.9	25.1
Farming, forestry, and fishing	0.6	0.5
Precision production, crafts, and repairs	2.6	3.0
Operators, fabricators, and laborers	18.7	15.8
Industrial category (%)		
Agriculture, forestry, and fisheries	0.7	0.6
Mining	0.2	0.1
Construction	0.5	0.8
Manufacturing	19.8	16.5
Transportation, communication, and other public utilities	5.7	6.2
Wholesale trade	1.4	1.9
Retail trade	9.6	10.7
Finance, insurance, and real estate	4.9	6.9
Business and repair services	2.4	3.8
Personal services	10.2	6.5
Professional and related services	36.4	37.2
Entertainment and recreation services	0.5	0.5
Public administration	7.8	8.3
Age (years)	39.8	40.1
Mean hourly wage (median)	6.30 (4.55)	9.98 (7.89)
Mean log hourly wage (median)	1.51 (1.52)	2.06 (2.07)
Real (standardized) wage (median)	8.69 (6.28)	8.06 (6.37)
N	15,670	17,382

Table 9.2 presents the results of a regression of logged nominal wages on the selected variables for each of the two years. The regression coefficients represent the change in earnings per unit change in the explanatory factor, controlling for all other variables in the equation. The human capital variables (years of schooling, college graduate, and years of experience) each had positive effects on African American women's hourly wages in both 1980 and 1990, and the size of the effects increased over the decade, although they were probably too small to cause any meaningful increase in black women's mean hourly wages.

There are a number of important differences between the 1980 and 1990 estimates. First, the effect of being never-married was negative and significant in 1990, but not in 1980. Second, the negative effect of having children, though significant in 1980, is even stronger in 1990. A test of the interaction effect of being never-married and having children, however, proved insignificant and was therefore excluded from the final model presented here. In other words, having children did not alter the effect of being never-married on earnings. Thus, this finding does not support some underclass theorists' contention that "single motherhood" has negatively affected African American women's wages. Marital status and fertility had additive effects on earnings, rather than multiplicative ones.

A number of occupational and industrial categories, not significant in 1980, were significant in 1990. Among the occupations, FFF exhibited a strong negative effect in 1990. In comparison, among the industries, MIN, TCP, WHL, FIR, and PUB had positive effects. Altogether, however, in 1990 these five industries represented only 22.9 percent of full-time employed African American women. By comparison, in 1990 MFG employed 16.5 percent of the sample. As predicted, employment in MFG had significant and positive effects on black women's earnings in both years and the effect was stronger in 1990. Moreover, outside of MIN and TCP—which together employed a mere 6.3 percent of the 1990 sample—MFG had the largest positive effect on earnings.

As predicted, public-sector employment had a significant and positive effect on black women's earnings in both 1980 and 1990. Nonetheless, the size of the effect was smaller than anticipated. By comparison, region had a large effect on earnings. In both 1980 and 1990, living outside the South had significant and positive effects on African American women's wages, perhaps reflecting the higher wages that workers earn in the Northeast, West, and Midwest to compensate for the higher costs of living outside the South. The magnitude of the regional effects changed from 1980 to 1990. By 1990, working in the West and Midwest had weaker positive effects while working in the Northeast had stronger positive effects.

Spatial distribution affected African American women in one other way. Residing outside metropolitan areas negatively affected their wages in both

Table 9.2. Understandardized Regression Estimates of Logged Hourly Wage among Black Women Workers Aged 25 to 64

Variable	1980		1990	
	B	SE B	B	SE B
Human capital				
Years of schooling	.029**	.003	0.35**	.003
College graduate	.266**	.026	.269**	.018
Years of experience	.014**	.002	.021**	.002
Experience squared[a]	−.023**	.004	−.027**	.004
Family structure				
Marital status (%)[b]				
Formerly married	.007	.013	−.015	.010
Never-married	−.003	.018	−.055**	.012
Number of children	−.007*	.003	−.019**	.003
Affirmative action				
Public sector	.069**	.017	.086**	.013
Restructuring				
Region (%)[c]				
West	.177**	.025	.154**	.016
Midwest	.180**	.017	.106**	.013
Northeast	.146**	.017	.228**	.015
Nonmetropolitan	−1.08**	.018	−.191**	.013
Occupational sergregation				
Occupational category[d]				
Technical, sales, and administrative	−.137**	.021	−.147**	.014
Services	−.333**	.023	−.387**	.016
Farming, forestry, and fishing	−.136	.132	−.313**	.089
Precision production, crafts, and repairs	−.239**	.043	−.156**	.030
Operators, fabricators, and laborers	−.260**	.029	−.314**	.021
Industrial category[e]				
Agriculture, forestry, and fisheries	−.097	.122	.067	.078
Mining	.192	.134	.351*	.139
Construction	.099	.082	.073	.050
Manufacturing	.107**	.025	.138**	.019
Transportation, communication, and other public utilities	.284**	.028	.305**	.020
Wholesale trade	−.022	.053	.103**	.034
Retail trade	−.144**	.024	−.106**	.017
Finance, insurance, and real estate	.021	.030	.094**	.020
Business and repair services	−.036	.041	−.035	.024
Personal services	−.180**	.024	−.129**	.020
Entertainment and recreation services	−.004	.084	.046	.060
Public administration	.030	.025	.102**	.019
Intercept	1.098**		1.460**	
Adjusted R^2	.154		.273	

[a]Values are multiplied by 10.
[b]Currently married was an omitted category.
[c]South was an omitted category.
[d]Managerial and professional specialty was an omitted category.
[e]Professional and related services was an omitted category.
*$p < .05$. **$p < .01$.

years, however the size of the effect grew between 1980 and 1990. Our results indicate that when it comes to earnings, urban black women have an advantage over their rural and small town counterparts. In the 1970s and 1980s, many manufacturers moved to small town and rural America, however black women seemed to have gained no earnings advantages from such relocations. These results challenge Hoffnar and Greene's (1995) conclusion that geography has no effects on black women's earnings, however their study compared city with suburban residence while this one compares metropolitan with non-metropolitan residence.

To examine how the variations observed in tables 9.1 and 9.2 contribute to the observed wage difference between 1980 and 1990, we conduct a decomposition analysis of the change in real wages. We can partition the wage difference into three segments: one portion deriving from differences in the levels of the selected explanatory characteristics (within group variation revolving around individual differences in human capital), another reflecting the payoff or returns to these characteristics (between group variation reflecting differential treatment), and a third representing differences in the intercept. Typically, the second and third components are combined to represent the "unexplained" contribution, or in this case, differences attributable to the way the market treated or evaluated the 1980 and 1990 samples (Jones and Kelley 1984). Contrary to the typical assumption that the unexplained sum measures "discrimination" in the labor market, we simply see it as representative of how different the labor market valued African American women's characteristics in 1980 than 1990.

Table 9.3 presents the results of the decomposition analysis. For each independent variable, we present the percentage of the overall gap explained by actual changes in the level of that variable, and in the remuneration (or returns) to the variable. Looking first at characteristics, we find that improvements in human capital (and particularly in years of schooling) as well as in occupational distribution (and, to a lesser extent, industrial distribution) worked to improve African American women's earnings between 1980 and 1990. Reductions in fertility also served to increase earnings, whereas changes to region, metropolitan residence, and marital status served to lower earnings. Not surprisingly, the decline in public sector employment described in table 9.1 also served to depreciate black women's earnings.

As far as the slopes or returns component is concerned, the returns to human capital, and particularly years of experience and schooling, worked in the direction of raising earnings. This finding is consistent with the notion that the demand for skilled labor increased over the period. The returns to industrial location also improved, as did the returns to public sector employment. On the other hand, changes in returns to net occupational distribution declined to offset the aforementioned improvements. There were also declines in the returns to occupational distribution suggesting, perhaps, that

Table 9.3. Decomposition of Real Wage Difference in Black Women, 1980 to 1990

	Percentage Explained by		
Variable	*Characteristics*	*Returns*	*Total*
Human capital			
Years of schooling	2.258	4.735	6.993
College graduate	0.606	0.025	0.631
Experience	0.007	8.504	8.511
Family structure			
Marital status	−0.271	−1.062	−1.333
Number of chilren	0.384	−2.805	−2.421
Affirmative action			
Public sector	−0.199	0.358	0.159
Restructuring			
Region	−0.698	−0.033	−0.731
Nonmetropolitan	−0.127	−0.775	−0.902
Occupational segregation			
Occupation	1.542	−1.871	−0.329
Industry	0.179	1.904	2.083
Total	3.680	8.979	12.659
Total explained by intercept		−11.659	
Variation	*Explained*	*Unexplained*	*Total*
Total	3.680	2.680	1.0

although the overall shifts in occupational distribution were positively related to earnings, a segment of the black female population may have shifted into occupations with very low remuneration. Moreover, the marital status distribution attracted greater wage penalty in 1990, as did both fertility and public sector employment. Similarly, the geographic distribution of the sample in 1990 was such that the returns were worse than for 1980.

Combining the coefficient and returns or slopes components, we see that the overall effect of human capital was to increase earnings. The same was true for industrial distribution and for public-sector employment, where the increased returns to such employment outweighed the drop in public-sector employment. All the other study variables had negative overall contributions to earnings, therefore they present viable explanations for the observed decline in wages. Fertility and marital status seem most important in the search for why African American women's earnings declined between 1980 and 1990. To a lesser extent, geographic distribution (both region and nonmetropolitan) and occupational distribution also contribute to the negative trend in earnings. Factoring in the sizable, negative intercept term, which reflects unmeasured variation, the net effect of all these changes is that there was a slight decline in real wages between 1980 and 1990.

DISCUSSION AND CONCLUSION

This study discloses some of the factors responsible for the change in the real wages of African American women from 1980 to 1990. The results of our analysis lead us to conclude that several, complex processes contributed to the changes in black women's earnings from 1980 to 1990. A clear paradox evident in the data is the fact that the decline occurred despite improvements in the human capital of black women. The considerably higher educational level of black women in 1990 did not offset the effects of other factors that contributed to the earnings drop. On the positive side, years of schooling yielded higher returns in 1990 than in 1980. Ironically, however, the returns to college graduation barely improved over the period. Years of work experience also paid off with higher returns in 1990 than in 1980, however most African American women did not gain from this improvement as the mean years of experience of working black women actually fell, albeit slightly, from 1980 to 1990.

Of all the measured factors, the family structure variables of marital status and fertility contribute most to the overall decline in wages. On the one hand, we find that the effects of being never-married were negative and significant in 1990 but not in 1980. On the other, we find that having children significantly and negatively affected black women's earnings in both 1980 and 1990 and that the earnings penalty associated with having children increased over time. Although black women had fewer children in 1990, cumulatively both fertility and marriage contributed negatively to the change in black women's earnings over the period.

The results of our analysis of family structure may reflect changes related to industrial restructuring and the allied job cutbacks and market recessions that occurred in the 1980s. First, African American women were more likely to be unmarried in 1990 than in 1980. As proposed by Wilson (1987) and others, the lower marriage rates may in part be a consequence of higher rates of unemployment and lower earnings among potential black male partners, supporting the underclass approach. Second, the effect of being never-married was negative in 1990 but not in 1980. It is plausible to think that the effect of having no male wage earner in the household is larger and more negative during those periods of recession that are characterized by both male and female earnings losses. In addition, we found no significant interaction effect between marital status and fertility on black women's earnings. In other words, the effects of marital status and fertility may be additive, rather than interactive. This finding would appear to contradict suggestions by underclass theorists that out-of-wedlock births to single mothers account for the lower earnings rates among black women in the 1980s. Changes in family structure negatively affected the earnings of African American women, but these family composition changes, at least among full-time workers, appear to have been induced by economic transformations rather than by individual attitudes and behavior.

Other structural factors included in our model do not appear to be responsible for the observed decline in earnings even though it is clear that black women's occupational distribution was affected by industrial restructuring. Although by 1990 the number of African American women in the traditional service occupations had gone down, fully a quarter of them remained concentrated in this area. Also, although the number of black women in managerial and professional jobs rose 4.6 percent to reach 21.8 percent, most black women remained concentrated in jobs at the lower end of the earnings scale. However, the decomposition analysis suggests that occupation had positive effects on wages across the period. For example, a sizable majority (58.9 percent) of African American women remained in SVC and TSA occupations although the relative proportions in each category shifted over time. Interestingly, the regression analysis showed that despite their gains in several occupations, in 1990 black women experienced earnings declines in at least four categories, and the decomposition analysis shows that black women actually experienced a decline in returns related to changes in their occupational distribution. Overall, the net contribution of occupation was negative albeit slight.

In contrast to occupational distribution, the contribution of industrial distribution was positive and substantial. Black women received higher returns as they increased their representation in several industries. Likewise, improvements in returns were substantial enough that the proportion of the earnings gap explained by returns to industrial distribution was almost 11 times higher than that explained by human capital characteristics. These gains may merely reflect the reality that, compared to all other race-gender groups, returns to black women were rock bottom prior to the 1970s and 1980s. Moreover, black women probably suffered from the 1980s shrinkage in the manufacturing sector, which traditionally offered them better pay than service-related jobs. Their representation in manufacturing dropped by 8 percent during the decade.

Geography had significant effects on black women's earnings in 1980 and 1990, possibly indicating the impact of restructuring. In both years, nonmetropolitan residents had lower earnings, but the effect was slightly larger in 1990 than in 1980. Also, living outside the South resulted in slightly higher earnings. These results challenge Hoffnar and Greene's (1995) conclusion that geographic space has no effects on black women's earnings, however their study compared city with suburban residence while this one compares metropolitan and nonmetropolitan residence.

Finally, African American women have viewed public-sector employment as a doorway to economic attainment. Yet, fewer of them were in the public sector in 1990 than in 1980. This may be a result of either cutbacks in government jobs and an expansion of opportunities in the private-sector or both. Interestingly, however, black women in public-sector employment received higher returns than their counterparts in the private sector. This is in line with other findings that blacks, as a group, fare better in public-sector jobs (Boyd 1993; Collins 1983). Further, the returns to public-sector employment improved over the period to more than offset the fall-off in public-sector employment. Thus, our findings support the notion that the public sector is a special niche that rewards African American women with higher returns for their characteristics than does the private sector. It appears that even in a period of anti-affirmative action policies, public-sector employment provided black women with better pay than the private sector.

In summary, the proportion of black women's earnings explained by their individual characteristics versus significant intercensal changes in returns to those characteristics indicates that it was changes in nonhuman capital factors that accounted for more of the earnings decline during the 1980s. However, it is clear that if human capital had not improved to the extent that it did, the condition of African American women would have been considerably worse.

Why is it that the returns to black women's characteristics varied so much from 1980 to 1990, and not always in a positive direction? Much of the observed decline in earnings can be traced to changes in the impact of marital status and fertility that occurred over the decade. This finding fits well with Budig and England's (2001) plausible explanations for a negative impact of motherhood, although our data do not give us the wherewithal to specify which are most salient in this case. It is possible, though, that for working black women lower productivity, discrimination, and/or selection into "mother-friendly" jobs might all be contributory factors. Also, past research supporting the significant contributions of structural factors leads us to suspect that other elements not specified in our model [such as government policies, continuing race and gender-based discrimination in the labor market (Browne 1999; Darity, Myers, and Chung 1998) and factors related to black women's location at the intersections of various stratification systems] played a significant role over the decade. Indeed, the evidence here is of a very large intercept effect, which measures variance in the outcome measure not explained by the selected variables. One example of a potential omitted explanatory factor comes from the growing body of work that documents that employer prejudices, stereotyping, and discrimination significantly constrain blacks' job access, pay, and promotion (Kennelly 1999; Moss and Tilly 2001; Neckerman and Kirschenman 1991).

Is it also possible that contrary to our presumptions, the quality, quantity, and consequences of employer discrimination changed from 1980 to 1990 and that this accounts for some of the large unexplained components that we found? Our study cannot answer this question definitively. It is possible, however, that anti-black sentiments increased during this period of affirmative action backlash. It is also possible that the 1980s backlash against poverty programs negatively affected black women's earnings and perhaps even more seriously for the unmarried and those with children. Kennelly (1999), for example, finds that many employers stereotype black working-class women as single mothers who have poor work ethics. Is there reason to think that such an effect may have increased over the decade of the 1980s? It certainly is not implausible, if we conceive of an increasingly stringent employment situation arising from the political cutbacks already described. In such an environment discrimination could become more pervasive. It is also feasible that in times of rising unemployment, economic hardships and dependents (especially children) stress parents and particularly single heads of households in ways that compromise their productivity at work or even their choices of jobs (Budig and England 2001). We encourage more in-depth studies of how family structure impacts employment and earnings. It will certainly be useful to understand whether employer and institutionalized discrimination in the hiring, promotion, and remuneration of black women are more salient than job choice or productivity as explanations.

Finally, we urge more research on what seems to be a bifurcation of the labor market experiences of African American women. While the mean wage of black women fell during the 1980s, the median real wage rose by 1.4 percent. These developments indicate a rise in the number of black women who fall in the lower end of the earnings distribution perhaps due to restructuring. This conclusion is reinforced by the finding that a sizable segment of this was redistributed into low paying occupations. It will be interesting to pursue the question of population bifurcation with richer data that enable a more detailed exploration of occupational change and that better reflect demand-driven processes. Corcoran's (1999) findings clearly suggest that different groups of women experience varying constraints and opportunities. This should be true even within race and future studies should examine different segments of the black female labor force, including the part-time and contingency workers who are perhaps most likely to slip into lower paying occupations. We also recommend cross-group comparisons to determine if the combined effects of the factors observed in this study are unique to black women.

NOTES

1. In 1980, 23.3 percent of African Americans lived in nonmetropolitan areas.
2. Of the nonagricultural industries, all but mining, manufacturing, and construction are "services-producing." The services occupational category falls within this

industry. Also, the agriculture, forestry, and fisheries industry includes services- and goods-producing sectors.

3. Clerical work includes telephone operators, data transcribers, stenographers, secretaries, administrative support staff, typists, mail clerks, cashiers, bank tellers, and similar work.

4. The Department of Labor counts as "full time" a minimum of 35 hours per week.

5. Hierarchical modeling would certainly have been preferred in analyses of this nature, if we had true multilevel data representing the different levels of intended measurement.

REFERENCES

Adelman, Robert, Chris Morett, and Stewart Tolnay. 2000. "Homeward Bound: The Return Migration of Southern-Born Black Women, 1940 to 1990." *Sociological Spectrum* 20:433–63.

Bernhardt, Annette, Martina Morris, and Mark S. Handcock. 1995. "Women's Gains or Men's Losses? A Closer Look at the Shrinking Gender Gap in Earnings." *American Journal of Sociology* 101:302–28.

Blau, Francine, and Andrea Beller. 1992. "Black-White Earnings over the 1970s and 1980s: Gender Differences in Trends." *Review of Economics and Statistics* 74:276–86.

Bound, John, and Laura Dresser. 1999. "Losing Ground: The Erosion of the Relative Earnings of African American Women during the 1980s." In *Latinas and African American Women at Work*, edited by I. Browne. New York: Russell Sage Foundation.

Boyd, Robert L. 1993. "Differences in the Earnings of Black Workers in the Private and Public Sectors." *Social Science Journal* 30:133–42.

Browne, Irene. 1999. "Latinas and African American Women in the U.S. Labor Market." In *Latinas and African American Women at Work*, edited by I. Browne. New York: Russell Sage Foundation.

———. 2000. "Opportunities Lost? Race, Industrial Restructuring, and Employment among Young Women Heading Households." *Social Forces* 78:907–29.

Budig, Michelle J., and Paula England. 2001. "The Wage Penalty for Motherhood." *American Sociological Review* 66:204–25.

Burbridge, Lynn C. 1994. "The Reliance of African-American Women on Government and Third-Sector Employment." *American Economic Review* 84:103–7.

Cancio, A. Silvia, T. David Evans, and David J. Maume, Jr. 1996. "Reconsidering the Declining Significance of Race: Racial Differences in Early Career Wages." *American Sociological Review* 61:541–56.

Collins, Sharon. 1997. *Black Corporate Executives*. Philadelphia: Temple University Press.

———. 1983. The making of the Black middle class. *Social Problems* 30:369–82.

Corcoran, Mary. 1999. "The Economic Progress of African American Women." In *Latinas and African American Women at Work*, edited by I. Browne. New York: Russell Sage Foundation.

Cotton, Jeremiah. 1988. "On the Decomposition of Wage Differentials." *Review of Economics and Statistics* 70:236–43.

———. 1989. "Opening the Wage Gap: The Decline in Black Economic Progress in the 1980s." *Social Science Quarterly* 70:803–19.

Cunningham, James S., and Nadja Zalokar. 1992. "The Economic Progress of Black Women, 1940–1980: Occupational Distribution and Relative Wages." *Industrial and Labor Relations Review* 45:540–55.

Darity, William A. Jr., Samuel L. Myers, and Chanjin Chung. 1998. "Racial Earnings Disparities and Family Structure." *Southern Economic Journal* 65:20–41.

DoDoo, F. Nii-Amoo, and Patricia Kasari. 1995. "Race and Female Occupational Location in America." *Journal of Black Studies* 25:465–74.

England, Paula, Lori Reid, and Barbara Kilbourne. 1996. "The Effect of Sex Composition of Jobs on Starting Wages in an Organization: Findings from the NLSY." *Demography* 33:511–21.

Fosu, Augustin Kwasi. 1992. "Occupational Mobility of Black Women, 1958–1981: The Impact of Post-1964 Anti-Discrimination Measures." *Industrial and Labor Relations Review* 45:281–94.

———. 1995. "Occupational Mobility and Post-1964 Earnings Gains by Black Women." *American Economic Review* 85:143–47.

Frey, William H. 1987. "Migration and Depopulation of the Metropolis: Regional Restructuring or Rural Renaissance?" *American Sociological Review* 52:240–57.

Glass, Jennifer, Marta Tienda, and Shelley A. Smith. 1988. "The Impact of Changing Employment Opportunity on Gender and Ethnic Earnings Inequality." *Social Science Research* 17:252–76.

Goldin, Claudia. 1997. "Career and Family: College Women Look to the Past." In *Gender and Family Issues in the Workplace*, edited by F. Blau and R. Ehrenberg. New York: Russell Sage foundation.

Goldin, Claudia, and Solomon Polachek. 1987. "Residual Differences by Sex: Perspectives on the Gender Gap in Earnings." *American Economic Review* 77:143–51.

Gwartney-Gibbs, Patricia A., and Patricia A. Taylor. 1986. "Black Women Workers' Earnings Progress in Three Industrial Sectors." *Sage* 3:20–25.

Hill, Martha. 1979. "The Wage Effects of Marital Stress and Children." *Journal of Human Resources* 14:579–94.

Hoffnar, Emily, and Michael Greene. 1995. "Residential Location and the Earnings of African American Women." *Review of Black Political Economy* 23:103–11.

Jones, F. L., and Jonathan Kelley. 1984. "Decomposing Differences between Groups: A Cautionary Note on Measuring Discrimination." *Sociological Methods and Research* 12:324–43.

Kasarda, John. 1989. "Urban Industrial Transition and the Underclass." *Annals of the American Academy of Political and Social Science* 501:26–47.

Kennelly, Ivy. 1999. "'That Single Mother Element': How White Employers Typify Black Women." *Gender & Society* 13:168–92.

Kilbourne, Barbara, Paula England, and Kurt Beron. 1994. "Effects of Individual, Occupational, and Industrial Characteristics on Earnings: Intersections of Race and Gender." *Social Forces* 72:1149–76.

King, Deborah. 1988. "Multiple Jeopardy, Multiple Consciousness: The Context of Black Feminist Ideology." *Signs: Journal of Women in Culture and Society* 18:1–43.

King, Mary. 1993. "Black Women's Breakthrough into Clerical Work: An Occupational Tipping Model." *Journal of Economic Issues* 27:1097–1125.

———. 1995. "Black Women's Labor Market Status: Occupational Segregation in the United States and Great Britain." *Review of Black Political Economy* 24:23–43.

Kletzer, Lori G. 1991. "Job Displacement, 1979–86: How Blacks Fared Relative to Whites." *Monthly Labor Review* 14:17–25.

———. 1995. "Black Women's Labor Market Status: Occupational Segregation in the United States and Great Britain." *Review of Black Political Economy* 24:23–43.

Korenman, Sanders, and David Neumark. 1991. "Marriage, Motherhood, and Wages." *Journal of Human Resources* 27:233–55.

Leonard, Jonathon. 1996. "Wage Disparities and Affirmative Action in the 1980s." *American Economic Review* 86:285–301.

Lundberg, Shelly, and Elaina Rose. 2000. "Parenthood and the Earnings of Married Men and Women." *Labour Economics* 7:689–710.

Moss, Philip, and Chris Tilly. 2001. *Stories Employers Tell: Race, Skill, and Hiring in America*. New York: Russell Sage Foundation.

Neckerman, Kathryn M., and Joleen Kirschenman. 1991. "Hiring Strategies, Racial Bias, and Inner-City Workers." *Social Problems* 38:433–47.

Reid, Lori. 1998. "Devaluing Women and Minorities: The Effects of Race/Ethnic and Sex Composition of Occupations on Wage Levels." *Work and Occupations* 25:511–36.

Reskin, Barbara. 1993. "Sex Segregation in the Workplace." *Annual Review of Sociology* 19:241–70.

Reskin, Barbara F., and Patricia A. Roos. 1990. *Job Queues, Gender Queues: Explaining Women's Inroads into Male Occupations*. Philadelphia: Temple University Press.

Simms, Margaret C., and Julianne M. Malveaux. 1986. *Slipping through the Cracks: The Status of Black Women*. New Brunswick, NJ: Transaction Books.

Smith, James P. 1979. "The Convergence to Racial Equality in Women's Wages." In *Women in the Labor Market*, edited by C. B. Lloyd, E. S. Andrews, and C. L. Gilroy. New York: Columbia University Press.

———. 1993. "Affirmative Action and the Racial Wage Gap." *American Economic Review* 83:79–84.

Spalter-Roth, Roberta, and Cynthia Deitch. 1998. "I Don't Feel Right Sized: I Feel Out-of-Work Sized." *Work and Occupations* 26:446–82.

Tienda, Marta, Shelley A. Smith, and Vilma Ortiz. 1987. "Industrial Restructuring, Gender Segregation and Sex Differences in Earnings." *American Sociological Review* 52:195–210.

U.S. Bureau of the Census. 1978. "A Statistical Portrait of Women in the United States: 1978." Washington: Current Population Reports, Special Studies, Series P-23, No. 100.

———. 2000. "The March Current Population Survey." Washington, DC: U.S. Department of Commerce.

U.S. Department of Agriculture. 1996, 1999, 2000. *Agriculture Fact Book*. Washington, DC: Government Printing Office.

U.S. Department of Labor. 1997. *Facts on Working Women*. Washington, DC: Women's Bureau.

Waldfogel, Jane. 1998. "Understanding the 'Family Gap' in Pay for Women with Children." *Journal of Economic Perspectives* 12:137–56.

Wilson, William J. 1980. *The Declining Significance of Race.* Chicago: University of Chicago.

———. 1987. *The Truly Disadvantaged.* Chicago: University of Chicago Press.

Xu, Wu, and Ann Leffler. 1992. "Gender and Race Effects on Occupational Prestige, Segregation, and Earnings." *Gender & Society* 6:376–92.

10

Stereotypes and Realities

Images of Black Women in the Labor Market

Irene Browne and Ivy Kennelly

As the chapters in this volume illustrate, opportunities for success in the U.S. labor market remain linked to gender and race, and black women continue to be among the most severely disadvantaged (Aldridge 1999; Corcoran and Parrott 1999). Earnings for black women are still lower than wages for black men, white women, and white men (England, Christopher, and Reid 1999). Opportunities for upward mobility are also restricted for black women; when they are able to secure positions of authority in the workplace, black women are most often placed in positions where they only supervise other black women (Browne, Tigges, and Press 2001).

Why do black women continue to remain at the bottom of the wage and authority hierarchy? Stratification in the labor market emerges through the interplay of labor supply, labor demand, and social processes that match workers to positions. The dynamics of this interplay are the source of heated debate among economists and sociologists (Bills 1992; Granovetter 1995). Theories of discrimination in particular stress that employer attitudes and practices are influenced by workers' gender and race, producing inequality through the matching process (Granovetter 1995; Rosenbaum and Binder 1997). Yet, very little is known about how employers actually perceive different groups in the labor force (Holzer 1996).

Black women in particular are absent from research on employer perceptions. Inquiries into how employers view black workers focus on black men, while studies of employer attitudes about women in the workforce focus on white women (Struyk, Turner, and Fix 1991; Kirschenman and Neckerman 1991; Neckerman and Kirschenman 1991; Moss and Tilly 1995a, b).[1] In

This chapter was originally published in *Latinas and African American Women at Work: Race, Gender, and Economic Inequality*, edited by I. Browne. New York: Russell Sage Foundation, 1999. The current version is slightly condensed.

addition, there is almost no research that compares employer perceptions to the actual pool of workers in local labor markets. Information on labor demand is uncoupled from labor supply, although theories of labor markets stress that demand and supply move together.

In this chapter, we address these gaps in the literature, and concentrate on how employers view black women workers. We address two questions: How do white employers perceive black women in the workforce? and How do these perceptions compare to profiles of the actual labor pool of black women in their local labor market?

We examine these questions by using a special dataset that allows us to contrast employer perceptions with experiences of a matched sample of women and men in the labor force. Members of 1,600 households in the Atlanta metropolitan area were surveyed, providing information on labor supply. From that sample, a subsample of their employers' names were collected. The employers were contacted and interviewed face-to-face. We are thus able to assess how well employers' views of black women workers correspond to the reports of those workers.

We cover theories in two separate fields—labor markets and cognitive psychology—that motivate our investigation. In the labor market literature, theories of statistical discrimination, status closure, and black feminism argue that employers will base perceptions on group status such as race and gender, shaping decisions about hiring and placing workers. The literature in cognitive psychology suggests that individuals regularly use popular stereotypes to form perceptions and filter information about individuals. We do not test these theories, but describe them to place our research in the context of the debates about black women in the labor market.

We then discuss how we use the employer in-depth interviews to investigate employers' views of black women in the labor force, and we compare the interviews with reports from the household surveys. Finally, we return to the theories to guide our interpretation of the results, and we discuss the relevance of our study to debates in scholarship on labor markets, particularly theories of discrimination.

EMPLOYER PERCEPTIONS AND THEORIES OF THE LABOR MARKET

Early neoclassical economic theory assumed that the decisions employers make about hiring, placement, and wages are based on individual workers' productivity in the context of overall labor supply and demand. Presumably, if gender and race were unrelated to productivity, these characteristics should not influence an employer's evaluation of the suitability of an individual for a particular position.

The New Information Economics recognized that there are costs to obtaining information about worker productivity, and incorporated this insight into economic theory. Economists propose the theory of "statistical discrimination" to explain why employers use gender and race in making decisions about workers in a competitive labor market. Because it is costly and time-consuming to assess the merits of every employee or potential employee individually, employers may decide whom their most desirable workers are by substituting the characteristics they associate with groups for information about individuals (Aigner and Cain 1977; Arrow 1972; Bielby and Baron 1986; Kirschenman and Neckerman 1991; Moss and Tilly 1991). If employers were able to obtain complete information on the skills and productivity of each job applicant, race and gender would presumably cease to be relevant in making hiring and placement decisions.

Generally, the theory of statistical discrimination assumes that employer perceptions of the workforce will be fairly accurate assessments of group differences—either in terms of means or variances (Aigner and Cain 1977; Bielby and Baron 1986; England 1992). Since mistaken assessments of worker capabilities can lead to a misfit between the worker and the job, and thus, low productivity, employers have an incentive to avoid basing decisions on inaccurate perceptions or stereotypes. (We define a "stereotype" as a "conventional and usually oversimplified conception or belief," *American Heritage Dictionary* 1987).[2] However, there is some debate over the extent to which systematic erroneous perception can be considered "statistical discrimination." We include both these "strong" and "weak" versions of the theory of statistical discrimination in our definition (Tomaskovic-Devey 1993).

Sociological theories of social closure argue that the stereotyping of workers on the basis of gender and race by white male employers is not simply a problem of incomplete information, but is an endemic feature of social institutions where one group attempts to maintain control over valued social resources (Ridgeway 1997; Squires 1977; Tomaskovic-Devey 1993). White men in powerful positions benefit from the social status hierarchy grounded in gender and race, and therefore attempt to reproduce that hierarchy (Blumer 1965; Jackman 1993; Lieberson 1980; Reskin and Roos 1990; Ridgeway 1997; Squires 1977; Tomaskovic-Devey 1993). These labor market benefits for white men include relatively higher wages, better chances for promotion, and greater job authority (Federal Glass Ceiling Commission 1995).

A number of theories of social closure can explain the position of African American women in the labor market (see Tomaskovic-Devey 1993 for a review of theories of social closure based on gender and race). Blumer's theory of "race relations" is one of the most well-developed, and it finds substantial empirical support (Bobo 1983, 1988; Bobo and Hutchings 1996; Bobo and Kluegel 1993). According to Blumer (1958; 1965), individuals form identities, allegiances, and normative ideas based on the economic and social position of their group. This resulting sense of "group position," grounded in existing economic and social conditions, generates perceptions of superiority and entitlement to coveted social and economic resources. Individuals who belong to a group that already receives societal benefits (i.e., whites) and who perceive an economic threat, such as competition for jobs from members of another group (i.e., blacks) will develop negative attitudes toward that group. These negative attitudes often crystallize into stereotypes, and then work to further rationalize the dominant groups' sense of superiority and entitlement.

Jackman (1993) argues that, while they legitimate the existing stratification in social institutions, stereotypes need not be negative to undergird status hierarchies. For instance, common stereotypes of women as nurturing and considerate are generally esteemed as feminine traits, but are still used to justify the concentration of women into lower-paying occupations where they may not have to be as "tough" or detached. Thus, employers do not simply invoke stereotypes to exclude individuals from the labor market. Rather, employers rely upon gender and racial stereotypes to sort individuals into different positions. White men are disproportionately allocated into jobs with the greatest rewards, while black women are restricted to positions with low earnings and little authority.

Black feminist theorists critique theories of gender inequality as well as theories of race stratification such as Blumer's for failing to consider how the dynamics of race and gender inequality operate simultaneously and interact (King 1988). Racial stereotypes are "gendered" in important ways, and stereotypic portrayals of women vary by race (Collins 1990; Essed 1991; Guy-Sheftall 1990; Landrine 1985; St. Jean and Feagin 1997). This combination of gender and racial stereotypes puts black women at a unique disadvantage in the labor market. Congruent with the position of social closure theorists, Collins (1990) argues that unequal power in the workplace enables employers to define black women in terms of pervasive stereotypes and use these "controlling images" to reinforce and legitimate the status quo.

Black feminist theory, theories of statistical discrimination, and social closure all suggest that employers have economic incentives to hold attitudes that are shaped by workers' group affiliations, particularly their gender and their race. These theories counter the assumptions inherent in older versions of orthodox economic theory that individual productivity will determine a worker's job and wages (England 1992). However, the theories differ in what they see as the main impetus for the influence of gender and race on employer perceptions of individual workers. Specifically, social closure and black feminist theories assume that the evaluations of black women workers made by white employers will be filtered through perceptual lenses that are biased. This assumption raises the question of how employer descriptions of black women workers compare to the actual labor pool.

THEORIES OF STEREOTYPING

Research in cognitive psychology suggests that the economic incentives for employers to stereotype described by theories of statistical discrimination, social closure, and black feminism may actually reinforce or exacerbate, rather than create, common perceptual processes. Individuals' perceptions are routinely selective and biased (Fiske and Taylor 1991; Hoffman and Hurst 1990). Because the capacity for information processing is limited, individuals focus upon selected aspects of their environment to organize the massive volumes of information they encounter daily. Social groups provide a readily accessible selection criteria that allow individuals to cognitively situate others in relation to "self" (Fiske and Taylor 1991). To further simplify the amount of information processed, individuals tend to make generalizations from their assumptions about social categories to specific individuals within those categories, leading to potential bias (Read 1983). Bias also arises from the tendency to make positive attributions about individuals perceived as "like oneself," and to attribute relatively more negative qualities to individuals perceived as "unlike oneself" (Pettigrew 1979). Once the generalizations and their concomitant evaluative labels are activated, individuals who fit those preconceived notions become more visible, and those who deviate from preconceived notions are considered "exceptions" (Heilman 1995). Through the cognitive processes that maintain our everyday perceptions of the social world, group differences are exaggerated, while diversity among individuals within groups is minimized (Fiske and Taylor 1991).

Stereotyping is thus a common facet of social interaction, as individuals tend to differentiate others in terms of social categories, and filter their perceptions and subsequent interactions on the basis of those categories (Jones 1981; Ridgeway 1997; Tajfel and Turner 1986). Gender is one of the primary social categories that individuals use to classify self and others for any interaction (Ridgeway 1997). Yet even though categorizing by gender is common, it can be disadvantageous to women in the workplace when it dictates what should be expected of them. "If the cultural construction of sex as a simplified, prior categorization system is related to its uses in interaction, then the cultural development of *gender stereotypes* is likely; these describe what behaviors can be expected from a person of a given category" (Ridgeway 1997:220–221. Italics are in the original). Stereotypes facilitate interaction by giving actors a cultural script based on an oversimplified, widely shared schema.[3]

Members of all groups are potentially subject not only to gender stereotyping, but also racial stereotyping, and stereotypes based on their combination of race and gender. Yet because most employers are white men, theories of stereotyping would suggest that employers will perceive workers who are not white men as being unlike themselves, making negative stereotypes of these workers prominent. Since black women are "others" to white men both in gender and race, negative stereotypes about black women may seem particu-larly salient to employers. This also raises the question of how employer per-ceptions compare to the profiles of the local labor force.

Because research on racial stereotypes in the workplace has almost always focused on men, and research on gender stereotypes has largely ignored racial variations, the perceptions and stereotypes specifically about black women in the workplace have not been adequately documented. No study systematically investigates the extent to which employer perceptions reflect the characteristics of labor supply. Yet theories of labor market disadvantage and theories of stereotyping such as Ridgeway's (1997) assume that employers are not objectively reporting patterns in the workforce and the actual prob-lems that they encounter with their employees. Instead, employers view groups of workers through perceptual lenses that contain biases. To illumi-nate these race- and gender-specific biases that white employers have of black women workers, we compare them with the patterns that actually exist in the labor market. Our study is a first step in uncovering the relationship between employer perceptions and the difficulty that black women face in the labor market.

METHODS

Studying employers' perceptions of black women presents a dilemma. Researchers know that white men are hired at greater rates and are paid higher wages than black women, white women, and black men of compara-ble education and training (England, Christopher, and Reid 1999; Smith 1997; Farkas et al. 1997). That is, race and gender—or characteristics associated with race and gender—are clearly influencing the process through which employ-ers sort workers into jobs. Yet, discovering the ways in which employers use gender and race as criteria in evaluating workers is a difficult feat. Even those employers with strong prejudices that lead them to systematically deny jobs to certain groups will be reluctant to openly state views that could be interpreted as "discriminatory."[4] Survey questions such as: "Do you think black workers are less skilled than white workers?" or "Do you prefer to hire white men for the higher-paying jobs?" might therefore yield little variation. Employers will say "no" or refuse to answer these potentially incriminating queries.

Employers are more likely to speak of race in circumspect or general ways that could not be construed as racist, and would not directly implicate them in unfair hiring practices. For instance, in conducting in-depth interviews with employers about a range of employment issues, Kirschenman and Neckerman (1991) found that employers did not often refer to race directly, but instead "coded" race in terms of space, using terms such as "the people from the inner-city" to refer to low-skilled black men.

In our study, we followed Kirschenman and Neckerman's (1991) strategy, using data from in-depth, open-ended, face-to-face interviews with employers. Employers were asked a series of questions about their personnel needs and their ability to find suitable workers to meet those needs. The survey design included questions that encouraged employers to speak about race and gender using their own frameworks, which gave them ample latitude to discuss their views of black women. While employers were asked about "blacks" in the labor force and "women" in the labor force, there were no questions specifically referring to "black women." Thus, when they spontaneously mentioned "black women" as a distinct group, employers were imposing their own race/gender schemas onto their descriptions of the labor force.

Employers discussed black women workers in response to questions such as:

- What skills and qualities do you look for in a worker for [sample job]?
- What are the main problems you face with your workforce, thinking specifically about [sample job]?
- We've talked to quite a few other managers who say there are significant differences between black and white workers, and I'm wondering what you think. Have you seen these differences? (Probe: We do know from other research that blacks and other minorities are doing badly in the labor market. Why do you think that is?) Do you see any differences between men and women? City and suburban workers?

When analyzing the responses to these and other questions in the interview transcripts to identify employer perceptions of black women, we watched for themes to emerge—opening our vision to those themes that resonated with the literature as well as those that were unexpected or new. What we found from this strategy was that many white employers easily characterized workers in terms of race and gender, and that these characterizations were consistent with theories of discrimination and stereotyping.

To analyze the interview transcripts we adopted a coding scheme approximating the open, axial, and selective coding strategies as laid out by Strauss and Corbin (1990). In the initial coding phases we noted and recorded repetitive themes in employers' descriptions of workers, guided by research literature and themes introduced by the employers themselves. We found at this stage that the concepts of "family" and "motherhood" came up often in white employers' discussions of women employees and applicants, but not as often and in different ways in their discussions of men. In further coding phases where we examined these concepts in different contexts than those we had originally seen, we realized that employers were not simply talking about their *men and women* employees differently, but that they also differentiated between *black and white women* employees and applicants. In descriptions of white women, many employers referred to "motherhood," but when speaking about black women, employers invoked the image of "single motherhood." We then reexamined the data to explore the prevalence of this image and search out deviant cases. Selective coding strategies allowed us to focus more specifically on the category of single motherhood and identify the contexts and ways in which it was used.

After the theme of single motherhood emerged, we found questions in the matched household survey of Atlanta residents with which we could compare the employer depictions of black women in the local labor market. The picture that employers painted of the labor market highlighted some dimensions of the local labor force but ignored other dimensions. In order to set the stage for our findings, we describe how we selected our sample of employers and households, and then present our results.

DATA

Our study site is the Atlanta metropolitan area, which encompasses the nine counties defined by the Atlanta Planning Department.[5] Atlanta enjoys the reputation of being the "city that's too busy to hate," where racial tolerance abounds and African Americans are welcomed into a flourishing economy. Many black Americans refer to the city as "the black Mecca," and approximately 24 percent of employed Atlantans are black (Jacobs 1996). Indeed, African Americans do encounter an array of opportunities in Atlanta that are unavailable in many other major cities in the United States. There is a large black middle class in Atlanta, and many blacks hold positions of political power. While it could be argued that whites in Atlanta, a Southern city, hold more negative racial attitudes than whites in the North, the evidence that Southerners are more prejudiced than Northerners is quite mixed (see Kuklinski, Cobb, and Gilens 1996 for a review). In fact, Atlanta's white residents appear to express slightly more tolerance toward blacks compared to whites in Detroit or Boston (Massagli forthcoming).

The data we use were collected as part of "The Multi-city Study of Urban Inequality" (MCSUI).[6] The study focuses on labor market inequality, residential segregation, and racial/ethnic attitudes (Browne et al. 1992). Study design involved three components, including interviews of household respondents, a telephone survey of employers, and face-to-face interviews with employers. We use data from the household survey and the in-depth interviews with employers in the Atlanta metropolitan area.

For the household survey, a representative sample of Atlanta households was drawn and one adult member from each sample household was interviewed face-to-face (Hall 1994).[7] The total N for the household survey was

1,528, which included 651 white respondents, 829 African Americans, and 49 respondents of "other" races.

Our sample of household respondents includes individuals between the ages of 21 and 64 who were in the labor force in 1992 or 1993, which is the labor pool that the employers encountered during the interview period. Since the employer interviews focused on jobs that required no more than a high school degree, we also provide information on men and women with a high school diploma or less education for comparison. The advantage of the full sample is that the numbers are relatively large, and they address the issue that in some cases the employer interviews referred to black workers in general rather than those in the sample job. In almost all cases, the patterns for the full sample and the low skill sample are the same.

The employers for the face-to-face interviews were drawn randomly from a list of employers who had been identified by respondents in the household survey. We thus obtained a matched sample of employers and paid workers with which to make our comparisons.

Two interviewers, a white woman and a white man, conducted structured, in-depth interviews with Atlanta employers in 45 firms from July 1994 to March 1995, obtaining a 75.0 percent completion rate in their final sample. The three persons targeted for interviews in each firm included the president or CEO of each firm, a human resource representative, and the direct supervisor of the job as named by the household respondent. Because some firms did not have each of the three targeted positions, and some potential respondents in each position refused to be interviewed, the average number of interviews per firm is 2.16. Of the 97 interview respondents, 57 percent are white men, 24 percent are white women, 12 percent are black men, 6 percent are black women and 1 percent are Asian women.

Only the responses of the 78 white employers are analyzed in the current analysis, since the relevant theories—social closure, black feminist, and stereotyping—assume that perceptions will differ systematically by race of the perceiver. In addition, there is strong evidence in the stereotyping literature that whites hold different perceptions of blacks than blacks hold of their own racial group.[8]

In our sample of "employers," 27 white respondents (34.6 percent) are presidents, CEOs, or related positions; 22 (28.2 percent) are human resource representatives; and 29 (37.2 percent) are supervisors of the sample job. Twenty-three white respondents (29.5 percent) are women, 55 (70.5 percent) are men.

Originally, the employer study was designed to test theories of industrial restructuring and the changing skill needs of employers for low-skill workers. Therefore, all of the sample jobs in the employer survey are positions considered "low skill," that is, requiring a high school diploma or less education. Common sample jobs include clerical worker, cashier, and sales representative. The average hourly wage for all jobs combined is $7.93, ranging from $4.25 (forklift operator) to $23.08 (salesperson).

WOMEN AS MOTHERS, BLACK WOMEN AS SINGLE MOTHERS

Employers' Perceptions

When employers talk about women workers, they often talk about mothers. Family responsibilities are one of the primary concerns employers have about women workers. Forty-two percent of the white employers mentioned parenthood and/or family when they discussed women, while this topic was only mentioned by seven employers when they talked about men. The topic of family and men, to these white employers, was about wages, since they assumed that men have the monetary responsibility of supporting their families. Only one employer indicated that men's responsibilities for their children could be problematic for them at work.

While white employers often brought up motherhood when they discussed their women employees and applicants, these employers were more specific when they referred to black women. Not only did they invoke the image of motherhood when talking about black women as mothers, they spoke about black women in terms of "single motherhood." Over one-third of white respondents used the single mother image at some point in their interviews when referring to black women, even though no questions specifically mentioning motherhood or single motherhood were included in the interview instrument. White employers spoke about "black women" differently from "women," which signifies that the category of "women" probably often means "white women." This indicates that not only is black women's gender salient to white employers, but their race is salient as well. The *combination* of gender and race creates perceptions of black women that are unique (Essed 1991; King 1988).

White employers did not make associations of single motherhood with any other gender and racial groups with near this frequency. Twelve percent of employers referred to either "white women" or "women" with no clear racial characterization as single mothers. No employers brought up the idea that black men or white men were single parents whose family responsibilities made their work in the paid labor force difficult.

Survey Data

How do these depictions of employed women as "mothers" and employed black women as "single mothers" compare to the actual characteristics of the local labor force? After all, motherhood remains one of the primary social roles for women, and the relatively high rates of single parenthood among black families is an abiding concern among scholars and policy makers.

Responses to the household survey reveal a disjuncture between employer depictions of most female workers—black or white—as "mothers" and the women in Atlanta's workforce. In fact, most women workers in our representative sample of households are not living in families with children under the age of 18. In our study an equal percentage (39%) of black and white women in the labor force had a child in their household at the time of the interview. Among the low-skilled, a slightly higher percentage of black women (41.2%) compared to white women (32.1%) are parents, but this difference is not statistically significant. Although these percentages are not small, they make it clear that not all or even most women in the labor force are mothers, despite employers' stereotypes.

The employed individuals who do have children under 18, maintained a pattern that is consistent with the remarks of employers; black women in our household survey are indeed more likely than white women to be single mothers. Almost 20 percent of our sample of black women in the labor force are single mothers, compared to about 5 percent of white women. The patterns are similar among the low-skilled respondents. Yet, while single motherhood is more common among the African Americans than the whites in our sample, note that the majority of black women in the labor force are *not* single mothers. Theories of statistical discrimination and research on stereotyping would explain these contrasts by arguing that employers attend to the information on black-white differences in family structure, rather than the actual levels of single motherhood for each group. (See original article for table summary of this data.)

MOTHERHOOD AND JOB PERFORMANCE

Employers' Perceptions

Employers' perceptions regarding women as "mothers" is important for understanding labor market stratification by gender, as employers often associated the role of mother with tardiness and absenteeism. One employer at an insurance company that employs a roughly equal number of men and women stated that,

> If I look at our attendance record I would in fact no doubt find that the people who have been documented and who have been terminated for attendance reasons were women, and those people are primarily out not because they're ill, but because kids are ill, or the husband is ill, or the parent. (Man; human resources manager; insurance company)

Another employer, a regional manager of sales representatives, posed a question he would like to ask applicants:

> Now, Ms. Jones, you're going to have somebody who can, y'know, if your children get sick I still need you to come to work here. So do you have somebody who can take care of those people? (Man; regional manager; pest control company)

He laments over how he "used to be able to ask that question as an employer. I can't ask that question anymore. It's against the law." Eighty-nine percent of workers in his firm are men; 100 percent of his sales representatives are men.

For many of the employers, the problems with job performance wrought by the pressures of motherhood were especially keen among *single* mothers. A dominant theme for employers who depicted black women as single mothers was that black women heading families alone are poor workers. However, some employers actually cast black single mothers as reliable workers. Although these images may seem contradictory, employers brought them up in ways that are not mutually exclusive.

According to some white employers, single black mothers have conflicting loyalties, which makes them poor workers. Since single mothers presumably have the greatest family responsibilities of all groups, employers assume that they will be late to work, distracted, and absent more often than others. One supervisor of clerical workers explained how single motherhood can be a difficult issue for her to manage:

> Many of the young ladies that report to me are single mothers. And, it's, . . . when a child is sick and they get a call from day care (and probably rightfully so) you find them extremely distracted. And sometimes even just unable to focus at all on the task at hand. It's very hard—how strict will you be with something like that? . . . The single-mother thing, I think, is huge. (Woman; supervisor; delivery company)

That "the single-mother thing is huge" is a view shared by a good number of employers. In the context of talking about the problems of the inner city, the interviewer asked this plant manager what the single biggest problem with his workers was. He replied, "I'd say single parent moms." When the interviewer asked why, he said simply, "Missing work. . . . When somebody's sick, they've got to go." (Man; plant manager; manufacturing plant)

Another employer made the connection between single motherhood and black women more explicit. This manager of laundry workers, all of whom were black and three-fourths of whom were women, brought up the term "family structure." When asked about his satisfaction with the available labor pool he said he was dissatisfied with applicants because they carried the markings of the inner-city "family structure"—meaning single black women with children. This employer then tied this assumed family structure to black women's job performance. The interviewer asked him, "Does that have an impact, does family structure have an impact on, on their job performance?" He replied, "I think it's everything. I think it's the major thing that we have here that's a problem." Then he generalized a bit further, and explained why single motherhood is so problematic in the paid labor force:

> Well, right off the bat you've got a, a child care problem. With a single mother, there's a, a child care problem. Of course obviously there's a big financial problem. . . . You're gonna have a, experience a higher absenteeism rate and tardiness rate because of the fact that the children obviously are very important and come first and there's a whole set of things that happen where the mother has to be, ah, y'know, off her job for one reason or another. So you have a work force where it's, it's a high rate of absenteeism. (Man; laundry/valet manager; hotel)

This employer, whose workforce is largely made up of black women, perceived the poor job performance of single mothers as his biggest perceived problem because of the absenteeism it creates. When the interviewer asked him if he had the same problems, like absenteeism, from men, he replied,

> Well, I have. The, . . . I realize that for the most part the men are not tied down with, with the kids. I know that. But yes, we have, have the same type of problems as far as basic work habits and coming to work with the men as we do with the ladies but it's for a different set of reasons I believe. [Interviewer: Do you have any idea what their reasoning is?] Well I think Black men has a very low self esteem level. (Man; laundry/valet manager; hotel)

This employer made it very clear that both men and women have absenteeism problems. Yet the problem he perceives to be the greatest is women's absenteeism, because of its association with single motherhood.

Seemingly in disagreement from the employers mentioned above, some white employers indicated that black single mothers were hard workers. This work ethic was not seen as a completely positive characteristic, however. Instead, half of the white employers who assumed that single mothers were desperate for their paychecks remarked that it was this desperation rather than a more noble force that made them work hard. For example, one employer compared his black employees to his white employees in this statement:

> the number of single parents in the inner city obviously is a much higher percentage. Those people absolutely have got to have income. They are supporting a family with one person running the household. From an ethic standpoint though, I would tell you it is more of a need to work than it is a real true work ethic. (Man; vice president for merchandising; grocery store)

This employer gave inner-city (read: black) single mothers credit for working hard, but simultaneously devalued this attribute because of its assumed source.

The same supervisor of laundry workers who was quoted above as saying that black women are the weakest link in his workforce because of their absenteeism problems, gave this somewhat disjointed answer when asked if he noticed any differences between his men and women workers:

> I think the ladies are much more responsible than the men for the most part, because I think they have more responsibilities. They have the burden of raising the family for the most part and the men don't. . . . I think that, um, off the record, that our welfare system promotes a single family, a single-parent family. I think, I think that's wrong. (Man; laundry/valet manager; hotel)

Although this employer was talking about the women who worked at his organization, he brought up their perceived single motherhood in the context of welfare, which would seem to refer to women outside the labor force. Stereotypes like this one surrounding single motherhood are often negative and can be used by white employers even when they do not directly apply to black women employees' situations. Thus, while employers give black women credit for being responsible because of their assumed heavy family load, they are associated with the negativity tied in with the single mother stereotype.

While the stereotype of the hardworking black single mother may arguably prompt employers to hire black women more than other groups (Kirschenman 1991), it seems more likely, based on the imagery employers used, that even the potential advantages in the matriarch stereotype are viewed negatively. It is even possible that employers feel that they can exploit black women, since the employers assume that single mothers are so desperate for their income.

These two images—the black woman as poor worker and the black woman as reliable worker—indicate that white employers do stereotype black women in a racialized and gendered way, and that the stereotype of black women is unique. The black woman is not "lazy" or "scary" like the black man (Kirschenman and Neckerman 1991), nor is she the secondary earner in a nuclear family like the white woman. The black woman, according to white Atlanta employers, is a single mother who is either reliable in a suspicious sort of way, or the most likely person to be late, distracted, and absent because of her childcare concerns.

While employers brought up single motherhood most often in a negative context, a handful of employers did not use this as a pejorative label, and instead remarked upon some of the ways they felt the workplace could change to accommodate the needs of single parents. An additional 6 percent of all white employers specifically noted that their places of employment practice some racist and sexist actions that they felt should not be tolerated.

MOTHERHOOD AND JOB PERFORMANCE

Survey Data

Employers state that their women employees often face conflicts between childcare and job responsibilities. Is this view reflected in the experiences of Atlanta's workforce? Individuals in the household survey sample who had children under the age of 18 in the household during the interview period were asked the following questions regarding potential childcare conflicts: "In the past 12 months, have concerns about childcare ever led you to: be late from work; be absent from work; change your hours?" Respondents could answer "yes" to any or all of these questions. We created an additional variable indicating whether a respondent answered "yes" to at least one of these questions.

Because most of the women in Atlanta's labor force are not raising children, the majority of women in the labor force do not face conflicts due to childcare responsibilities (Tables 10.1 and 10.2). Only 17 percent of black women and 21 percent of white women report that concerns over childcare led them to be late, absent, or to change hours of work at least once over the past year (table 10.1). Among the low-skilled, black women were slightly more likely than white women to face conflicts between job demands and childcare needs, but this difference is not statistically significant. Black women do face childcare conflicts significantly more often than black men, however. Thus, although black women are over three times more likely than white women to be single mothers, black female headship is not necessarily leading to higher levels of work conflicts for black women as measured by our survey questions.

Employers' perceptions of black women as "single mothers" and therefore "poor workers" clearly carry negative connotations. Yet it is possible that employers' perception that single mothers are the group most likely to be late, distracted, or absent from their jobs is an accurate assessment. The paid labor market is not structured around a single parent's needs, or even a married parent's needs. The survey data enable us to address this question, and examine the employers' assumptions that because they are single mothers, black women have the greatest conflicts between work responsibilities and childcare needs.

Even among women with children, black women are not more likely than white women to have conflicts between work and childcare responsibilities. Table 10.2 indicates that employers are correct in assuming that women who have children in their household often face difficulties that can potentially

Table 10.1.   Conflicts between Job and Childcare among Employed Respondents, by Gender and Race

	Women		Men	
	Black	*White*	*Black*	*White*
In the past 12 months, have concerns about childcare ever caused you to . . .				
Total sample:				
Be late for work	9.1%	9.9%	7.1%	6.8%
Be absent from work	13.2%	15.3%	7.7%	8.3%
Change hours	7.2%	10.4%	7.7%	5.9%
Any of the above	17.0%	21.3%	10.7%	11.7%
N:	317	202	195	205
Low-skill sample:				
Be late for work	10.0%	4.9%	2.9%*	5.1%
Be absent from work	15.3%	12.5%	4.9%*	6.4%
Change hours	4.0%	6.2%	5.8%	3.8%
Any of the above	18.7%	14.8%	8.7%*	9.9%
N:	149	81	103	78

Significance tests are comparisons with estimates for African American women: $^*p < .05$. $^{**}p < .01$.

affect job performance. Among women with children below age 18 in our sample, a relatively high percentage of both black and white women reported problems with childcare that led to tardiness, absences, or changes in work hours. Yet it is striking that black women were no more likely than white women to report work conflicts arising from childcare concerns. Forty-three percent of black mothers compared to about 54 percent of white mothers reported that they were late, absent from their job, or changed hours due to childcare concerns (this difference is not statistically significant).

In addition, white men with children are equally as likely as black women with children to face conflicts between childcare responsibilities and work demands. Our data reveal that childcare presents difficulties for a sizable minority of fathers. About 41 percent of white fathers and 31 percent of black fathers reported that concerns with childcare led them to be late, absent, or change hours of work. Yet, employer perceptions of male workers excluded the demands of fatherhood completely. Although a higher proportion of black women than white women in the low-skill sample state that childcare concerns made them late for work, this difference is not statistically significant. Given the lack of overall significance for any of the estimates, the patterns for the total sample and the low-skill sample are the same in table 10.3.

Table 10.2. Job and Childcare Conflicts among Employed Respondents with Children under 18, by Gender and Race of Respondent

	Women		Men	
	Black	*White*	*Black*	*White*
In the past 12 months, have concerns about childcare ever caused you to . . .				
Total sample:				
Be late for work	23.6%	25.0%	20.6%	24.1%
Be absent from work	34.1%	38.8%	22.4%	29.3%
Change hours	18.9%	26.3%	22.4%	20.7%
Any of the above	43.2%	53.8%	30.9%	40.7%
N:	125	80	68	59
Low-skill sample:				
Be late from work	24.6%	15.4%	10.7%	16.0%
Be absent for work	37.7%	38.5%	17.9%	20.0%
Change hours	9.8%	19.2%	21.4%	11.5%
Any of the above	45.2%	46.2%	32.1%	28.0%
N:	61	26	28	25

Significance tests are comparisons with estimates for African American women: *p < .05. **p < .01

Our data suggest that employer perceptions of black women do not reflect the characteristics of Atlanta's labor force in a simple way. Employers invoke images of black women as single mothers who face constant conflicts between their responsibilities at home and at work. While black women are more likely than white women to be the sole family head, the majority of black women in the labor force are not single mothers, even among the low-skilled. Further, the data indicate that employers may be incorrect in assuming that higher rates of single headship among black women lead to more protracted difficulties with balancing home and family.

This second finding is puzzling. After all, it seems reasonable to assume that the absence of a second adult in the household would place additional childcare burdens on single mothers. We suspect that the ability to balance work and childcare is so difficult and precarious for single mothers, that only those who are successfully able to make adequate arrangements are in the labor force (Edin and Harris 1999). Another explanation could rest in the kinship relationships that black women may form with family members and neighbors. Researchers have documented that black women may develop a community of "other mothers" and "fictive kin" to help each other with the burdens associated with balancing work for pay outside the home and work without pay inside the home (Collins 1990; Stack 1974; Troester 1984; hooks 1984). The prevalence of this type of support network may make the presence or absence of a biological father less important in determining the ability of black women to resolve conflicts between childcare needs and the demands of their job.

Finally, it is possible that black women face constraints from childcare responsibilities more times over the course of a year compared to white women. Our survey questions ask only whether the respondent has been late, absent from work, or changed hours "at least once" during the previous 12 months. Thus, among those who answered "yes" to these questions, we do not know how often these difficulties occurred.

DISCUSSION

When asked to discuss their employment needs and the problems that they encounter in meeting their needs, many white employers invoke specific imagery in relation to black women. These white employers describe black women in the workforce as "single mothers," whose difficulties lead them to be either poor workers or desperate yet reliable workers.

Our data from the matched sample of employed Atlanta employers and workers highlight the ways in which employer perceptions are, at best, selective, and at worst, inaccurate. Theories of status closure, stereotyping, and black feminism provide insight toward interpreting our results. As employers use stereotypes to formulate impressions of their labor pool based on gender and race, it appears that they accentuate some patterns while ignoring others. Employers discuss black women workers as "single mothers" who bring the problems related to childcare responsibilities to work, although the majority of black women in the labor force are not single parents. Black women's assumed single motherhood is salient to employers, while employers do not seem to notice men's childcare responsibilities or the potential conflicts with paid work that these responsibilities can create for members of any gender or racial group. Group differences among paid workers are highlighted and exaggerated in employer descriptions.

These perceptions reflect attitudes that are prevalent in dominant U.S. culture. The stereotype of black women as single mothers carries negative connotations for employers. Status closure theory and black feminist theory would argue that the unfavorable image of black single motherhood is used as a trope by employers to keep black women in the lowest-paid positions. Indeed, the "black matriarch" has been a central theme within mainstream white culture since slavery. white clergy and intellectuals writing at the turn-of-the-century characterized black mothers as "immoral" women who caused problems within the black family and were responsible for the "deterioration of the black community" (Guy-Sheftall 1990). In the 1960s, Moynihan (1965) specifically cited the "matriarchal" family as the predominant black family structure and argued that its pathological and emasculating consequences were the source of black men's economic distress. Other recent depictions of the black matriarch include the impoverished single woman whose work ethic is not an adequate model for her children (Collins 1990).

Theories of statistical discrimination would disagree that employer perceptions are motivated by attempts to maintain status hierarchies and regulate access to social and economic rewards on the basis of gender and race. Rather, white employers are just being rational. Given a woman applicant and a man applicant, the odds are higher that the woman rather than the man will be shouldering childcare obligations that could interfere with her job performance. Given a white woman applicant and a black woman applicant, the odds are higher that the black woman rather than the white woman will be a single mother. Note that these "rational" decisions still lead to systematic disadvantage for black women in the labor market, as these women are evaluated in terms of "average" differences between groups rather than individual merit.

Our data do not allow us to differentiate between the motivations behind employer perceptions. What our study does provide is a test of the basic assumptions common to theories of statistical discrimination, social closure, black feminism, and stereotyping: that is, that employers evaluate workers on the basis of gender and race, and that there are discernable patterns to these evaluations. Further, we show that these patterns in employer perceptions do not follow the contours of the labor force in a simple or straightforward manner.

In suggesting that employers may be filtering their perceptions of black women through preexisting stereotypes, we do not mean to downplay the difficulties that black women who *are* single mothers encounter as the sole providers for their families. What our data suggest is that employers are apt to focus upon this status as the "defining characteristic" of black women, regardless of its accuracy. Small differences in the population can become exaggerated when filtered through employers' gendered and racialized perceptions. Those employed black women who are not mothers of young children or who have actually resolved conflicts between childcare and paid work are less visible to employers than black women who fit the common cultural stereotype of the "matriarch." The literature on stereotyping suggests that regardless of her family status, any black woman is susceptible to an employer's negative image of the black woman as single mother.

Regardless of which of the theories best describe the underlying mechanism shaping employer perceptions, all of the theories imply processes of systematic discrimination against black women in the labor market. Our findings are therefore especially pertinent amid the current judicial and legislative trend to do away with policies of affirmative action that attempt to counteract the prejudicial attitudes that factor into hiring, firing, promotion, and wage rate decisions. The MCSUI data indicate that EEO is not enough to guard against employers' negative prejudicial images of specific groups of workers, and that affirmative action policies continue to be necessary, especially for black women. Further, the study suggests that despite employers' formal proclamations of nondiscrimination, the potential for discrimination lurks within the everyday practices of organizational life. Clearly, the next step in the research agenda is to demonstrate the extent to which employer perceptions work to keep black women at the bottom of the labor market reward structure.

NOTES

1. As noted by Berry in the foreward to the volume, *All the Women Are White, All the Blacks Are Men, Some of Us Are Brave* (Hull, Scott, and Smith 1982), the "invisibility" of black women is common throughout social science research, although the pattern is slowly changing.

2. The literature on stereotyping includes a wide range of definitions and debates. We use a definition that does not privilege a particular theory or assume that stereotypes are necessarily negative, consensual, or false (see Miller 1982 for a review of these definitional debates). Instead, we see stereotypes as oversimplified generalizations about a group.

3. The degree to which gender stereotypes are activated depends on the organizational features of the firm, the context of the interaction, and the other salient identities, such as race (Kanter 1977; Ridgeway 1997). In her landmark study, Kanter (1977) argued that stereotyping on the basis of gender (and, by extension, race) will vary with the requirements of the job, access to power and mobility, and the relative size of gender and race groups. Individuals who are "tokens" within an organization will be more likely to be stereotyped by coworkers.

4. In one telephone survey of employers, a pilot study showed that employers were not responsive to direct questions about black-white differences in skills and abilities (Holzer 1996; personal communication).

5. These counties are: Clayton, Cobb, DeKalb, Douglas, Fayette, Fulton, Gwinett, Henry, and Rockdale.

6. This study is also being carried out in Boston, Los Angeles, and Detroit.

7. Specifically, the household sample is a multistage, stratified area-probability design of the nine-county Atlanta Metropolitan Area. Areas (census tracts) with a high proportion of low-income persons and African American residents were oversampled. The total completion rate was 75 percent. See Johnson, Oliver, and Bobo (1994) for a complete description of the study design.

8. We plan to investigate the related question about differences in perceptions of black employees by white and black employers in a subsequent paper. In the current paper, we are concerned with establishing how white employers perceive black women, and comparing these perceptions to our household survey responses.

REFERENCES

Aigner, Dennis J., and Glen C. Cain. 1977. "Statistical Theories of Discrimination in Labor Markets." *Industrial Labor and Relations Review* 30:175–87.

Aldridge, Delores P. 1999. "Black Women in the New World Order: Toward a Fit in the Economic Marketplace." Pp. 357–79 in *Latinas and African-American Women at Work: Race, Gender, and Economic Inequality,* edited by Irene Browne. New York: Russell Sage Foundation.

Arrow, Kenneth. 1972. "Models of Job Discrimination." Pp. 83–102 in *Racial Discrimination in Economic Life*, edited by A. Pascal. Lexington, MA: Lexington Books, Heath.

Bielby, William T., and James N. Baron. 1986. "Men and Women at Work: Sex Segregation and Statistical Discrimination." *American Journal of Sociology* 91(4): 800–37.

Bills, David B. 1992. "A Survey of Employer Surveys: What We Know about Labor Markets from Talking with Bosses." *Research in Social Stratification and Mobility* 11:3–31.

Blumer, Herbert. 1958. "Race Prejudice as a Sense of Group Position." *Pacific Sociological Review* 1:3–7.

Blumer, Herbert. 1965. "Industrialization and Race Relations." Pp. 228–29 in *Industrialization and Race Relations: A Symposium*, edited by G. Hunter. New York: Oxford University Press.

Bobo, Lawrence. 1983. "Whites' Opposition to Busing: Symbolic Racism or Realistic Group Conflict?" *Journal of Personality and Social Psychology* 45:1196–1210.

Bobo, Lawrence. 1988. "Group Conflict, Prejudice, and the Paradox of Contemporary Racial Attitudes." Pp. 85–114 in *Eliminating Racism: Profiles in Controversy*, edited by Phyllis A. Katz and Dalmas A. Taylor. New York: Plenum Press.

Bobo, Lawrence, and Vincent L. Hutchings. 1996. "Perceptions of Racial Group Competition: Extending Blumer's Theory of Groups Position to a Multiracial Social Context." *American Sociological Review* 61:951–72.

Bobo, Lawrence, and James R. Kluegel. 1993. "Opposition to Race-Targeting: Self-Interest, Stratification Ideology, or Racial Attitudes?" *American Sociological Review* 58(4): 443–64.

Browne, Irene, Leann Tigges, and Julie Press. 2001. "Inequality through Labor Markets, Firms, and Families: Race, Ethnicity, and Wages among Women in Three Cities." In *The Multi-City Study of Urban Inequality*, edited by Alice O'Connor, Michael Massagli, and Larry Bobo. New York: Russell Sage Foundation.

Collins, Patricia Hill. 1990. *Black Feminist Thought*. London: Unwin Hyman.

Corcoran, Mary, Colleen M. Heflin, and Belinda L. Reyes. 1999. "The Economic Progress of Mexican and Puerto Rican Women." Pp. 105–38 in *Latinas and African-American Women at Work: Race, Gender, and Economic Inequality*, edited by Irene Browne. New York: Russell Sage Foundation.

Edin, Kathryn, and Kathleen Mullan Harris. 1999. "Getting Off and Staying Off: Race Differences in the Work Route Off Welfare." Pp. 270–301 in *Race, Gender, and Economic Inequality: Latina and African American Women at Work*, edited by Irene Browne. New York: Russell Sage Foundation.

England, Paula. 1992. *Comparable Worth: Theories and Evidence*. New York: Aldine de Gruyter.

England, Paula, Karen Christopher, and Lori L. Reid. 1999. "Gender, Race, Ethnicity, and Wages." Pp. 139–82 in *Latinas and African American Women at Work: Race, Gender, and Economic Inequality*, edited by Irene Browne. New York: Russell Sage Foundation.

Essed, Philomena. 1991. *Understanding Everyday Racism: An Interdisciplinary Theory*. Newbury Park, CA: Sage.

Farkas, Georga, Paula England, Keven Vicknair, and Barbara Stanek Kilbourne. 1997. "Cognitive Skill, Skill Demands of Jobs, and Earnings among Young European American, African American, and Mexican American Workers." *Social Forces* 75(3): 913–40.

Federal Glass Ceiling Commission. 1995. *Good for Business: Making Full Use of the Nation's Human Capital*. Washington, DC: U.S. Government Printing Office.

Fiske, S. T., and S. E. Taylor. 1991. *Social Cognition*. New York: McGraw-Hill.

Granovetter, Mark. 1995. *Getting a Job, 2nd Ed*. Chicago: University of Chicago Press.

Guy-Sheftall, Beverly. 1990. *Daughters of Sorrow: Attitudes woward Black Women, 1880–1920*. Brooklyn, NY: Carlson Publishers.

Heilman, Madeline. 1995. "Sex Stereotypes and Their Effects in the Workplace: What We Know and What We Don't Know." *Journal of Social Behavior and Personality* 10:3–26.

Higginbotham, Elizabeth, and Lynn Weber. 1999. "Perceptions of Workplace Discrimination among Black and White Professional-Managerial Women." Pp. 327–56 in *Latinas and African American Women at Work: Race, Gender, and Economic Inequality*, edited by Irene Browne. New York: Russell Sage Foundation.

Hoffman, Curt, and Nancy Hurst. 1990. "Gender Stereotypes: Perception or Rationalization?" *Journal of Personality and Social Psychology* 58(2): 197–208.

Holzer, Harry. 1996. *What Employers Want*. New York: The Russell Sage Foundation.

Holzer, Harry. 1997. Personal Communication.

hooks, bell. 1984. *Feminist Theory: From Margin to Center*. Boston: South End Press.

Hull, Gloria T., Patricia Bell Scott, and Barbara Smith, editors. 1982. *All the Women Are White, All the Blacks Are Men, But Some of Us Are Brave: Black Women's Studies*. Old Westbury, NY: Feminist Press.

Jackman, Mary. 1993. *The Velvet Glove*. Berkeley: University of California Press.

Jacobs, Jerry. 1996. "Why Gender Composition but Not Racial Composition Reduces Occupational Earnings: An Analysis of Local Labor Markets." *Sociological Focus*. 29(3): 209–30.

Johnson, James H. Jr., Melvin L. Oliver, and Lawrence D. Bobo. 1994. "Understanding the Contours of Deepening Urban Inequality: Theoretical Design of a Multi-city Study." *Urban Geography* 15(1): 77–89.

Jones, Russell. 1981. "Perceiving Other People: Stereotyping as a Process of Social Cognition." Pp. 41–91 in *The Eye of the Beholder: Contemporary Issues in Stereotyping*, edited by Arthur G. Miller. New York Praeger.

Kanter, Rosabeth Moss. 1993. *Men and Women of the Corporation*. New York: Basic Books.

King, Deborah. 1988. "Multiple Jeopardy: The Context of a Black Feminist Ideology." *Signs* 14:42–72.

Kirschenman, Joleen. 1991. "Gender within Race in the Labor Market." Paper presented at the Urban Poverty and Family Life Conference, University of Chicago.

Kirschenman, Joleen, and Kathryn M. Neckerman. 1991. "'We'd Love to Hire Them, But . . .': The Meaning of Race for Employers." Pp. 203–32 in The *Urban Underclass,* edited by Christopher Jencks and Paul E. Peterson. Washington, DC: Brookings.

Kuklinski, James H., Michael D. Cobb, and Martin Gilens. 1996. "Racial Attitudes and the 'New South.'" Working Paper #49. Institute of Government and Public Affairs. University of Illinois.

Landrine, Hope. 1985. "Race * Class Stereotypes of Women." *Sex Roles* 13:65–75.

Lieberson, Stanley. 1980. *A Piece of the Pie.* Berkeley: University of California Press

Miller, Arthur G. 1982. "Historical and Contemporary Perspectives on Stereotyping." Pp. 1–40 in *The Eye of the Beholder: Contemporary Issues in Stereotyping,* edited by Arthur G. Miller. New York: Praeger.

Moss, Philip, and Chris Tilly. 1991. "Why Black Men Are Doing Worse in the Labor Market: A Review of Supply-Side and Demand-Side Explanations." New York: Social Science Research Council.

Moss, Philip, and Chris Tilly. 1995a. "'Soft Skills and Race: An Investigation of Black Men's Employment Problems." Working Paper #80. New York: Russell Sage Foundation.

Moss, Phillip, and Chris Tilly. 1995b. "Raised Hurdles for Black Men: Evidence from Interviews with Employers." Working Paper A#81. New York: Russell Sage Foundation.

Moynihan, Daniel Patrick. 1965. *The Negro Family: The Case for National Action.* Washington, DC: Office of Policy Planning and Research, U.S. Department of Labor.

Neckerman, Kathryn M., and Joleen Kirschenman. 1991. "Hiring Strategies, Racial Bias, and Inner-City Workers." *Social Problems* 38(4): 433–47.

Pettigrew, Thomas F. 1979. "The Ultimate Attribution Error: Extending Allport's Cognitive Analysis of Prejudice." *Personality and Social Psychology Bulletin* 5:461–76.

Raheim, Salome, and Catherine Alter. 1995. *Final Evaluation Report: The Self-Employment Investment Demonstration.* Washington, DC: Corporation for Enterprise Development.

Raheim, Salome, and Donald Yarbrough. 1996. "Evaluating Microenterprise Programs: Issues and Lessons Learned." *Journal of Developmental Entrepreneurship* 1(2): 87–103.

Read, Stephen J. 1983. "Once Is Enough: Causal Reasoning from a Single Instance." *Journal of Personality and Social Psychology* 45:323–34.

Reskin, Barbara, and Patricia A. Roos. 1990. *Job Queues, Gender Queues: Explaining Women's Inroads into Male Occupations.* Philadelphia: Temple University Press.

Ridgeway, Cecilia. 1997. "Interaction and the Conservation of Gender Inequality: Considering Employment." *American Sociological Review* 62:218–35.

Rosenbaum, James E., and Amy Binder. 1997. "Do Employers Really Need More Educated Youth?" *Sociology of Education* 70:68–85.

Servon, Lisa. 1997. "Microenterprise Programs in U.S. Inner-Cities: Economic Development or Social Welfare?" *Economic Development Quarterly* I:166–80.

Servon, Lisa. 1998, "Why Pursue Self-Employment? The Range of Options for Disadvantaged Entrepreneurs." Presented at annual meeting of the Association of Collegiate Schools of Planning, Pasadena, CA, (October).

Servon, Lisa. 1999. *Bootstrap Capital: The Potential and Limits of U.S. Microenterprise Programs*. Washington, DC: Brookings.

Servon, Lisa, and Timothy Bates. 1998. "Microenterprise as an Exit Route from Poverty: Recommendations for Programs and Policy Makers." *Journal of Urban Affairs* 20(4): 419–41.

Severens, C. Alexander, and Amy Kays. 1997. *1996 Directory of U.S. Microenterprise Programs*. Washington DC: Aspen Institute.

Smith, Ryan A. 1997. "Race, Income, and Authority at Work: A Cross-Temporal Analysis of Black and White Men (1972–1994)." *Social Problems* 44(1): 19–37.

Squires, Gregory. 1977. "Education, Jobs, and Inequality: Functional and Conflict Models of Social Stratification in the United States." *Social Problems* 24:436–50.

Stack, Carol D. 1974. *All Our Kin: Strategies for Survival in a Black Community*. New York: Harper & Row.

St. Jean, Yanick, and Joe Feagin. 1997. "Black Women, Sexism, and Racism: Experiencing Double Jeopardy." Pp. 157–80 in *Everyday Sexism in the Third Millennium*, edited by Carol Rambo Ronai, Barbara Zsembik, and Joe R. Feagin. New York: Routledge.

Strauss, Anselm, and Juliet Corbin. 1990. *Basics of Qualitative Research: Grounded Theory Procedures and Techniques*. Newbury Park, CA: Sage.

Struyk R. J., M. A. Turner, and M. Fix. 1991. *Opportunities Diminished: Discrimination in Hiring*. Washington, DC: Urban Institute.

Tajfel, Henri, and Jonathan Turner. 1986. "The Social Identity Theory of Intergroup Behavior." Pp. 7–24 in *Psychology of Intergroup Relations*, edited by Stephen Worchel and William Austen. Chicago: Nelson Hall.

Tomaskovic-Devey, Donald. 1993. *Gender and Racial Inequality at Work: The Sources and Consequences of Job Segregation*. Ithaca, NY: ILR Press.

Troester, Rosalie Riegle. 1984. "Turbulence and Tenderness: Mothers, Daughters, and 'Other mothers' in Paule Marshall's Brown Girl, Brownstones." *Sage: A Scholarly Journal on Black Women* 1:2:13–16.

Part Three: Gendered Racism and Labor Market Experience

**"Racial Differences in Labor Market Outcomes among Men,"
by Harry J. Holzer.**

1. Discuss historic (between 1940 and 1990) differences in the wages of white men and African American men? What accounts for the gains toward parity made by black men during these decades?
2. Describe the specific labor markets trends that have adversely affected black men's employment. What role has education played?
3. Given the extension of equal opportunity and affirmative action laws, is racial discrimination still a factor? Give specific evidence for your answer.
4. How does residential segregation by race affect employment opportunities?
5. What policies does Holzer recommend for improving the economic standing of black men?

"Reversal of Fortune: Explaining the Decline in Black Women's Earnings," by Yvonne D. Newsome and F. Nii-Amoo DoDoo

1. Explain human capital theory. Based on this theory, should black women's employment status be improving? Why?
2. How has the labor market position of black women been affected by economic restructuring by occupational segregation?
3. Have black women benefited from affirmative action policies? Give evidence.
4. How has the occupational status of black women changed between 1980 and 1990?
5. What two factors do Newsome and Dodoo find more responsible for their declining status in the labor market?

"Stereotypes and Realities: Images of Black Women in the Labor Market," by Irene Browne and Ivy Kennelly

1. Explain neoclassical economic theory.
2. In contrast to neoclassical economic theory, feminist theory, the theory of statistical discrimination, and social closure theory offer alternative explanations of the labor market experience. Explain these alternative theories.
3. What do Browne and Kennelly mean when they say that racial stereotypes are "gendered?" Give examples.
4. Why is stereotyping so commonplace, especially in the labor market?
5. What are the dominant perceptions of black women among employers, and how do these perceptions differ from reality?

IV

NEW VALUES, NEW DIRECTIONS

Our final section of the volume contains two chapters describing business ownership as an option for African Americans. Since economic restructuring muted equal opportunity legislation, African American public sector employees experienced considerable job loss and insecurity. State budgetary constraints due in some respects to restructuring led many of these employees to look for new avenues to make a living; so they have turned toward self-employment. Durr, Lyons, and Lichtenstein discuss the skill set development needs of African Americans in an urban context as entrepreneurs. Fairlie and Meyer discuss the convergence of and white rates of self-employment in the twentieth century.

11

Identifying the Unique Needs of the Urban Entrepreneurs

African Americans Skill Set Development

Marlese Durr, Thomas S. Lyons, and Gregg Lichtenstein

1. INTRODUCTION

U.S. cities have had a tendency to develop outward from their centers. This is the result of a variety of economic, socioeconomic, transportation, and land use regulation activities and policies, discussions of which are beyond the scope of this chapter. Suffice it to say that the modern-day result of these activities and policies are what some have called the "doughnut city": a lifeless central core surrounded by an ever-expanding ring of development out into the city's hinterlands.

From the late 1950s to the present, as the postindustrial economy and social changes took hold, large numbers of African Americans became inhabitants of U.S. inner cities (Massey and Denton, 1993). Because of the historical segregation between white and African American communities, each developed businesses intended to serve their own communities. As white businesses moved to suburbia, African American businesses remained within the cities, but were unable to capture white clientele left behind, or those now living in the suburbs, rendering them unable to engage in business expansion or new business formation throughout the city.

Therefore, within the cities, two business communities exist: one white and one black; one expanding and growing in line with the postindustrial economy and one continuing to experience low rates of business creation and survival (Bendick and Egan, 1991). African Americans, many of whom lacked educational experiences associated with economic and enterprise development were excluded from being considered as potential investors/partners in

This chapter was originally published in *Race & Society* 2(2): 75–90, 2001.

community-wide efforts to encourage and sustain economic development (Lyons, Lichtenstein, and Ckhatre 1995; Herring, Horton, and Thomas 1996). The massive disinvestment in the city's urban core has left that part of the metropolitan region a wasteland, (e.g., dilapidated business storefronts, ghost-like business areas) with high rates of unemployment, deteriorating housing stock, high rates of crime, and staggering social problems. The inner-cities became a location in which few if any investors with capital sought to launch new enterprises because the people who live in these areas are those who literally cannot afford to escape, and are typically members of minority groups, particularly African Americans, possessing little economic and political power.

Goldsmith and Randolph (1992) advise that local economic development should emphasize the connections between political empowerment and economic development, and do battle against racial discrimination. This implies that U.S. public policy should not only look at the rehabilitation of cities, but at equal distribution of income to lessen poverty through a reconstructed economy and society, which will compete effectively across communities in the United States and overseas. Acknowledging that vast improvements have taken place in federal budgets for cities, new and expanded programs must be designed and become mandated within social and industrial policies to generate employment and education and provide skills for human growth and welfare which meet all citizens' needs.

Porter (1995) describes inner-cities as places where residents possess a natural advantage for economic development because of their central location, local market demand, integration of regional clusters, and building costs. He maintains that these assets encourage the growth and formation of companies, which can exploit these advantages, and take root in the inner-city. But, this model does not necessarily place African Americans within the calculus of small business development or expansion. As a potential solution to this problem, many such communities have begun to engage in enterprise development. We define enterprise development as the intervention in the free market economic system for the purpose of assisting entrepreneurs in creating and growing successful new businesses. The needs of entrepreneurs are largely determined by the context in which the entrepreneur operates. Entrepreneurs in rural environments face very different obstacles to their success than do their counterparts in urban contexts. In the same vein, urban entrepreneurs have different needs than do suburban entrepreneurs because of deficiencies in African American entrepreneurial skill level and limited network contacts within the community-wide enterprise economy (Lyons, Lichtenstein, and Ckhatre 1995).

Unlike the historical past, where racial discrimination played a major role in business investment and development for African Americans, contemporary constraints to investment within these communities are grounded in economic shifts over the past three decades, which reduced employment opportunities, limiting expansion of, or eliminating, their employment bases or decreasing their revenue bases. In tandem with these structural changes, African Americans receive limited opportunities for entrepreneurial mentoring to shore up skills and experiences associated with operating a business (Lyons, Lichtenstein, and Ckhatre 1995; Herring, Horton, and Thomas 1996).

To meet the needs of this community and enhance its development, a skill set for successful entrepreneurship must be developed. However, before a discussion of the skill needs of urban entrepreneurs can be undertaken, it is necessary to define several basic terms and concepts: entrepreneur, resource, obstacle, need, practices, within the framework of developing enterprises of the inner-city.

Entrepreneur

A person with an idea for a new and innovative product or service who starts an enterprise for the purpose of selling that good or service. This is distinct from a franchisee who starts a business that sells someone else's product or service. While about 65 percent of all enterprises started by entrepreneurs in the United States fail sometime during their first three to five years, only about 2 percent of all franchises do so (Dunn and Bradstreet, 1992). Franchises provide their own support systems for franchisees; a benefit entrepreneurs do not enjoy. It is this latter circumstance that helps to justify enterprise development programs.

Resource

Something either tangible or intangible that an entrepreneur requires to successfully launch and sustain her/his enterprise. Resources may include business ideas, physical commodities, skills or competencies, and a market. (A more complete discussion of resources required by entrepreneurs can be found later in this chapter.)

Obstacle

A barrier that stands between an entrepreneur and a resource that he/she requires.

Need

The point where an entrepreneur requires assistance in overcoming an obstacle to her/his ability to obtain a resource.

Practice

An activity, method, or technique used by an enterprise development program to assist an entrepreneur in meeting her/his need(s).

Program

A strategically assembled set of practices.

2. PRACTICES VS. PROGRAMS

National, state, and local governments have attempted numerous interventions over the years in an effort to revitalize the economies of U.S. urban cores, with only limited success. Those interventions have tended to follow one of two strategies. The first is an effort to attract outside investment. This has generally focused on initiatives to encourage major corporations to locate facilities in the urban core to create jobs for local residents and provide needed services. Examples of this strategy are many and include programs to bring major chain supermarkets into the inner-city or to provide financial incentives to encourage manufacturers to build new plants in these communities. Critics of these programs point out that they tend to "colonize" urban communities by using their low-wage workforce to generate profits that are exported to the corporation in question's home offices.

The second general urban economic development strategy has been an attempt to foster local, community-based economic activity and investment. Its focus is on enterprise development, as opposed to business attraction. This strategy includes a host of programs that are presently in good currency, among them enterprise and empowerment zones, empowerment business incubation programs, micro-lending programs, community banking, cooperatives, minority business development centers, etc. While the jury is still out on the effectiveness of these newer approaches to urban enterprise development, already researchers are finding that these programs suffer from a basic misunderstanding on the ability part of their users and are too often poorly implemented (Bearse, 1998; Servon and Bates, 1998; Reynolds and white, 1999).

The basic problem with these approaches is that they are treated as "generic" programs designed to fit any enterprise development situation. The focus is on structure, or form, as opposed to the function of the program. For example, in business incubation the objective is to create the most effective incubator: one, it is assumed, that will be successful in all contexts and under all circumstances. Thus, the focus is on the optimal size of the incubator facility, the appropriate number and type of client entrepreneurs, the most desirable mix of pre-packaged service offerings, etc. It is believed that this model incubator can then be superimposed on any landscape with positive results; yet, the fact remains that incubation programs in the United States are closing their doors at a rate of one per month (Meeder, 1996). Why? Because different contexts provide different obstacles to entrepreneurship. Rather than permitting structure to dictate function in creating enterprise development programs, enterprise developers should follow the advice of the late architect Louis Sullivan, who maintained that "form must follow function"; the mechanisms used to meet these obstacles must be tailored to the context. This raises the question, "What is the function of enterprise development?" The answer can be simply stated as "helping entrepreneurs to overcome the obstacles they face to obtaining the resources necessary to successfully launch and sustain their new businesses." Once this function is clear, then the form, or structure, the enterprise development program must take is self-revealing. It becomes a strategically assembled set of activities, methods, techniques, etc. (i.e., practices) that are tailored to meet the needs of the specific entrepreneurs it serves. In this way, the enterprise development program is context-specific and, therefore, relevant. Its chances for success are greatly enhanced as well.

An entrepreneur who operates in an urban context in the United States faces obstacles that are unique to that environment and that individual. These obstacles stem from the conditions of poverty, isolation, racism, and crime, among others that exist there. Any enterprise development program that is used in the urban context must employ practices that are specifically designed to mitigate these obstacles: to help the urban entrepreneur hurdle them to get to the resources he/she needs. In essence, then, what is being advocated here is an approach to urban enterprise development that is **"practice-based,"** as opposed to program-based. Successful practices must be viewed as building blocks for developing successful programs. To put it another way, the program becomes the "house that the practices built," permitting the kind of flexibility needed to meet the challenges of enterprise development in the complex and constantly changing global economy and in any given context.

3. THE RESOURCE REQUIREMENTS OF THE URBAN ENTREPRENEUR

The resources required for successful entrepreneurship can be categorized into four major types: (1) a business concept; (2) physical resources; (3) core competencies and skills; and (4) market(s).

Business Concept

A business concept is an innovative idea for a product or service that will meet a need or demand in the market. It is the first resource that any successful entrepreneur requires. It must be a well-considered, viable, salable idea.

Physical resources

Physical resources include a variety of important inputs for the operation and growth of the enterprise. They include necessary supplies/raw materials;

space for offices and/or production activities; plant and equipment, including the technology that goes into the equipment; and money or financial capital.

Core competencies and skills

Core competencies and skills are a set of skills that the entrepreneur and her/his employees must possess in order to successfully operate and develop the enterprise and provide value to its customers. They are intangibles that include management skills (e.g., planning, supervising, organizing, and directing); technical and operational skills (i.e., those skills required to produce the service or product offered by the enterprise); marketing and sales skills (i.e., the ability to identify markets and exploit them); financial skills (e.g., investment); legal skills; administrative skills (e.g., accounting, human resource development); and higher-order skills (e.g., problem-solving and learning).

Market-Related Resources

Market-related resources are those that are associated with the potential and actual customer base of the enterprise. Among these is the product or service. That is, what the business produces and delivers to the customer. Another market-related resource is the customers, themselves. Yet another is the set of distribution channels for promoting, merchandising, and selling the product or service. Finally, the means of transporting, or delivering, the product or service to the customer is a market-related resource.

These are resources that virtually "*all*" entrepreneurs require no matter what business they are in, or the context in which they operate that business. Some of these resources they already possess. Others they must obtain if they hope to be successful. It is, of course, this latter set of resources with which enterprise development programs must be concerned. Because these are resources that all entrepreneurs require to successfully create and sustain their enterprises, this list applies to urban entrepreneurs as well as those operating in other contexts. It is this basic set of resources that each urban entrepreneur must either possess or obtain. It is the set of obstacles to obtaining the resources not already in the entrepreneur's possession that are unique to the urban context.

4. OBSTACLES FACED BY THE URBAN ENTREPRENEUR: THE U.S. EXPERIENCE

Obtaining required resources is not necessarily automatic for entrepreneurs (Lichtenstein and Lyons, 1996). They often face obstacles, or barriers, to their acquisition. There are nine generic obstacles commonly encountered by entrepreneurs. These nine obstacles can be further categorized into two types: resource accessibility obstacles and entrepreneurial capacity obstacles. Resource accessibility obstacles are those that impact resource supply, while entrepreneurial capacity obstacles affect the entrepreneur's own ability to acquire and use required resources. In and of themselves, these obstacles are neither positive nor negative. Their ultimate impact rests with each individual entrepreneur's attitude toward, and response to, them.

5. RESOURCE ACCESSIBILITY OBSTACLES

There are four resource accessibility obstacles: availability, visibility, afford-ability, and transaction barriers. The **availability** obstacle can be character-ized as any situation in which the required resource does not exist, is not available in a usable form, is not available in sufficient quantity, or is not of acceptable quality to the entrepreneur. A lack of availability may also manifest itself in terms of distance, both actual and perceived. The latter refers to situa-tions in which the entrepreneur is isolated by race, by misunderstanding, or by operating in a place that is perceived as dangerous.

A lack of **visibility** refers to an obstacle created when those responsible for providing and managing a resource fail to adequately inform entrepreneurs of its existence. This can take a variety of forms. Some resource providers simply do not publicize information on the availability or quality of the resource. In other instances, information may be disseminated, but not in a form that is readily understandable or accessible to the entrepreneur. In still other cases, the information may be inaccurate. Whether or not an entrepreneur will use certain information often depends on the degree to which he/she trusts the source. Entrepreneurs commonly rely on their own personal channels (i.e., friends, relatives, etc.) for information and advice, regardless of the actual competence of these advisers. Enterprise development assistance providers are, all too often, guilty of contributing to the visibility obstacle.

The authors recently attended a workshop designed to bring minority entrepreneurs and economic development resource providers together. At one point, a resource provider rattled off a lengthy list of services that her agency offered to new enterprises. The entrepreneurs present reacted by ask-ing why they were not aware of the availability of these services. The resource provider, somewhat defensively, replied that her agency did not have the funding to advertise its services.

The **affordability** obstacle comes into play when the resource carries a price that places it beyond the reach of the entrepreneur. While affordability is a relative concept, it is a fact that most new enterprises lack the financial wherewithal to pay for expensive management and technical consultation, among other resources. The fourth resource accessibility obstacle is the **trans-**

action barrier. This is an obstacle that has to do with the exchange that must take place in order to acquire a resource. There are a host of potential transaction barriers. Some have to do with the way in which a resource is provided, and include laborious application or permitting processes, business hours that are inconvenient for the busy schedules of entrepreneurs, and language and cultural barriers to obtaining certain resources. Some come about as a result of the entrepreneur's circumstances, for example day care for working mothers. Still other transaction barriers have to do with the way in which entrepreneurs are perceived by resource providers. These may stem from prejudices based on educational status, level of experience, and race or ethnicity. One other type of transaction barrier is that which is commonly caused by a fragmented approach to providing resources for enterprise development. Many enterprise development programs operate independently of one another, creating incompatible requirements and standards, and confusion on the part of client entrepreneurs.

6. ENTREPRENEURIAL CAPACITY OBSTACLES

The remaining five generic obstacles to entrepreneurship are the entrepreneurial capacity obstacles. Even if resources are available, visible, and affordable, and there are no barriers to the exchange process, the individual entrepreneur may be impaired in her/his ability to use them. This may be due to problems with the entrepreneur's own individual self-awareness, accountability, emotional coping ability, skill, and creativity. These obstacles, without question, are the least understood and most ignored by enterprise development programs. They are psychological and developmental in nature, and they represent the true complexity of entrepreneurship. Millions of dollars have been spent over the years on enterprise development activities, and yet failure rates among new businesses remain high. At least part of the explanation for this situation may lie in the fact that the vast majority of enterprise development resources have been targeted at the resource availability obstacles to entrepreneurship at the expense of the entrepreneurial capacity obstacles.

The **self-awareness** obstacle has to do with the entrepreneur not being aware that he/she has a problem or requires a given resource. This lack of awareness may be a product of incompetence, inexperience, or misperception. Whatever the cause, the enterprise development objective must be to make the entrepreneur aware. Until this is done, he/she cannot begin to understand what service or resource is needed. An example is offered from a business incubation program in the United States. One of the program's clients operates her own housekeeping service. Despite the fact that her client list was steadily growing, her business was not realizing a profit. She was working harder than ever and had nothing to show for it. In frustration, she went to the incubation program manager. He sat down and went through her financial materials with her. They discovered that she was not selling her service at a price that would do more than merely cover her expenses, explaining her lack of profit. The manager helped her adjust her prices appropriately, and her business became a great success. Due to her inexperience, this entrepreneur was unable to recognize the source of her problem. She originally thought she needed more capital; however, if the incubation program had simply made her a loan, it would not have solved her problem or, ultimately, have saved her business.

A lack of **accountability** is another obstacle to entrepreneurship. In this situation, the entrepreneur refuses to take responsibility for resolving her/his problem. This may take the form of simply ignoring the problem, denying its existence, or pointing the finger of blame elsewhere. Final accountability for an enterprise's success or failure lies with the entrepreneur. Successful entrepreneurship involves, among other things, the willingness and ability to take personal responsibility for one's mistakes and to listen to, and learn from, others.

Some entrepreneurs are emotionally unable to cope with one or more of their problems. Typically, this obstacle manifests itself as a difficulty in accepting advice, a fear that someone will steal an idea, an inability to admit a weakness, a lack of confidence, a lack of inspiration or motivation, risk aversion, impatience, arrogance, or worry. Emotions can be channeled either positively or negatively. Recognizing and overcoming emotional obstacles is very difficult. This makes it very tempting for enterprise development programs to avoid or ignore them. Doing so, however, is a mistake that could undermine any and all positive efforts on other fronts.

The **capability** obstacle involves a lack of skill on the part of the entrepreneur in using a given resource or pursuing particular activities. That is, the fact that a resource is available to an entrepreneur does not necessarily mean that he/she is able to use it, or the fact that he/she is aware of a resource requirement does not guarantee that the entrepreneur will know how to go about getting it. A new enterprise may be given a loan as start-up capital, but its proprietor may not know how to properly manage the money. It might also be the case that the entrepreneur is aware that additional financial capital is needed but has no idea where to get it or who to ask for help in finding out.

A lack of **creativity** arises when an entrepreneur is unable to generate a creative solution to a problem at hand. This is not a reference to a lack of business acumen or management skills; it has to do with a limited capacity for innovative problem solving. To address a problem by applying existing solutions is a management activity. To eliminate the problem by reframing the conditions that cause it is creative, and the stuff of true entrepreneurship. It turns "intractable" problems, by conventional wisdom, into those that can be solved. An entrepreneur who is not resourceful and creative is probably not

Obstacles	(1) Availability	(2) Visibility	(3) Affordability	(4) Transaction Barriers	(5) Self-Awareness	(6) Accountability	(7) Emotions	(8) Capability	(9) Creativity
Required Resources									
I. Business Concept									
II. Physical Resources Supplies/Raw Materials Space Equipment/Plant Money/Capital									
III. Core Competencies/Skills Managerial/Technical/Operational Marketing/Sales Financial Legal Administrative Second-Order Skills									
IV. Market Product or Service Customers Distribution Channels Transportation									

Source: Gregg A. Lichtenstein and Thomas S. Lyons. 1996. Incubating New Enterprises: A Guide to Successful Practice. Washington DC : Aspen Institute

Figure 11.1.   Diagnosing Entrepreneurial Needs

an entrepreneur at all. A creative approach to problem-solving can be learned. Enterprise development programs must understand that helping entrepreneurs is about more than merely giving them the resources they lack. It is about assisting them to develop new solutions to the problems they face.

Our discussion has centered on obstacles to entrepreneurship that are general in nature and they apply to entrepreneurial activities that take place in any context. But, in reality, specific obstacles faced by entrepreneurs are highly context-specific, especifically for African Americans, we will now shift to those obstacles presented by the urban context, as defined, in the United States.

URBAN ENTREPRENEURSHIP BARRIERS

We are currently engaged in research that examines, among other things, the obstacles faced by African American entrepreneurs operating in inner-city environments. The following discussion stems from preliminary results of that research. The managers of 27 of 41 empowerment business incubation programs, located in cities throughout the United States, were interviewed regarding the unique obstacles that their client entrepreneurs face. The comments of these incubation program managers were organized into a set of "obstacle scenarios": generalized descriptions of eight barriers to urban entrepreneurship. Then, each scenario was analyzed and categorized according to the typology of resource requirements and obstacles described above. Finally, a few strategically applied practices for overcoming identified obstacles are presented for each scenario.

Lack of Access to Capital

This was the most frequently cited obstacle to minority entrepreneurship in inner-city communities. While responding incubation program managers acknowledged that this is a barrier faced by most entrepreneurs, regardless of race or gender, it is especially acute for minority entrepreneurs. Banks are highly reluctant to make loans to this latter group. Chief among the reasons given for turning down minority business loan applicants are lack of collateral and a bad credit history. Furthermore, inner-city entrepreneurs tend to lack sufficient personal savings, family backing, or friends who are capable of helping them financially—all of which are resources commonly used by majority entrepreneurs.

Obviously the required resource in question in this scenario is a physical resource: money or capital. Initially, the principal obstacle would appear to be a lack of availability: for urban minority entrepreneurs' capital is nonexistent or not available in sufficient quantity. However, this may actually involve an affordability barrier: the capital is unaffordable due to collateral requirements or interest charges. A transaction barrier may be involved as well: the entrepreneur lacks the credit history to get access to the capital, even if he/she has the collateral and can pay the interest. Furthermore, the entrepreneur could be facing a capability barrier in that he/she may not know where to get help with a money problem. Finally, the real problem could be a creativity obstacle. The urban entrepreneur may lack the entrepreneurial ability to reframe the problem and create a nontraditional solution to the problem of insufficient capital.

The survey identified several practices that responding incubation programs have adopted to address these obstacles. Three programs have established an incubator-based micro-loan program, available exclusively to clients. Another program has linked itself to the local economic development corporation which makes loans to clients at low interest rates, with minimal collateral requirements. Once clients have successfully obtained and paid off these loans, their probability of obtaining a bank loan increases substantially.

A third responding incubation program refers its clients to a city-sponsored business loan program that encourages applications from minority entrepreneurs. Still another respondent has created what it calls a Lenders Partnership Program, in which the incubator partners with local banks to provide loans to incubator clients up to $100,000 for five years at an interest rate of prime +3 percent. In several instances, programs try to improve clients' chances of getting a bank loan by evaluating their loan applications and business plans before they are submitted and offering advice for the applications' and plans' improvement.

Lack of Business and Technical Skills

The second most frequently identified obstacle to entrepreneurship in the inner-city was the fact that would-be entrepreneurs are highly deficient in the business and technical skills necessary for innovation, business formation, and business development over the long term. Some managers attribute the fact that this problem is more acute in minority communities than among the general populace to "prior treatment and customs," as one manager put it, that have set minority would-be entrepreneurs behind. Other managers suggest that the problem that enterprise development programs must attempt to solve is that most minority entrepreneurs really do not know where to go for help in developing the skills they need or obtaining appropriate consultation. While the list of needed skills cited by responding incubation program managers covers a wide variety of competencies, a lack of skills in decision making, business planning, and general business acumen were featured.

This general barrier suggests availability, visibility, affordability, transaction, and capability barriers to obtaining core competencies/skills. In particular, the assertion that minority entrepreneurs do not know where to go to get these skills suggests that visibility and capability obstacles may be particularly onerous. Comments by incubation program managers also imply that isolation, race, and other factors may stand as barriers to making the transaction for obtaining business and technical skills. This suggests an emotional coping element as well.

Most of the minority-focused incubation programs contacted offer business and technical assistance and consultation to their clients at the incubator facility. Much of this assistance is provided free of charge. Some is provided by incubation program staff, through training sessions and one-on-one counseling, but other forms of assistance are provided by outside experts/consultants who are brought on site. One program utilizes corporate sponsors to cover the cost of offering the training. Several programs hold regular meetings, seminars, workshops, training programs, etc. where incubator clients are addressed by outside experts. In one case, the incubation program takes advantage of its proximity to a major state university by partnering with the latter to offer an eight-week course on entrepreneurial development.

Difficulty in Establishing Markets

Minority entrepreneurs have difficulty finding markets for their goods or services, especially outside of their own communities. In some cases, they do not have the necessary contacts. In most cases, however, it is difficult for them to become suppliers to majority-owned corporations because they are often not taken seriously as business people. This latter issue of a lack of serious recognition by majority-owned firms, and by society in general, was a recurring observation by the minority-focused incubation program managers interviewed.

The required resource described in this scenario is a market, particularly the establishment of customers and distribution channels. The key obstacle to markets might be perceived as availability: the markets are out there, but they are not available in sufficient quantity to minority entrepreneurs. This might also be viewed as a transaction barrier in that the markets exist, but minority status prevents the entrepreneur from being taken seriously as a supplier to that market. The frustration engendered by this situation may yield emotional obstacles in the form of low self-esteem, lack of motivation, and negatively channeled anger. It could also result in a lack of accountability.

One incubation program in the survey group has addressed this obstacle by establishing a quarterly roundtable session involving clients and prospective buyers. Another program links its clients to the city's Minority Enterprise, Inc. program which arranges contacts with prospective buyers. Yet another approach is the creation of a network of firms that have successfully graduated from the incubation program and are operating on their own. The graduates are then linked to current tenant entrepreneurs, providing valuable market contacts later. Finally, one minority-focused incubation program offers customized marketing services to its client firms.

Personal Problems

Because inner-city minority entrepreneurs are often low-income and are many times caught up in the social problems that are common to their communities, they are inclined to have more personal problems than do other entrepreneurs. This tends to interfere with their ability to successfully start and sustain a business. These problems may range from poor health to single parents with the need for child care assistance. The principal resource involved here is core competencies/skills: those skills an entrepreneur needs to successfully operate a business. Certainly, personal problems could present emotional barriers to obtaining these competencies. Personal problems may also yield a lack of self-awareness and accountability.

The survey of minority-focused incubation programs identified three interesting practices aimed at obstacles. In one case, the incubator manager is a certified counselor, who provides personal advice and support to its clients. In another, the incubation program sponsors a weekly radio talk show, of which the program manager is the host, which interviews various experts on entrepreneurship and business development. The show is designed to offer hope and encouragement to entrepreneurs by providing them with ideas for solving their business problems. It is also hoped that the radio show will encourage those individuals who might otherwise feel they lack what it takes to be a successful entrepreneur to consider starting a business.

In a very different vein, one minority-focused incubation program manager addresses this obstacle through a "tough love" approach. He believes in creating an environment that avoids the perpetuation of dependency. He offers, as he puts it, no "freebies," no subsidies, and accepts no excuses.

Lack of Role Models

Minority entrepreneurs must often break new ground on their own, with few if any role models or mentors. This appears to be particularly true for African American entrepreneurs. As one responding incubator manager noted, this obstacle can also be linked to the lack of business and technical skills obstacle (described above). This circumstance only serves to lessen the probability of success.

The resource to be accessed in this scenario is core competencies/skills. The obstacle to accessing these skills is often the lack of availability of minority role models for showing the way: they simply do not exist in an adequate quantity. Despite this, there are instances in which role models or mentors do exist but entrepreneurs are unaware of them, or vice versa. This constitutes a visibility obstacle that requires a third party to intervene and link the two parties in some way.

Increasingly, only a few of the respondent incubation programs directly address this obstacle. This may suggest a deficiency in minority business incubation that needs to be addressed. Only further research can verify this potential problem. Both programs that address this obstacle do so through the practice of providing mentoring programs to incubation clients. In some cases, the program manager serves as a mentor. In others, volunteers from the business community play this role, holding monthly meetings with their protégés. Finally, one program requires its clients to join local business organizations.

Reluctance to Approach Established Sources of Assistance

Some responding incubation program managers asserted that many minority entrepreneurs are not comfortable with approaching business assistance sources (e.g., banks, government agencies, etc.) in the city. In some cases, this is due to past experiences with these sources. As one program manager put it, "they get bounced back and forth, unable to find the right person to deal with in the agency." In other cases, the entrepreneurs feel that they lack the necessary credibility to get the help they need.

The required resources encompassed by this scenario include physical, core competencies/skills, and market. The sources of assistance in question may supply some or all of these. The reasons for the reluctance described above suggest several obstacles. The reluctance, itself, stands as a transaction barrier to obtaining resources and may also stem from a variety of transaction barriers including prejudices relating to race, educational status, and level of experience. Emotions may also be involved. Feelings of a lack of credibility suggest a self-awareness obstacle.

The incubation programs in the survey assist their clients in overcoming these obstacles in several ways. Most of the respondents stated that they offer referral services that help to put the client directly in touch with the party that can best assist them. The programs surveyed also offer certain in-house services that allow the client to obtain assistance without leaving the incubation facility and at low or no cost. One incubation program manager stated that they will accompany clients to assistance providers, if requested. One program has started what it calls its Small Business Clinic. This program brings assistance providers to the clients, at no cost to the latter. It allows for one-on-one interaction between client and provider as well. Still another incubation program has established an elaborate collaboration with federal, state, and local partners to create, among other things, an entrepreneurship development center for its minority clients.

Isolation

The relative isolation from the rest of the metropolitan area in which inner-city minority residents tend to live is said to act as a barrier to entrepreneurship as well. This condition serves to make it more difficult to stay abreast of new developments, access resources, and develop markets, among other things. The isolation scenario embodies business concept, physical location, core competencies/skills, and market resources. Isolation can yield a lack of visibility and capability regarding new ideas, technologies, sources of information, etc. It can also make resources less available and less affordable. Finally, isolation, itself, is a transaction barrier to the acquisition of resources in the four categories.

Those practices described above that involve networking minority clients with the wider community can serve to overcome these obstacles. In addition, one incubation program has developed an information clearinghouse, designed to heighten the awareness of its clients by giving them access to information on resources available through the larger community. Another program encourages its tenant entrepreneurs to form business partnerships among themselves to strengthen their ability to compete for resources in the larger community.

Forced to be Entrepreneurial

The limited skills of many inner-city minority employees make them vulnerable to cyclical fluctuations in hiring and to the down-sizing that has characterized the globalization of the economy. They are often the "last hired and first fired," as one incubation program manager put it. Many find that their only option is to start a business; however, they are not necessarily equipped to do so, nor are they necessarily so inclined. At this point, many other obstacle scenarios described above come to bear.

This predicament creates self-awareness, emotional coping, capability, and creativity obstacles to obtaining resources in all four resource categories. It places highly inexperienced individuals into a difficult situation. They may not know where to turn for help, or be able to effectively use the assistance they receive. Thinking entrepreneurially will, most likely, require a complete reorientation for them. They present the ultimate challenge to enterprise development programs. Virtually all the practices sketched out above can provide some help to minority entrepreneurs facing this obstacle; however, it will take a combination of such practices assembled strategically and applied synergistically to successfully mitigate this barrier. Figure 11.2 provides a summary of the diagnosis and treatment practices discussed in detail above.

Conclusion: Urban Enterprise Development as Entrepreneurial Skill-Building

Urban entrepreneurs face a unique and difficult set of obstacles to obtaining the resources they need to be successful. Traditional enterprise development strategies either ignore these obstacles altogether or attempt to treat them with prepackaged solutions that address, at best, only some portion of the true problem. In medical terms, a prescription is made without a true diagnosis.

By looking at urban entrepreneurial needs in terms of required resources and obstacles to obtaining those resources, a complete diagnosis of the problem can be made. Then, the appropriate remedy can be prescribed. The matrix in figure 11.1 is a graphic representation of the relationship between resource needs and obstacles. It serves as a diagnostic tool that enterprise

BARRIERS	RESOURCES	OBSTACLES	PRACTICES
1. Lack of Access to Capital	Money or Financial Capital	Ability to obtain capital	• Incubator-based Micro-loan Programs • Network with city Loan Programs • Partnerships with local banks
2. Business and Technical Skills	Securing Business and Technical Assistance in decision making, business planning, debt collection, and general business acumen	Business isolation, race, emotional coping elements	• Free-in-house Training • Corporate Sponsorship • University Partnerships
3. Establishing Markets	Establishment of customers and distribution channels	Markets are not available to minority entrepreneurs, lack of motivation, negatively channeled anger	• Quarterly Roundtable with prospective clients and buyers • Marketing Networks • Customized Marketing Service
4. Personal Problems	Skills to successfully start and sustain a small business	Personal problems may present emotional barriers to obtaining these skills, may also yield a lack of self-awareness	• Managers as Certified Counselors • A weekly radio talk show • Tough Love
5. Lack of Role Models	Access to minority role models who can show the way, a person to link these parties	Deficiency in minority incubation programs, programs do not address this obstacle	• Mentoring Programs
6. Reluctance to approach Established Sources	Capital support from banks, government agencies, etc.	They get bounced back and forth unable to find the right persons to deal with in the agency, feeling they lack the necessary credibility to obtain serious help	• Direct Referral • In-house Services • Accompany client to Service Providers
7. Isolation	Staying abreast of new developments, access to resources, development of markets	Lack of awareness about new ideas and technologies, sources of information, etc.	• Networking • Information Clearinghouse Partnerships
8. Forced to be Entrepreneurial	Start their own business	Inexperienced persons in business situations, thinking entrepreneurial requires a new orientation	• All of the Above practices

Figure 11.2. Summary of the Diagnostic and Treatment of Identified Barriers to Inner-City Entrepreneurship

development practitioners can use to better understand how to treat the problems of local entrepreneurs. Its flexibility permits the practitioner to apply it to any context, much as was done above in analyzing the obstacles faced by those entrepreneurs that operate in urban, inner-city environments. Once the problem(s) has been identified, solutions that address themselves specifically to that problem can be sought, or developed. For the purposes of this discussion, these individual solutions are being called "practices." They are the component activities of a successful urban enterprise development program. When one looks at these problems, or obstacles, more closely it becomes apparent that overcoming them requires entrepreneurial skill that must be mastered. These skills are of four types (Gerber, 1995; Lyons, Lichtenstein, and Ckharte 1995):

(1) **Technical Skills**—which have to do with the entrepreneur's core business (e.g., computer software design skills, carpentry skills, cooking or baking skills, and so forth);

(2) **Managerial Skills**—which focus on the entrepreneur's learned abilities relative to organizing and operating a business;

(3) **Entrepreneurial Skills**—which relates to the entrepreneur's ability to develop innovative solutions to problems; and

(4) **Personal Maturity Skills**—which are required to meet the obstacles on the right-hand.

The practice of urban enterprise development service providers if strategically applied can help African American entrepreneurs to develop these skill sets and enhance their opportunity for business success. In this way, enterprise development becomes a tool not only for economic enhancement, but for these entrepreneurs' individual and community empowerment as well.

REFERENCES

Bearse, P. A. 1998. "A Question of Evaluation: NBIA's Impact Assessment of Business Incubators." *Economic Development Quarterly* 12(4): 322–54.

Bates, T. 1995. "Why Do Minority Business Development Programs Generate So Little Minority Business Development?" *Economic Development Quarterly* 9(1): 3–14.

Bendick Jr., M., and M. L. Egan. 1991. *Business Development in the Inner-City: Enterprise with Community Links*. New York: Community Development Research Center, Graduate School of Management and Urban Policy, New School for Social Research.

Blair, J. P., and R. Premus. 1992. "Location Theory." In R. D. Bingham and R. Mier, *Theories of Local Economic Development: Perspectives from across the Disciplines*. Newbury Park, CA: Sage.

Butler, J. S. 1991. *Entrepreneurship and Self-Help among Black Americans*. Albany: State University of New York Press.

Dunn and Bradstreet Business Report. 1992.

Gerber, M. E. 1995. *The E-myth Revisited.* New York: Harper Business.

Goldsmith, W. W., and L. A. Randolph, L. A. 1992. "Ghetto economic development." In R. D. Bingham and R. Mier, *Theories of Local Economic Development: Perspectives from across the Disciplines.*

Herring, C., H. D. Horton, and M. Thomas. 1996. "Inner-city Entrepreneurship: Is Self-Employment a Cure for Poverty?" Unpublished paper.

Horton, H. D. 1988. "Occupational Differentiation and Black Entrepreneurship: A Sociodemographic Analysis." *National Journal of Sociology* 2:187–202.

Lichtenstein, G. A., and T. S. Lyons. 1996. *Incubating New Enterprises: A guide to Successful Practice.* Washington, DC: Aspen Institute.

Logan, J. R., and H. Molotch. 1987. *Urban Fortunes: the Political Economy of Place.* Berkeley: University of California Press.

Lyons, T. S., G. A. Lichtenstein, and C. Sumedha. 1996. "Identifying Obstacles to Minority Entrepreneurship and Creating Enterprise Development to Overcome Them." ACSP-AESOP Joint International Conference, Toronto, Ontario, Canada, July.

Lyons, T. S., G. A. Lichtenstein, and S. Ckhatre. 1995. "Surmounting Barriers to Inner-City Minority Entrepreneurship: The Role of Business Incubation." Conference of the Association of Collegiate Schools of Planning, Detroit, MI, October 19–22.

Lyons, T. S. 1990. *Birthing Economic Development: How Effective Are Michigan's Business Incubators?* Athens, OH: National Business Incubation Association.

Massey, D. S., and N. A. Denton. 1993. *American Apartheid: The Segregation and Making of the Underclass.* Cambridge, MA: Harvard University Press.

Meeder, R. 1996. Presentation to SPEDD Inc., Louisville, Kentucky.

Petersen, P. E. 1981. *City Limits.* Chicago: University of Chicago Press.

Porter, M. E. 1995. "The Competitive Advantage of the Inner-City." *Harvard Business Review,* May–June 56–71.

Reynolds, P. D., and S. B. White. 1997. *The Entrepreneurial Process: Economic Growth, Men, Women, and Minorities.* Westport: Quorum Books.

Servon, L. J., and T. D. Bates. 1998. "Microenterprise as an Exit Route from Poverty: Recommendations for Program and Policy Makers." *Urban Affairs Quarterly* 20, (1): 419–41.

Sharp, E. B., and M. G. Bath. 1992. "Citizenship and Economic Development." In R. D. Bingham and R. Mier, *Theories of Local Economic Development: Perspectives from across the Disciplines.* Newbury Park, CA: Sage.

Stone, C. N. 1984. "City Politics and Economic Development: The Political Economy Perspective." *Journal of Politics* 46(1): 286–99.

12

Trends in Self-Employment among White and Black Men during the Twentieth Century

Robert W. Fairlie and Bruce D. Meyer

INTRODUCTION

The decline in self-employment during this century is one of the major historical trends in the U.S. labor market. The fraction of white male workers that was self-employed fell from one in six in 1910 to one in ten in 1970. It is also striking that this trend stopped and reversed itself between 1970 and 1990 as the self-employment rate rose from 10.0 percent to 11.4 percent. Given the magnitude of these changes in self-employment, surprisingly very little research has documented the changes and identified their causes. Trends in black self-employment have been studied even less, despite much recent interest in the lack of black-owned businesses and frequent conjectures about historical levels of self-employment and their causes. We use census microdata covering most of the twentieth century to document the trends in self-employment among both white and black men and to explore some proposed explanations.

An examination of long-term trends in self-employment is important for several reasons. First, it has been argued that small businesses create a large share of new jobs in the economy, are an important source of innovation, and have an important effect on political decisions in the United States (Birch 1979; Davis, Haltiwanger, and Schuh 1996; Glazer and Moynihan 1970; Brown, Hamilton, and Medoff 1990). Second, many academics and policy makers view self-employment as a route out of poverty and as an alternative to unemployment or potential discrimination in the labor market (Glazer and

This chapter was originally published in the *Journal of Human Resources* 34(4): 643–69. The current version is slightly condensed.

Moynihan 1970; Light 1972, 1979; Sowell 1981; Moore 1983; U.S. Department of Labor 1992). Third, the institutional environment in which the self-employed work differs in important ways from that of wage/salary workers. The self-employed are not subject to the usual labor contracts and their consequent incentives, and they either do not receive, or purchase for themselves, fringe benefits provided by employers, such as health insurance and pensions. Past research has argued that the self-employed have a different return to education, will have a different age-earnings profile, and have more variability in hours worked than wage/salary workers (Wolpin 1977; Lazear and Moore 1984; Rettenmaier 1996). Finally, the self-employed are often singled out in the formation of public policy. They face different income tax treatment and are frequently excluded from social insurance programs.

Past studies have examined trends in white or total self-employment during various periods of the twentieth century; these studies, however, have generally been limited by their reliance on published aggregate data and their use of a short time period (Phillips 1962; Becker 1984; Blau 1987; Aronson 1991). Several social scientists near the middle of this century, documented the decline in self-employment over the first half of the century and predicted that it would continue to decline (Weber 1958; Mills 1951; Phillips 1962). The clearest statement comes from Phillips (1962, p. 1) who reports that "the proportion of self-employed persons in the American labor force has been declining for many decades. This trend will no doubt persist in the future." A few studies have focused on the recent rise in self-employment; only one of these studies, however, includes an empirical analysis of its potential causes. Blau (1987) finds that changes in technology, industrial structure, tax rates, and social security retirement benefits contributed to the rise in self-employment from 1973 to 1982. We test some of these explanations using census microdata covering a longer time period.

Although several recent studies have documented and analyzed the causes of the low rate of self-employment among blacks in the United States, none of these studies have examined the trend over the twentieth century (Bates 1987; Borjas and Bronars 1989; Meyer 1990; Fairlie 1999; Fairlie and Meyer 1996). In the past few years, many news articles and editorials have referred to estimates from the Survey of Minority-Owned Business Enterprise (SMOBE) that show a large increase in the number of black-owned businesses over the last 20 years.[1] On the contrary, estimates that we present in this chapter indicate that the black self-employment rate has not appreciably changed relative to the white self-employment rate over the last 20 years or, for that matter, over the last 80 years. The issue of convergence in racial self-employment rates is of special interest because many early researchers emphasized the role that lack of traditions and past inexperience in business played in creating low rates of business ownership among blacks (DuBois 1899; Myrdal 1944; Cayton and Drake 1946; Frazier 1957).

Using census microdata, we first examine potential causes of the long-term decline in the white male self-employment rate from 1910 to 1970 and the reversal of this trend after 1970. We also briefly examine recent Current Population Survey (CPS) data. Our main findings are as follows:

1. We find little support for a few recently proposed explanations for the rise in self-employment.
   (a) Self-employment has risen sharply even for those groups unlikely to be affected by social security retirement incentives.
   (b) Changes in immigration levels or immigrant self-employment rates cannot explain a significant portion of the recent upturn in white self-employment.
2. The long-term decline in the self-employment rate reflects declining rates within nearly all industries. Technological change favoring capital-intensive, large-scale production may be responsible for this trend. The long-term decline, however, was weakened somewhat by a shift in total employment toward high self-employment industries.
3. The recent increase in the self-employment rate was caused by an end to the overall decline in self-employment within industries and the continuing shift of overall employment from low self-employment industries, such as manufacturing, toward high self-employment industries, such as construction, professional, and business and repair services. We also find offsetting increases and decreases in self-employment across a few industries. These findings are consistent with changes in consumer demand, increased global competition, and changes in technology driving the recent upturn in self-employment.

We also explore the factors contributing to the trend in the black male self-employment rate. We focus on the trend in black self-employment relative to white self-employment. The main findings from this analysis are as follows:

1. The self-employment rate of black men relative to white men remained roughly constant from 1910 to 1990 (at a level of approximately one-third the white rate).
2. The large gap between the black and the white self-employment rates is due to the lower self-employment rates of blacks in all industries and not due to the concentration of blacks in low self-employment rate industries.
3. We find that major demographic changes that occurred during the twentieth century, such as the Great Black Migration and the racial convergence in educational attainment, did not have large effects on the racial self-employment rate gap.
4. Evidence from simulations using a simple intergenerational model of self-employment suggests that, if not for continuing factors reducing

black self-employment, racial convergence in self-employment rates would occur within a few generations.

II. DATA

This study uses individual data from eight decennial censuses of population: 1910, 1920, and 1940 through 1990. A public-use sample is not currently available for the 1930 census. We use random samples of the population for each year to obtain approximately 40,000 individuals of each race if more than that many are available. Further details and the exact samples used are described in Fairlie and Meyer (1999). The CPS data that we briefly examine at the end of the chapter are described in Section V.

The final sample that we use for each of the census years only includes respondents who meet several restrictions. First, we only include men in this analysis because the study of female self-employment is complicated by overall changes in labor force participation, education, and the fertility of women that are beyond the scope of this chapter. Second, consistent with previous studies of self-employment, we exclude individuals who work in agriculture. Third, we restrict our samples to include individuals who are between the ages of 16 and 64 (unless noted otherwise) and who report working at least 15 hours during the week prior to the interview and at least 14 weeks during the year prior to the interview. In 1910 and 1920, however, we do not impose the hours and weeks worked restrictions because these variables are not available.

We distinguish between self-employment and wage/salary work based on the individual's response to the class of worker question found on each of the included censuses. The self-employed in our study are those individuals who report primarily being an employer, working on their own account, or being self-employed with their own incorporated or no incorporated business. For example, in 1990 the relevant choices on the census questionnaire were "SELF-EMPLOYED in own NOT INCORPORATED business, professional practice, or farm" and "SELF-EMPLOYED in own INCORPORATED business, professional practice, or farm" (U.S. Bureau of the Census 1993: E-15).

III. RESULTS FOR WHITE MEN

In this section, we document the patterns and analyze the causes of changes in self-employment rates for white men over the twentieth century. The white male self-employment rate decreased steadily from its highest point in 1910 (16.0 percent) to its lowest point in 1970 (10.0 percent). In 1970, the downward trend in the self-employment rate ended and began a climb to 11.4 percent in 1990. If we limit the sample to full-time, full-year workers, we find a nearly identical pattern. The similar patterns rule out the possibility that either underemployment or disguised unemployment is the driving force behind the major changes in self-employment during the twentieth century (Lebergott 1964; Carter and Sutch 1994).

We now explore explanations for the pattern of white self-employment over this century with an emphasis on hypotheses regarding the recent upturn. These explanations have been proposed in past studies or are suggested by research on the determinants of self-employment. (See original article for table summary of data.)

A. Older Workers and Population Aging

Quinn (1980) and Fuchs (1982) find that self-employment is much more common among older workers. They argue that high rates of self-employment among older workers are due to the large number of wage/salary workers who switch to self-employment near the end of their careers as a form of partial retirement and the lower likelihood of self-employed workers fully retiring near the end of their careers. These two studies also point out that higher returns to retirement may induce higher rates of self-employment among the elderly population because the self-employed can partially retire and still receive benefits. These observations suggest that changing self-employment rates and employment shares for the elderly could be a substantial part of aggregate self-employment trends. The results indicate that the self-employment rate among workers aged 55–64 decreased more from 1910 to 1970 and increased more from 1970 to 1990 than did the rate among workers aged 16–54. The effects of these changes on the trend in the aggregate rate were small, however, largely because this age group represented only a small part of the total workforce throughout the twentieth century. Another interesting finding is that the share of the workforce aged 55–64 increased 7.7 percentage points between 1910 and 1970 and decreased 4.2 percentage points between 1970 and 1990. These changes in the employment share of older workers, who have high self-employment rates, thus worked to diminish both the long-term decline and the recent increase in the aggregate self-employment rate.

The net effect of the trend in elderly self-employment rates and the changes in elderly employment shares on the trend in the aggregate self-employment rate was small because those aged 55–64 represented just over 11 percent of employment in 1990. Furthermore, the self-employment rate among workers aged 16–54 experienced nearly the same 6.0 percentage point decrease from 1910 to 1970 and a slightly larger 1.6 percentage point increase from 1970 to 1990 than occurred in the aggregate self-employment rate. To conclude, these findings indicate that the long-term decline and the recent upturn in the aggregate white self-employment rate cannot be explained by changes in either the self-employment rate of older workers or the share of the workforce that is older.

B. Immigration

Recent studies of self-employment, such as Borjas (1986), Light and Sanchez (1987), Yuengert (1995), and Fairlie and Meyer (1996), find that immigrants have higher self-employment rates than comparable natives. We explore whether changes in immigration patterns or changes in immigrant self-employment rates over the twentieth century contributed to the trend in self-employment among white men. Remember that our self-employment rates are for white men, and thus exclude the large number of Asian immigrants since the passage of the Immigration Reform Act of 1965. The small immigrant percentage of the white male workforce during most of the twentieth century suggests that immigrants cannot account for a large part of the aggregate trend. When one examines the trend in the white native self-employment rate, it is evident that this trend is similar to the trend in the white aggregate rate. In fact, the decrease in the white native rate from 1910 to 1990 was 0.60 percentage points larger than the decrease for the aggregate rate, and the increase from 1970 to 1990 was only 0.08 percentage points smaller.[2] From 1970 to 1990, the faster increase in self-employment among immigrants accounts for only 5.7 percent of the increase in the white self-employment rate, and there was essentially no change in the percentage of the workforce that was immigrants. To conclude, patterns of immigration and immigrant self-employment cannot explain the long-term decline in white self-employment or its recent upturn. Immigration dampened the decline in self-employment from 1910 to 1970 and contributed only slightly to the recent upturn.

C. Industry Decompositions

We now examine patterns of self-employment across industries. We report self-employment rates and employment shares by industry for white male workers in each available census year. Major changes in both self-employment rates within industries and employment shares across industries occurred during the last 80 years.

To identify the relative importance of changes in industry self-employment rates and shares in creating the trend in the aggregate self-employment rate, we perform a decomposition. (See table summary of data in original article.)

The results indicate that the long-term decline from 1910 to 1970 in the self-employment rate was due primarily to a decrease in self-employment rates within nearly all industries. The within-industry decline, however, was somewhat counterbalanced by a shift in overall employment toward high self-employment industries. The importance of the within-industry decline can be seen in the large contribution (of the same sign as the change in the aggregate self-employment rate) from changes in self-employment rates within industries from 1910 to 1970 and the smaller contribution (of the opposite sign) from changes in employment shares. The increase in self-employment from 1970 to 1990 was caused by an end to the decline in the self-employment rate within most industries and the continuing shift in overall employment toward high self-employment industries.

Increases in the self-employment rate within construction, manufacturing, transportation, and FIRE exerted upward pressure on the aggregate self-employment rate from 1970 to 1990. However, the large decrease in the self-employment rate within trade and the smaller decrease within personal services acted to diminish the overall increase in self-employment.

In summary, we find that the long-term decline in self-employment earlier in this century was primarily due to declining rates of self-employment within almost all industries. These patterns are consistent with technological change favoring capital-intensive, large-scale production during this period (see Blau 1987).[3] In comparison, we find that the recent upturn in the aggregate self-employment rate was mainly due to an industrial shift from low to high self-employment industries. The industrial shift toward high self-employment industries may be due to factors such as changes in consumer demand, increased global competition, and changes in technology. Our findings, however, do not allow us to disentangle the effects of each of these factors on the trend in the aggregate self-employment rate.

IV. RESULTS FOR BLACK MEN

We now examine trends in black self-employment during the twentieth century. A few recent studies document and explore causes of the low rate of self-employment among black men. Using various data sources, these studies generally find that black men are one-third as likely to be self-employed as white men. Low levels of education, low asset levels, smaller probabilities of having self-employed fathers, and consumer discrimination are found to contribute to the lack of self-employment among black men. In addition to the recent studies, the main historical studies argue that the absence of black traditions in the field of business enterprise is a major cause of the low level of black self-employment. We examine whether several of these hypotheses can explain the pattern of black self-employment relative to white self-employment during the twentieth century.

From 1910 to 1990, the black self-employment rate generally followed the same time pattern as the white self-employment rate. The main difference was that the decline in black self-employment continued until 1980 and reversed only after 1980. The similar trends in the racial self-employment rates resulted in a roughly constant black/white ratio during the past 80 years. These trends in the self-employment rates and the black/white ratio remain essentially unchanged when we include only full-time, full-year workers. In most years, conditioning on full-time employment increases the white self-employment rate and decreases the black self-employment rate. The changes, however, are small and thus do not substantially alter the black/white ratio in any of the census years.

The constancy of the black/white ratio is surprising in light of the substantial gains blacks have made in education, earnings, and civil rights during the twentieth century (Smith and Welch 1989) and the numerous government programs created to promote minority business ownership (Balkin 1989). We now investigate several possible explanations.

A. Industry Analyses

Although black and white overall self-employment rates did not converge during the twentieth century, there may have been a convergence in racial self-employment rates within some industries during this period. The most striking finding is that black men had substantially lower self-employment rates within all industries and census years. Transportation and Business and Repair Services are the only industries in which the black self-employment rate was consistently greater than 50 percent of the white rate. The finding of low black rates in all industries indicates that the large racial gap in self-employment throughout the century was primarily due to low black self-employment rates within industries and not due to an overrepresentation of blacks in low self-employment rate industries. In fact, the largest positive contribution from racial differences in industry distributions to the black/white gap in aggregate self-employment rates in any censuses year is 11.6 percent.[4] Another interesting finding is that the trends in the black/white ratio for most industries were roughly flat over the century.

Although a comparison of these estimates to the white employment shares reveals some convergence in racial industry distributions, the results indicate that blacks and whites mainly experienced growths and declines in the same industries over the century. The direct contribution of relative changes over time in racial industry distributions is 0.1 to 13.5 percent of the 1990 black/white self-employment rate gap.[5] The industrial changes of the U.S. workforce from 1910 to 1990 apparently did not alter the racial gap in the aggregate self-employment rate. Clearly, the similar levels and trends in the black/white self-employment rate ratios across industries were responsible for this finding.

Overall, the findings from this analysis demonstrate that the large gap between the black and the white self-employment rate during the twentieth century was due to the fact that blacks had lower self-employment rates in all industries and not due to blacks being overrepresented in low self-employment rate industries. Furthermore, the similar trends of blacks and whites in self-employment rates within industries and employment shares across industries contributed to the constancy in the black/white ratio of the aggregate self-employment rate.

B. Education, Migration, and other Demographic Factors

We now examine the influence of demographic factors on the racial trends in self-employment. During the twentieth century, the U.S. labor force experienced major geographical, age, and educational shifts. Although the black self-employment rate remained relatively low during the century, these demographic changes may have had large offsetting effects on the difference between white and black self-employment rates. To explore the importance of demographic factors, we employ the decomposition methodology used by Smith and Welch (1989)[6] in their study of trends in racial earnings differences. The decomposition is a dynamic generalization of the familiar method of decomposing intergroup differences in a dependent variable into those due to different observable characteristics across groups and those due to different returns to characteristics across groups.

We calculate separate contributions from age, family characteristics, education, and region. (See original article for calculations.) The decomposition results for the change between any two census years (1940 to 1990, for example) can be calculated by summing the included decadal decomposition results.[7] In the underlying regressions, we include a constant, age, age squared, and dummy variables for marriage, presence of children, three educational categories (high school graduate, some college, and college graduate), and eight census divisions.[8] The difference between the white and black self-employment rates was large in each census year and experienced only minor changes during this period. Although the changes in the racial gap were small from 1940 to 1990, individual demographic variables may have had large effects on the trend in the gap. We first examine the effect of these variables during the period from 1940 to 1960.

One of the most important demographic changes occurring during the twentieth century was the large exodus of blacks from rural areas in the South to urban areas in the North from 1915 to 1960, known as the Great Black Migration. Using our sample of workers in nonagricultural industries, we find that the percentage of black workers living in the South fell from 68 percent in 1940 to 52 percent in 1960, whereas the percentage of whites living in the South increased slightly over the same period. Our decomposition results indicate that this relative regional shift increased the racial gap during this period somewhat as evidenced by the positive estimates of (i) for 1940 through 1960 that sum to just under 0.6 percentage points. The small positive direct effect of the Great Black Migration due to the lower self-employment rates in the North that increased the racial gap was more than offset by the fact that blacks were moving into regions with smaller racial gaps in self-employment and that self-employment was increasing in the regions overrepresented by blacks. Evidence of these latter factors, which worked to reduce the racial gap, are provided by the negative estimates of contributions (ii) and (iii) which sum to just over 0.6 percentage points for this period. All of the effects, however, were small, implying that the major regional shifts that occurred during this period of time had little effect on black self-employment relative to white self-employment.

During the 1940s and 1950s, racial trends in age, family characteristics, and educational distributions also had little effect on changes in the racial self-employment rate gap. These findings are less surprising, however, as the racial difference in mean values of these variables did not change substantially during this period. There is some evidence that the relative trends in self-employment across educational levels were favorable to less-educated blacks.

We now examine the period from 1960 to 1990. Perhaps the most important demographic change that occurred during this period was the substantial increase in black educational levels relative to those of whites. The percentage of the white male workforce that was high school graduates grew from 51.1 percent in 1960, to 85.8 percent in 1990. In comparison, 25.4 percent of employed black men were high school graduates in 1960 increasing to 74.7 percent in 1990. Past research and our regression estimates indicate that the probability of self-employment increases with education. Therefore, we expect the relative increase in black educational levels to reduce the racial gap in the self-employment rate (holding other factors constant). Our decomposition estimates indicate, however, that the relative racial trends in educational attainment had only a minor effect on changes in the racial gap.

Examining the other contributions from education, we find that the educational improvements made by blacks placed them in educational categories that had larger racial self-employment rate gaps. Rising self-employment rates among less-educated workers over time reduced the racial gap. Overall, the racial trends in education did not have a large effect on the trend in the racial self-employment rate gap from 1960 to 1990. Furthermore, none of the included variables provide large contributions to changes in the racial gap during this period.

Our results indicate that trends in demographic factors, including the Great Black Migration and the racial convergence in education levels, did not have large effects on the trend in the racial gap in the self-employment rate.[9] We therefore conclude that the constancy of the racial gap in self-employment was not due to offsetting influences of important racial trends in demographic factors.

C. Past Self-Employment Experience

Past studies such as DuBois (1899), and later Myrdal (1944), Cayton and Drake (1946), and Frazier (1957) identify the lack of black traditions in business enterprise, in large part due to slavery, as a major cause of low levels of black business ownership at the time of their analyses. We take this argument about past experience to mean that lack of past experience in self-employment per se is the cause of current low rates. We do not take this argument to include other human and physical capital as well as intangibles that are passed intergenerationally. To examine whether this story can explain the lack of convergence of the black rate to the white rate over this century, we begin by examining the microdata evidence on intergenerational links in self-employment. After having seen that these links are strong, we then do two things. First, we construct a simple model of serial correlation in self-employment rates using evidence from the earlier microdata work. We use this model to approximate the speed with which the effects of the initial low black self-employment rate would fade, in the absence of other forces reducing black self-employment. Second, we examine if younger cohorts of blacks are more likely to be self-employed as would be expected if other forces reducing black self-employment had only recently diminished.

Recent studies have used nationally representative surveys to examine the extent of the intergenerational correlation in self-employment, finding that an individual who had a self-employed parent is about two to three times as likely to be self-employed as someone who did not have a self-employed parent.[10] This intergenerational relationship is substantial, but whether or not it can explain the constancy of the black/white ratio over time requires some modeling.

Calculations using our intergenerational model of self-employment indicate that an initial lack of business experience cannot explain the current low levels of black self-employment without major changes in our assumptions. Substantial deviations from the steady-state assumption and the assumed white self-employment rate are of little quantitative importance for the convergence calculations. The assumption that, if changed, could substantially alter the results is the assumption that business experience is passed from parents to children. It seems likely that parents are the major influence, but other sources of information on acceptable careers and the means to attain them are probably also important (uncles, cousins, neighbors, and so on). However, as long as parents are the major influence, convergence would occur reasonably quickly. The discrepancy is due to forces that reduce current black self-employment besides the initial conditions of low black self-employment. The empirical finding of a constant black/white self-employment ratio over the twentieth century implies that there are continuing factors that depress the black self-employment rate. These factors could be discrimination, or they could be skills, capital, and intangibles that are passed intergenerationally.

We also examine whether more recent generations of blacks have higher relative self-employment rates than older generations. There is no clear evidence of an improvement in relative self-employment rates among younger generations of blacks. Although the youngest cohort has the largest black/white ratio in 1990, the second and third youngest cohorts have low ratios in both 1980 and 1990. The figure also indicates that the black/white ratio does not change substantially as each synthetic cohort ages.

V. A BRIEF COMPARISON TO NUMBERS FROM THE CURRENT POPULATION SURVEY (CPS)

The focus of this chapter is the nature and determinants of long-term trends in self-employment over the twentieth century. The only data available for this purpose are the decennial censuses. The census datasets are also large enough to allow disaggregation of the population in ways that facilitate explaining the changes. In this section, we use annual CPS data since 1966 to examine trends in the last few years and to determine more precisely when declines or increases began. We undertake this analysis, in part, because other research has found a decline in self-employment in recent years (Blanchflower 1998) or emphasized recent increases in the number of black owned businesses (U.S. Small Business Administration 1999). The evidence here suggests that the censuses provide an accurate picture of recent trends in self-employment.

The CPS numbers suggest that the white male rate fell slightly through the late 1960s and early 1970s and then rose through 1992 or 1993. Since 1993 or 1994 the white self-employment rate appears to have fallen slightly. The black male rate has followed a similar pattern, though there is less suggestion of a fall in recent years until 1997 when the rate drops substantially. The black/white ratio appears to have been fairly steady at between 0.3 and 0.4 during the years of comparable data. Overall, the changes in recent years do not appear large and the earlier patterns agree closely with those in the census data.

VI. CONCLUSION

In our analysis of 1910 and 1940 to 1990 Census microdata, we find that the white male self-employment rate fell from 16.0 percent in 1910 to 10.0 percent in 1970, then rose to 11.4 percent in 1990. We have ruled out a number of possible explanations for the long-term decline and recent upturn in the white self-employment rate. In particular, we find that social security, the age distribution of the workforce, and immigration do not explain the trends in self-employment. We do find, however, that the long-term decline was mainly due to declining self-employment rates within nearly all industries, and the recent upturn was mainly due to a shift of overall employment to high self-employment industries. These findings are consistent with technological change favoring capital-intensive, large-scale production during the period from 1910 to 1970, and changes in consumer demand, increased global competition and changes in technology favorable to self-employment during the period from 1970 to 1990.

We find that the self-employment rate of black men relative to white men remained roughly constant from 1910 to 1990. Substantially lower black self-employment rates were found in all industries and census years. Major demographic changes occurring during the twentieth century, such as the Great Black Migration and the racial convergence in educational attainment, did not have large effects on the racial self-employment rate gap. We show using a simple intergenerational model of self-employment that, if not for continuing factors reducing black self-employment, racial convergence in self-employment rates should occur in only a couple of generations. We also do not find higher relative self-employment rates among more recent cohorts of black men than among older cohorts. With available data, we cannot carefully examine the role that other factors, such as asset differences, consumer and lending discrimination, and risk aversion, have played in causing the absence of convergence of the black and white self-employment rates during this century.

NOTES

1. For example, see "Black-Owned Firms in U.S. Are Increasing at Rapid Rate," *Wall Street Journal,* September 12, 1990, p. B2.

2. From 1940 to 1970, however, the large decrease in the immigrant self-employment rate and the declining share of the workforce that was immigrant contributed to the decline in the aggregate self-employment rate over this period. The decrease in the white native self-employment rate was 0.94 percentage points smaller than the decrease in the white aggregate rate (accounting for 24.5 percent of the decrease in the aggregate rate).

3. Blau (1987) finds that a measure of technology (total factor productivity weighted by self-employment and wage/salary industry distributions) explains a large portion of the increase in aggregate self-employment from 1973 to 1982. Changes in his measure of technology, however, may also be due to demand-induced changes in industry structure. He concludes that "the source of the favorable shift in TFP for the self-employed is uncertain."

4. The contribution from racial differences in industry distributions in year t is [Multiple line equation(s) cannot be converted to ASCII text]. The contributions are generally smaller using black self-employment rates as weights.

5. These contributions are using black and white self-employment rates, respectively.

6. Smith and Welch (1989) argue for using the white or majority parameter estimates because these estimates more closely resemble market prices of attributes. We also calculated decompositions using black as the base race and obtained similar results.

7. The interpretation of this term for specific subsets of variables is problematic, because it is sensitive to the choice of excluded category. Therefore, we only report the total contribution of this component for all of the variables.

8. The coefficient estimates from these regressions generally have the anticipated signs. We find that self-employment increases with age, education level, and living in the Pacific division.

9. These results are robust to using blacks as the base race in equation 9 and including industry controls in the underlying regressions.

10. Fairlie (1999) finds that having a self-employed father increases the transition rate into self-employment by 55 percent and decreases the exit rate by 76 percent. Under a constant hazard assumption, the resulting probability of self-employment increases by 72 percent. Dunn and Holtz-Eakin (2000) find that the self-employment rate of children of self-employed parents varies from under two to almost three times that of children of parents who are not self-employed. Hout and Rosen (1997) find that having a self-employed father roughly doubles the probability of self-employment.

11. If we assume, instead, that the initial black rate is zero then the black rate achieves 82 percent of the white rate after one generation and 97 percent of the white rate after two generations.

12. In a thorough analysis of the redesign using the parallel survey, Polivka and Miller (1998) conclude that the redesign raised the self-employment rate of men by about one-half of a percentage point. However, the parallel survey seems to have two drawbacks. The sample used for the parallel survey does not appear to have the same characteristics as the regular CPS sample, and interviewer procedures were different. In particular, the interviewers had lower caseloads, and the interviews were longer and were supervised more carefully.

REFERENCES

Aldrich, Howard E., and Roger Waldinger. 1990. "Ethnicity and Entrepreneurship." *Annual Review of Sociology* 16(1):111–35.

Aronson, Robert L. 1991. *Self-Employment: A Labor Market Perspective*. Ithaca, NY: ILR Press.

Balkin, Steven. 1989. *Self-Employment for Low-Income People*. New York: Praeger.

Bates, Timothy. 1987. "Self-Employed Minorities: Traits and Trends." *Social Science Quarterly* 68(3): 539–51.

Becker, Eugene H. 1984. "Self-Employed Workers: An Update to 1983." *Monthly Labor Review* 107(7):14–18.

Birch, David. 1979. *The Job Creation Process*. Cambridge, MA: MIT Program on Neighborhood and Regional Change.

Blanchflower, David G. 1998. "Self-employment in OECD Countries." Working Paper. Hanover, NH: Dartmouth College.

Blau, David M. 1987. "A Time-Series Analysis of Self-Employment in the United States." *Journal of Political Economy* 95(3): 445–67.

Borjas, George. 1986. "The Self-Employment Experience of Immigrants," *Journal of Human Resources* 21(4): 487–506.

Borjas, George, and Stephen Bronars. 1989. "Consumer Discrimination and Self-Employment." *Journal of Political Economy* 97(3): 581–605.

Brown, Charles, James Hamilton, and James Medoff. 1990. *Employers Large and Small*. Cambridge, MA: Harvard University Press.

Carter, Susan B., and Richard Sutch. 1994. "Self-Employment in the Age of Big Business: Toward an Appreciation of an American Labor Market Institution." Working Papers on the History of Retirement, History of Retirement Project. University of California.

Cayton, Horace R., and St. Clair Drake. 1946. *Black Metropolis*. London: Jonathan Cape.

Cohany, Sharon, Anne Polivka, and Jennifer Rothgeb. 1994. "Revisions in the Current Population Survey Effective January 1994." *Employment and Earnings* 41(2): 13–37.

Davis, Steven J., John C. Haltiwanger, and Scott Schuh. 1996. *Job Creation and Destruction*. Cambridge, MA: MIT Press.

DuBois, W. E. B. 1899. *The Philadelphia Negro*. Philadelphia: University of Pennsylvania.

Dunn, Thomas A., and Douglas J. Holtz-Eakin. 2000. "Financial Capital, Human Capital, and the Transition to Self-Employment: Evidence from Intergenerational Links." *Journal of Labor Economics* 18(2): 282–305.

Evans, David, and Linda Leighton. 1989. "Some Empirical Aspects of Entrepreneurship." *American Economic Review* 79(3): 519–35.

Fairlie, Robert W. 1999. "The Absence of the African-American Owned Business: An Analysis of the Dynamics of Self-Employment." *Journal of Labor Economics* 17(1): 80–108.

Fairlie, Robert W., and Bruce D. Meyer. 1996. "Ethnic and Racial Self-Employment Differences and Possible Explanations." *Journal of Human Resources* 31(4): 757–93.

Fairlie, Robert W., and Bruce D. Meyer. 1999. "Trends in Self-Employment Among White and Black Men: 1910–1990." National Bureau of Economic Research Working Paper No. 7182. Cambridge, MA: NBER.

Frazier, E. Franklin. 1957. *The Negro in the United States*, 2nd Ed. New York: Macmillan.

Fuchs, Victor R. 1982. "Self-Employment and Labor Force Participation of Older Males." *Journal of Human Resources* 17(3): 339–57.

Glazer, Nathan, and Daniel P. Moynihan. 1970. *Beyond the Melting Pot, 2nd Edition*. Cambridge, MA: MIT Press.

Hout, Michael, and Harvey Rosen. 2000. "Self-Employment, Family Background, and Race." *Journal of Human Resources* 35(4): 670–92.

Lazear, Edward P., and Robert L. Moore. 1984. "Incentives, Productivity, and Labor Contracts." *Quarterly Journal of Economics* 99(3): 275–96.

Lebergott, Stanley. 1964. *Manpower in Economic Growth: The American Record Since 1800.* New York: McGraw-Hill.

Light, Ivan. 1972. *Ethnic Enterprise in America.* Berkeley: University of California Press.

———. 1979. "Disadvantaged Minorities in Self Employment." *International Journal of Comparative Sociology* 20(1–2): 31–45.

Light, Ivan, and Angel A. Sanchez. 1987. "Immigrant Entrepreneurs in 272 SMSAs." *Sociological Perspectives* 30(4): 373–99.

Meyer, Bruce D. 1990. "Why Are There So Few Black Entrepreneurs?" National Bureau of Economic Research Working Paper No. 3537. Cambridge, MA: NBER.

Mills, C. Wright. 1951. *White Collar.* New York: Oxford University Press.

Moore, Robert L. 1983. "Employer Discrimination: Evidence from Self-Employed Workers." *Review of Economics and Statistics* 65(3): 496–501.

Myrdal, Gunnar. 1944. *An American Dilemma.* New York: Harper and Brothers.

Phillips, Joseph D. 1962. *The Self-Employed in the United States.* Urbana: University of Illinois.

Polivka, Anne E., and Stephen M. Miller. 1998. "The CPS After the Redesign: Refocusing the Economic Lens." In *Labor Statistics Measurement Issues,* ed. John Haltiwanger, Marilyn E. Manser, and Robert Topel, 249–86. Chicago: University of Chicago Press.

Quinn, Joseph. 1980. "Labor Force Participation of Older Self-Employed Workers," *Social Security Bulletin* 43(4): 17–28.

Rettenmaier, Andrew J. 1996. "A Little or a Lot: Self-Employment and Hours of Work." Paper presented at the Society of Labor Economists Annual Meeting, Chicago.

Smith, James P., and Finis R. Welch. 1989. "Black Economic Progress after Myrdal." *Journal of Economic Literature* 27(2): 519–64.

Sowell, Thomas. 1981. *Markets and Minorities.* New York: Basic Books.

Thurman, Wallace. 1929. *The Blacker the Berry: A Novel of Negro Life.* New York: Macmillan.

U.S. Bureau of the Census. 1993. *Census of Population and Housing, 1990.* Public Use Microdata Sample U.S. Technical Documentation. Washington, DC: GPO.

U.S. Department of Labor. 1992. *Self-Employment Programs for Unemployed Workers.* Unemployment Insurance Occasional Paper 92–2. Washington, DC: GPO.

U.S. Small Business Administration. 1999. *Minorities in Business. Office of Advocacy.* Washington, DC: GPO.

Weber, Max. 1958. *The Protestant Ethic and the Spirit of Capitalism.* New York: Scribner.

Wolpin, Kenneth I. 1977. "Education and Screening." *American Economic Review* 67(5): 949–58.

Yuengert, Andrew M. 1995. "Testing Hypotheses of Immigrant Self-Employment." *Journal of Human Resources* 30(1): 194–204

Part Four:
New Values, New Directions

"Identifying the Unique Needs of the Urban Entrepreneurs: African Americans Skill Set Development," by Marlese Durr, Thomas S. Lyons, and Gregg Lichtenstein

1. Describe what the authors mean by skill set development for urban entrepreneurs.
2. What are the drawbacks for African American small business owners in developing clientele?
3. Describe factors which continue to hamper African Americans in growing a larger clientele within major urban areas?

"Trends in Self-Employment among White and Black Men during the Twentieth Century," by Robert W. Fairlie and Bruce D. Meyer

1. Why are long-term studies of self-employment important?
2. How do age and immigrant status affect patterns of self-employment among white men?
3. Overall, how do rates of self-employment differ between white men and black men?
4. What factors contribute to the low level of self-employment among black men?

Index

Contributors

Eduardo Bonilla-Silva is a professor at Duke University. His research focuses on racial stratification and race relations.

Karen W. Brewster is an associate professor of sociology at Florida State University and a Research Associate at the Center for Demography and Population Health. Her research focuses on health and inequality.

Irene Browne is an associate professor at Emory University. She has written extensively in the area of gender inequality.

F. Nii-Amoo DoDoo is a professor at Pennsylvania State University of Maryland, and his research centers on issues of race and inequality.

Marlese Durr is an associate professor at Wright State University. She studies racial inequality and labor market issues that affect African Americans.

Robert W. Fairlie is a member of the Department of Economics at the University of California—Santa Cruz.

Cedric Herring is a professor of sociology at the University of Illinois at Chicago. He studies race, discrimination, labor markets, and public policy.

Shirley A. Hill is a professor in the Department of Sociology at the University of Kansas. She studies race, family, and health care issues.

Harry J. Holzer is a professor of public policy at Georgetown University. His research focuses on low-wage labor markets and the problems of minority workers in urban areas.

Andrea G. Hunter is an associate professor at the University of North Carolina—Greensboro. She focuses on cultural strategies in black families, gender construction and ideology, and racial diversity.

Verna Keith is an associate professor at Arizona State University. Her research focuses on race, mental health, and aging.

Ivy Kennelly is an assistant professor of sociology at George Washington University. She studies the theoretical interdependencies of race, class, and gender as a system of inequality and oppression.

Gregg Lichtenstein is president of Collaborative Strategies, a consulting firm that specializes in launching new ventures and alliances.

Thomas S. Lyons is in the Department of Urban and Public Affairs at the University of Louisville in Kentucky.

Bruce D. Meyer is in the Harris School of Public Policy at the University of Chicago.

Stephanie Moller is an assistant professor at the University of North Carolina—Charlotte, where she studies poverty, stratification, political sociology, and education.

Yvonne D. Newsome is an associate professor at Agnes Scott College. She studies race and ethnic identity, race relations, and the sociology of education.

Irene Padavic is a professor at Florida State University. She studies race, gender-based inequalities, and labor market experiences and practices.

Maxine D. Thompson is an associate professor at North Carolina State University. She studies medical sociology, social psychology, and social inequalities.